"十三五"普通高等教育汽车服务工程专业规划教材

汽车服务工程专业英语

(第二版)

于明进 主 编

人民交通出版社股份有限公司
China Communications Press Co.,Ltd.

内 容 提 要

本书由汽车服务工程专业教学指导委员会组织编写,主要内容包括汽车构造与基本原理、汽车检测与维修、汽车营销与售后服务、汽车保险、汽车评估、新能源与车联网技术六个单元。内容模块化,有利于按需施教;附参考译文和词汇表,便于教学和自学。

本书供汽车服务工程专业和其他相关汽车专业本科教学使用。

图书在版编目(CIP)数据

汽车服务工程专业英语 / 于明进主编. —2 版. —北京:
人民交通出版社股份有限公司, 2017.5
ISBN 978-7-114-13739-6

Ⅰ.①汽… Ⅱ.①于… Ⅲ.①汽车工业—销售管理—商业服务—英语 Ⅳ.①F407.471.5

中国版本图书馆 CIP 数据核字(2017)第 068992 号

"十三五"普通高等教育汽车服务工程专业规划教材

书　　名:	汽车服务工程专业英语(第二版)
著 作 者:	于明进
责任编辑:	李　良　曹　静
出版发行:	人民交通出版社股份有限公司
地　　址:	(100011)北京市朝阳区安定门外外馆斜街 3 号
网　　址:	http://www.ccpress.com.cn
销售电话:	(010)59757973
总 经 销:	人民交通出版社股份有限公司发行部
经　　销:	各地新华书店
印　　刷:	北京市密东印刷有限公司
开　　本:	787×1092　1/16
印　　张:	12.75
字　　数:	306 千
版　　次:	2008 年 8 月　第 1 版
	2017 年 5 月　第 2 版
印　　次:	2019 年 11 月　第 2 版　第 2 次印刷　累计第 6 次印刷
书　　号:	ISBN 978-7-114-13739-6
定　　价:	28.00 元

(有印刷、装订质量问题的图书由本公司负责调换)

"十三五"普通高等教育汽车服务工程专业规划教材编委会

主任委员：许洪国(吉林大学)

副主任委员：

张国方(武汉理工大学)　　　储江伟(东北林业大学)
简晓春(重庆交通大学)　　　王生昌(长安大学)
李岳林(长沙理工大学)　　　肖生发(湖北汽车工业学院)
关志伟(天津职业技术师范大学)　付百学(黑龙江工程学院)

委员：

杨志发(吉林大学)　　　　　杜丹丰(东北林业大学)
赵长利(山东交通学院)　　　唐　岚(西华大学)
李耀平(昆明理工大学)　　　林谋有(南昌工程学院)
李国庆(江苏理工学院)　　　路玉峰(齐鲁工业大学)
周水庭(厦门理工学院)　　　宋年秀(青岛理工大学)
方祖华(上海师范大学)　　　郭健忠(武汉科技大学)
黄　玮(天津职业技术师范大学)　邬志军(皖西学院)
姚层林(武汉商学院)　　　　田茂盛(重庆交通大学)
李素华(江汉大学)　　　　　夏基胜(盐城工学院)
刘志强(长沙理工大学)　　　孟利清(西南林业大学)
陈文刚(西南林业大学)　　　王　飞(安阳工学院)
廖抒华(广西科技大学)　　　李军政(湖南农业大学)
程文明(江西科技学院)　　　鲁植雄(南京农业大学)
钟　勇(福建工程学院)　　　张新峰(长安大学)
彭小龙(南京工业大学浦江学院)　姜连勃(深圳大学)
陈庆樟(常熟理工学院)　　　迟瑞娟(中国农业大学)
田玉东(上海电机学院)　　　赵　伟(河南科技大学)
陈无畏(合肥工业大学)　　　左付山(南京林业大学)
马其华(上海工程技术大学)　王国富(桂林航天工业大学)

秘书处：李　斌　夏　韡　李　良

前言
Qianyan

本书由汽车服务工程专业教学指导委员会组织编写，供汽车服务工程专业和其他相关汽车专业本科教学使用。

根据汽车市场和汽车技术的发展，结合应用型本科高校人才培养方案的改革，考虑汽车服务工程专业的就业和发展方向，本书编写组对汽车服务工程专业英语进行了修订。本次修订删减了部分陈旧的内容，增加了新能源汽车和车联网技术的内容，并将其单独作为一个单元。本书主要特色如下：

（1）专业方向明确，针对性强。本书紧密结合汽车服务工程专业的培养目标编写，包括六个单元，内容涉及汽车构造与基本原理、汽车检测与维修、汽车营销与售后服务、汽车保险、汽车评估、新能源汽车和车联网技术六个方面。以使学生熟悉汽车服务工程专业常用英语词汇，初步掌握有关知识的英语表达方法，培养专业翻译能力。

（2）内容新颖、翻译准确。课文主要选自国内外相关领域的最新英语科技资料，既包含基本知识，又包含汽车最新技术。各单元参考译文全部经专业老师审阅修改，保证翻译准确，专业术语规范。

（3）结构安排合理，便于教学。注意与公共英语以及专业课的衔接，课文难度由浅入深、各单元所涉及的专业知识与所学专业课相对应，系统性强；内容弹性化、模块化，有利于按需施教。对课文中的语法难点、专业词汇和短语进行注释，并给出复习思考题和参考译文，最后附总词汇表，便于教学和自学。

本次修订工作由于明进、赵培全、杨君、韩广德、刘新磊等老师完成。

本书编写及修订过程中，参阅了国内外有关的书籍杂志和网页，得到了中国重汽集团公司、山东交通学院汽车工程学院及有关老师和长安大学陈焕江老师的大力支持和帮助。在此表示衷心感谢。

本书疏漏和不妥之处，恳请读者指正，以便今后改进。

本书编写组
2017 年 2 月

Contents 目 录

Unit 1　Fundamentals of Automobile ································· 1
　Lesson 1　Structure of Automobile ································· 1
　Lesson 2　Basics of Four-stroke Cycle Engine ······················ 6
　Lesson 3　Fuel Injection Systems of Gasoline Engine ·············· 12
　Lesson 4　Variable Valve Timing ·································· 17
　Lesson 5　Transmission ··· 23
　Lesson 6　Brakes ··· 29
Unit 2　Inspecting and Maintenance of Automobile ················ 34
　Lesson 7　Automobile System Diagnosis ···························· 34
　Lesson 8　Automobile Maintenance ································· 40
　Lesson 9　Engine Maintenance ····································· 46
　Lesson 10　The Check Engine Light ································ 52
　Lesson 11　Safety and Performance Testers ························ 59
Unit 3　Sell Automobile ··· 66
　Lesson 12　The 5W's of World Class Customer Service Training ····· 66
　Lesson 13　Leader of Heavy Truck ································· 72
　Lesson 14　The Character of CROWN ································ 79
　Lesson 15　The Sample of Export Trade Contracts Text ············· 84
　Lesson 16　Notes to A Motor Vehicle Owner ························ 90
　Lesson 17　Auto Market Assault ··································· 95
Unit 4　Automobile Insurance ···································· 101
　Lesson 18　Property Insurance Contract ·························· 101
　Lesson 19　Auto Insurance Basics ································ 106
　Lesson 20　The Benefits with An Auto Insurance Contract ········· 112
　Lesson 21　The Cover for Your Car ······························· 117
　Lesson 22　The Legal Responsibilities to Third Parties ·········· 123
Unit 5　Assessment of Automobile ································ 131
　Lesson 23　New Car Assessment Program ··························· 131
　Lesson 24　Estimating for Automobile Repair ····················· 135
　Lesson 25　Assessment of Labor Hour Cost ························ 141

Lesson 26　Actual Cash Value of Automobile ………………………………………… 144
Unit 6　New Eenergy Vehicle and Connected Vehicle Technology ……………… 149
　Lesson 27　The Electric Vehicles and Hybrid Power ……………………………… 149
　Lesson 28　Plug-in Hybrid Electric Vehicle ………………………………………… 155
　Lesson 29　Basic Knowledge of Electric Vehicle …………………………………… 159
　Lesson 30　Paris Show Points the Way to the Future of Electric Cars …………… 164
　Lesson 31　The Car of the Future: It Talks, It Thinks, and It Can Drive Itself …… 169
　Lesson 32　The First Internet Vehicle ………………………………………………… 173
Vocabulary ……………………………………………………………………………… 177
References ……………………………………………………………………………… 196

Unit 1 Fundamentals of Automobile

Lesson 1 Structure of Automobile

In order to study automobiles, it is important to review the basic parts of an automobile. See Fig. 1-1. An automobile can be subdivided into several major categories: the body and frame, the engine or power source, the chassis and the electrical equipment.

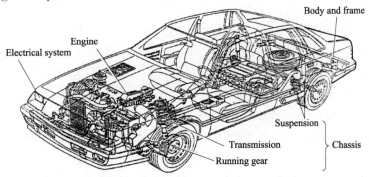

Fig. 1-1 Basic parts of an automobile

1. Body and Frame

The body and frame section is the basic foundation of an automobile. All other components and systems are attached to the body and frame. The frame supports the automobile body, engine, and the driveline. Fig. 1-2 illustrates the body and frame of a typical automobile.

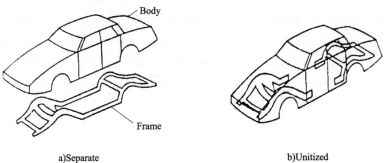

Fig. 1-2 Body and frame

There are two types of body and frame configuration. The separate body and frame construction illustrated in Fig. 1-2a) has been used for a long time. The second type of construction is called the unitized body. See Fig. 1-2b). This type of vehicle is designed with the frame and body in one unit. The unitized body is used in most cars today.

2. Engine

The engine is used to power the vehicle. The engine is also called the power source or motor. The word "motor" is defined as that which imparts motion. So a motor can be any device that produces power. However, the power source in the automobile is usually referred to as the engine.

Most automobiles use the gasoline engine as a power source. However, other power sources are being tested and introduced every year. For example, the diesel engine is also being used as a power source today, and has been used in commercial vehicles widely. In addition, some automotive engineers predict the use of gas turbines and Stifling engines for future power sources in the automobile.

Most automobiles use the reciprocating piston or Otto cycle engine. However, certain car manufactures also offer rotary design engines as an optional power source. Although the rotary engine now used on certain vehicles looks similar to the reciprocating piston engine, internally there are many differences. [1]

The engine is typically located in the front of the vehicle. But some vehicles have rear engines. In addition, certain manufactures have developed engines that are placed in the middle of the body and frame.

Most of engines are designed with several supporting technical systems. These include: the fuel system, the ignition system, the starting and charging system, the lubricating system, the cooling system, the air intake and exhaust system, the pollution control system.

The fuel system is designed to mix the air and fuel in the engine. This mix will produce an efficient combustion process. The ignition system is designed to ignite the air and fuel that has been mixed. The starting and charging system is designed to start the engine and to keep the battery charged during operation. The lubricating system is designed to keep all engine moving parts lubricated so that friction is reduced internally. The cooling system is designed to keep the engine at the most efficient operating temperature. The air intake system is designed to get air into the engine efficiently and without dirt. The exhaust system is designed to clean the exhaust gases and to reduce the sound of the exhaust noise. The pollution control system is designed to reduce various emissions from the engine including carbon monoxide, nitrogen oxide (oxides of nitrogen), and hydrocarbons.

3. Chassis

The chassis consists of the transmission, the running gear and the suspension system. It is shown in Fig. 1-3.

The transmission is defined as those components that transmit the power from the engine to the wheels. This action will propel the vehicle in a forward or reverse direction. The transmission includes components such as the clutch, gearbox, drive shaft, differential, and halfshafts etc.

There are two methods in which the transmission can be designed: the rear wheel driveline system and the front wheel driveline system. In rear wheel driveline system, the engine is in the front of the body and frame. The power is then transmitted to the rear of the vehicle for propulsion. The front wheel driveline system is used on most cars today. In this system the engine is in the front of the vehicle. The driveline can be also in the front of a vehicle. Both systems have advantages and disadvantages and are equally reliable in their operation.

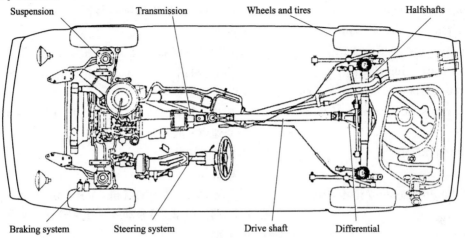

Fig. 1-3 Chassis of a car

The running gear consists of the wheels, tires, braking system and steering system. The braking system is used to reduce the speed of the vehicle and hold it stationary as necessary. The steering system is used to provide the means by which the vehicle is directionally turned.

The suspension system on the automobile includes such components as the springs, shock absorbers, struts, torsion bars, axles, and connecting linkages. These components are designed to support the body and frame, the engine, and the driveline on the road. Without suspension system, the comfort and ease of driving would be reduced. The springs and torsion bars are attached to the axles of the vehicle. The two types of springs commonly used are leaf spring and coil spring. Torsion bars are made of long spring steel rods. One end of the rod is connected to the frame, while the other end is connected to the movable parts of the axles. As the axles move up and down, the rod is twisted and acts as a spring. Shock absorbers are used to slow down the upward and downward movement of the vehicle. This action occurs when the car goes over a rough road. The axles and connecting linkages are those components that connect the springs, torsion bars, and shock absorbers to the vehicle frame and to the wheels.

4. Electrical Equipment

The electrical equipment mainly comprises the battery, alternator, lights, instrumentation, electrical devices and electronic control systems etc.

New Words

subdivide [ˈsʌbdiˈvaid] vt. 细分(细区分,再划分,重分,叠分,分小类)

frame [freim] n. 骨架结构,框架,框子;【机】架,座身;(人或物的)骨骼,身躯

chassis [ˈʃæsi] n. (pl. chassis, chassises)底盘,底架,底板[座]

configuration [kənˌfigjuˈreiʃən] n. 结构,布局,形态[计算机]配置

impart [imˈpɑːt] v. 给予(尤指抽象事物),传授,告知

turbine [ˈtəːbin, -bain] n. 涡轮

reciprocate [riˈsiprəkeit] v. 互换,交换,报答,【机】使往复运动;上下移动

lubricate [ˈluːbrikeit] v. 润滑,涂油

hydrocarbon [ˌhaidrouˈkɑːbən] n. 烃,碳氢化合物

transmission [trænzˈmiʃ(ə)n] n. 传递;移转;传播;传播之物;【机】传动装置;变速器;联动机件

clutch [klʌtʃ] v. 抓住,攥住;
n. 离合器

differential [ˌdifəˈrenʃ(ə)l] adj. 差别的,微分的,【机,物】差动的,差速的;
n.【数】微分;【机】差动;差动齿轮;差速器

halfshaft n. 半轴

driveline n. 传动系统,驱动管路

friction [ˈfrikʃən] n. 摩擦,摩擦力

tire [ˈtaiə] n. 轮胎

strut [strʌt] n. 高视阔步,支柱
v. 抗压材趾高气扬地走,用支柱支撑

torsion [ˈtɔːʃən] n. 扭,捻,捻率,【物】【机】扭转,转矩

alternator [ˈɔltəːˌneitər] n. 交流发电机

Phrases and Expressions

drive shaft 传动轴
running gear 行走装置,行驶系
carbon monoxide 一氧化碳
nitrogen oxide 氮氧化物

Notes to the Text

[1] Although the rotary engine now used on certain vehicles looks similar to the reciprocating piston engine, internally there are many differences.

虽然现在某些汽车使用的转子式发动机与往复活塞式发动机看起来转子式相似,但本质上有许多不同。

Review Questions

1. What does an modern automobile consist of?

2. Do you know what differences there are between a rotary engine and a reciprocating piston engine?

3. What systems or components are included in the automobile chassis?

4. What are the main functions of the braking system in an automobile?

5. Please list the main components that the suspension system on an automobile includes.

参考译文

第一单元　汽车基本原理

第一课　汽车的构造

为了研究汽车,了解汽车的基本组成是非常重要的。如图1-1所示,汽车被分为几大主要部分:车身和车架,发动机或动力源,底盘和电气设备。

1. 车身和车架

车身和车架是汽车的基本构成部分。其他所有部件和系统都与车身和车架相连。车架支撑着车身、发动机、传动系、行驶系。典型车辆的车身和车架如图1-2所示。

车身和车架的结构有两种类型,分离式车身和车架已使用了很长时间,如图1-2a)所示。第二种被称为整体式车身,车辆的车身和车架设计成一体,如图1-2b)所示。整体式车身在今天的大多乘用车中使用。

2. 发动机

发动机为汽车提供动力,因此发动机又被称为动力源或马达。马达是产生运动的源泉,因此马达可以是提供动力的任何装置,但是,汽车的动力源通常是指发动机。

大多数汽车使用汽油发动机作为动力源,但是每年都有其他动力源被试验和引进。比如,今天的柴油发动机也被当作动力源,已经广泛应用于商用车。另外,有些汽车工程师预测将来燃气轮机和斯特林发动机也将被作为汽车的动力源。

许多汽车使用往复活塞式或奥托循环发动机,但是,有些汽车制造商提供转子式发动机作为任选的动力源。虽然现在某些汽车使用的转子式发动机与往复活塞式发动机看起来转子式相似,但本质上有许多不同。

发动机一般置于汽车前部,但是也有一些汽车采用后置发动机。另外,还有一些制造商已开发了中置发动机(即发动机),置于车身和车架的中部。

绝大多数发动机都有几个专门的系统,包括:燃料供给系统、点火系统、起动和充电系统、润滑系统、冷却系统、进气和排气系统、排放控制系统。

燃料供给系统在发动机内将空气和燃油混合,混合气将产生高效的燃烧过程。点火系统的作用是将混合的空气和燃油点燃。起动和充电系统的作用是起动发动机和在运行期间为蓄电池充电。润滑系统的作用是保持发动机运动件之间的润滑,减少内部摩擦。冷却系统的作用是保持发动机在高效的运行温度下工作。进气系统的作用是使洁净的空气高效地进入发动机,排气系统的作用是排出废气、减小排气噪声。排放控制系统的作用是减少发动机各种排放物,包括CO、NO_x和HC。

3. 底盘

底盘由传动系统、行驶系统、悬架组成,如图 1-3 所示。

传动系统是指那些将发动机动力传给车轮的部件,其作用是驱动汽车前进或倒车。传动系统包括离合器、变速器、传动轴、差速器和半轴等。

传动系统有两种设计方法:后轮驱动系统和前轮驱动系统。后轮驱动系统,发动机置于车身和车架的前部,动力传到汽车后轴产生驱动。目前许多汽车使用前轮驱动系统,这种系统发动机置于汽车的前部,传动装置也在前部。这两种系统都各自存在优缺点,运行时可靠性相差不大。

行驶系统由车轮、轮胎和控制汽车的制动系统、转向系统组成。制动系统用来使车辆减速,必要时使车辆保持静止。转向系统用来实现车辆转向。

汽车的悬架系统包括悬架弹簧、减振器、导向机构、扭力杆、车轴、连接装置。这些部件的作用是支撑车身和车架、发动机、连接装置。没有悬架系统,乘坐的舒适性就会变差。弹簧和扭力杆与车桥相连,常用的两种弹簧是钢板弹簧和螺旋弹簧。扭力杆由长弹簧钢棒制成,一端与车架相连,而另一端与车桥的活动部件相连。随着车轴上下活动,扭力杆被扭转起弹簧作用。减振器的作用是缓冲汽车的上下振动,这种作用在恶劣的行驶条件下就发挥出来。车桥和连接装置是将弹簧、扭力杆、减振器与车架和车轮相连接的那些部件。

4. 电气设备

电气设备主要包括蓄电池、交流发电机、灯光、仪表、电动装置和电子控制系统等。

Lesson 2 Basics of Four-stroke Cycle Engine

The fundamental parts of the conventional engine are shown in simple diagrammatic form in Fig. 2-1 which shows a cross-section through the cylinder, piston and connecting rod of the engine. In the figure, a flywheel is mounted on the end of the crankshaft and the crank is of the double-web type with a bearing on each side of the crank.

1. Cylinder

The ideal form consists of a plain cylindrical barrel in which the piston slides, the movement of the piston or "stroke" being, in some cases, somewhat longer than the bore, but tending to equality or even less. [1] This is known as the stroke:bore ratio.

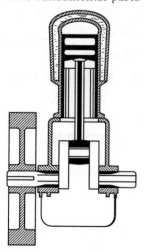

Fig. 2-1
A cross-section of the engine

The upper end consists of a combustion or "clearance" space in which the ignition and combustion of the charge take place. In practice, it is necessary to depart from the ideal hemispherical shape in order to accommodate the valves, sparking plug, etc., and to control the process of combustion.

2. Piston

The usual form of piston for internal combustion engines is an inverted bucket-shape, machined to a close (but free sliding) fit in the cylinder barrel. Gas tightness is secured by means of flexible "piston rings" fitting closely in grooves turned in the upper part of the piston.

The pressure of the gases is transmitted to the upper end of the connecting rod through the "gudgeon pin" on which the "small end" of the connecting rod is free to swing.

3. Connecting Rod

The connecting rod transmits the piston load to the crank, causing the latter to turn, thus converting the reciprocating motion of the piston into a rotary motion of the crankshaft. The lower end, or "big end", of the connecting rod turns on the crank pin.

4. Crankshaft

In the great majority of internal combustion engines this is of the double-web type, the crank pin, webs and shaft being usually formed from a solid forging. The shaft turns in two or more main bearings (depending on the number and arrangement of the cylinders) mounted in the main frame or "crankcase" of the engine.

5. Flywheel

At one end the crankshaft carries a heavy flywheel, the function of which is to absorb the variations in impulse transmitted to the shaft by the gas and inertia loads and to drive the pistons over the dead points and idle strokes. [2] In motor vehicles the flywheel usually forms one member of the clutch through which the power is transmitted to the road wheels.

The foregoing are the fundamental and essential parts by which the power developed by the combustion is caused to give rotation to the crankshaft, the mechanism described being that of the single-acting engine, because a useful impulse is transmitted to the crankshaft while the piston moves in one direction only. [3]

It is now necessary to describe the sequence of operations by which the combustible charge is introduced, ignited, burned and finally discharged after it has completed its work.

There are two important cycles or operations in practical use, namely, the "four-stroke", or "Otto" cycle as it is sometimes called (after the name of the German engineer who first applied it in practice), and the "two-stroke", or "Clerk" cycle, which owed its early development largely to Sir Dugald Clerk. The cycles take their names from the number of single piston strokes which are necessary to complete a single sequence of operations, which is repeated continuously so long as the engine works.

The first named, "four-storke" cycle, is by far the most widely adopted except for small motorcycle and motor boat engines, and for large diesels. Though "four-storke" cycle leads to greater mechanical complication in the engine, it shows higher thermal efficiency, and therefore greater economy in fuel.

Fig. 2-2 shows in a diagrammatic manner a four-stroke engine cylinder provided with two valves of the "mushroom" or "poppet" type. The cylinder is shown horizontal for convenience.

The inlet valve communicates through a throttle valve with the air filter, from which air is drawn. The exhaust valve communicates with the silencer through which the burnt gases are discharged to the atmosphere. These valves are opened and closed at suitable intervals by mechanisms.

The four strokes of the complete cycle are shown at Fig. 2-2a),b),c) and d).

Below the diagrams of the cylinder are shown the corresponding portions of what is known as the indicator diagram, that is to say, a diagram which shows the variation of pressure of the gases in the cylinder throughout the cycle. In practice such diagrams can be automatically recorded when the engine is running by a piece of apparatus known as an indicator, of which there are many types.

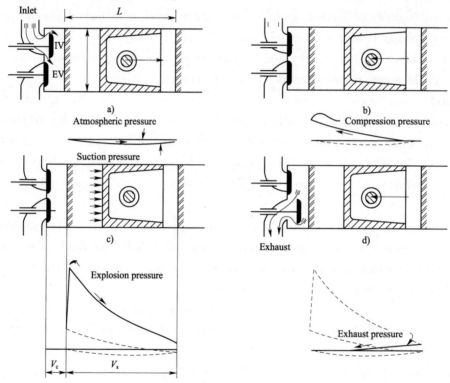

Fig. 2-2 The four storkes of the complete cycle

The four strokes of the cycle are as follows.

(a)Induction stroke—exhaust valve closed, inlet valve open.

The momentum imparted to the flywheel during previous cycles or rotation by hand or by starter motor, causes the connecting rod to draw the piston outwards, setting up a partial vacuum which sucks in a new charge of mixture from the intake manifold. The pressure will be below atmospheric pressure by an amount which depends upon the speed of the engine and the throttle opening.

(b)Compression stroke—both valves closed.

The piston returns, still driven by the momentum of the flywheel, and compresses the charge into the combustion head of the cylinder. The pressure rises to an amount which depends on the "compression ratio", that is, the ratio of the full volume of the cylinder when the piston is at the outer end of its stroke to the volume of the clearance space when the piston is at the inner (or upper) end. [4] In ordinary petrol engines this ratio is usually between 8 and 10 and the pressure at the end of compression is about 0. 8 to 1. 1 MPa, with full throttle opening.

(c)Combustion or working stroke—both valves closed.

Just before the end of the compression stroke, ignition of the charge is effected by means of an electric spark, and a rapid rise of temperature and pressure occurs inside the cylinder. Combustion is completed while the piston is practically at rest, and is followed by the expansion of the hot gases as the piston moves outwards. The pressure of the gases drives the piston forward and turns the crankshaft thus propelling the car against the external resistances and restoring to the flywheel the momentum lost during the idle strokes. The pressure falls as the volume increases.

(d)Exhaust stroke—inlet valve closed; exhaust valve open.

The piston returns, again driven by the momentum of the flywheel, and discharges the spent gases through the exhaust valve. The pressure will be slightly above atmospheric pressure by an amount depending on the resistance to flow offered by the exhaust valve and silencer.

It will thus be seen that there is only one working stroke for every four piston strokes, or every two revolutions of the crankshaft, the remaining three strokes being referred to as idle strokes, though they form an indispensable part of the cycle. This has led engineers to search for a cycle which would reduce the proportion of idle strokes, the various forms of the two-stroke engine being the result. The correspondingly larger number of useful strokes per unit of time increases the power output relative to size of engine, but increases thermal loading.

New Words

inverted [in'və:tid]	adj. 反向的,倒转的
foregoing [fɔː'gəuiŋ]	adj. 前面的,先前的,前述的
fundamental [fʌndə'mentl]	adj. 基本的,根本的
symmetrical [si'metrikəl]	adj. 对称的
stuffing ['stʌfiŋ]	n. 填塞物,填料
accommodate [ə'kɔmədeit]	v. 使适应,调节,和解
groove [gru:v]	n. 凹槽,惯例
inertia [i'nə:ʃjə]	n. 惯性,惰性
thermal ['θə:məl]	adj. 热的,热量的
mushroom ['mʌʃrum]	n. 草,蘑菇
vaporizer ['veipəraizə]	n. 气化器
indicator ['indikeitə]	n. 指示器,指示剂
momentum [məu'mentəm]	n. 动力,动量
idle ['aidl]	adj. 懒惰的,停顿的,(机器)空转的

Phrases and Expressions

gudgeon pin　　　　　　　　　　活塞销
piston ring　　　　　　　　　　活塞环

Notes to the Text

[1] The ideal form consists of a plain cylindrical barrel in which the piston slides, the movement of the piston or "stroke" being, in some cases, somewhat longer than the bore, but tending to equality or even less.

汽缸的理想形状是一个平滑圆柱桶,活塞在里面运动。在某些情况下,活塞的运动行程或冲程会大于汽缸直径,但趋于相等,甚至小于缸径。

[2] At one end the crankshaft carries a heavy flywheel, the function of which is to absorb the variations in impulse transmitted to the shaft by the gas and inertia loads and to drive the pistons over the dead points and idle strokes.

曲轴的一端安装一个很重的飞轮,飞轮的作用是吸收由做功气体和惯性载荷引起的传递给曲轴的各种冲力,并进而驱动活塞越过上下止点和不做功的冲程。

[3] The foregoing are the fundamental and essential parts by which the power developed by the combustion is caused to give rotation to the crankshaft, the mechanism described being that of the single-acting engine, because a useful impulse is transmitted to the crankshaft while the piston moves in one direction only.

前面所描述的都是些基本的、必不可少的部件。燃烧产生的动力通过这些部件传递给曲轴,使其旋转。因为只有当活塞向一个方向运动时,才能将有用的冲力传递给曲轴,这也是单作用式发动机的原理。

[4] The pressure rises to an amount which depends on the "compression ratio", that is, the ratio of the full volume of the cylinder when the piston is at the outer end of its stroke to the volume of the clearance space when the piston is at the inner (or upper) end.

压力升高的程度与压缩比有关。压缩比是指活塞处于下止点时的汽缸容积与活塞处于上止点时的余隙容积之比。

Review Questions

1. Please list the fundamental parts of the conventional engine.
2. What are the main functions of the fundamental parts of the conventional engine?
3. Do you know the cycles or operations in practical use?
4. What are the four strokes of a conventional engine complete cycle?
5. Please talk about the working principle of the four strokes.

参考译文

第二课　四冲程发动机基础

传统发动机的基本组成部分如图 2-1 所示,图 2-1 是从发动机的汽缸、活塞、连杆中间剖开的剖视图。图中，飞轮安装在曲轴的末端，曲柄采用双曲拐方式每侧均由一个轴承支撑。

1. 汽缸

汽缸的理想形状是一个平滑圆柱桶，活塞在里面运动。在某些情况下，活塞的运动行程或冲程会大于汽缸直径，但趋于相等，甚至小于缸径。这就是所谓的行程—缸径比。

汽缸的上部形成燃烧室或余隙容积，可燃混合气的点火及燃烧都在这里进行。在实际应用中，为便于安装气门和火花塞等以及有效控制燃烧进程，燃烧室的形状并非是理想的半球形。

2. 活塞

内燃机常用的活塞形式是倒置的圆桶形，加工后和汽缸形成紧密配合（但可以自由滑动），气体的密封由装于活塞头部环槽中的弹性活塞环来保证。

气体的压力通过活塞销传递给连杆顶端，而连杆的小头可以在活塞销上自由摆动。

3. 连杆

连杆把活塞上的载荷传递给曲轴，使曲轴旋转，结果把活塞往复运动转换为曲轴的旋转运动。连杆底端或大端在曲柄销上旋转。

4. 曲轴

对于绝大部分内燃机而言，曲轴是双辐板形式，通常曲柄销、辐板和轴由实心锻件锻造而成。曲轴在发动机缸体或曲轴箱内的两个或多个主轴承中旋转（由汽缸的数目及布置情况决定）。

5. 飞轮

曲轴的一端安装一个很重的飞轮，飞轮的作用是吸收由做功气体和惯性载荷引起的传递给曲轴的各种冲力，并进而驱动活塞越过上下止点和不做功的冲程。在汽车上，飞轮往往作为离合器的一个部件，发动机的动力通过飞轮传递给车轮。

前面所描述的都是些基本的，必不可少的部件。燃烧产生的动力通过这些部件传递给曲轴，使其旋转。因为只有当活塞向一个方向运动时，才能将一个有用的冲力传递给曲轴，这也是单作用式发动机的原理。

现在有必要描述一下可燃混合气的导入、点燃、燃烧以及工作结束后的排气这一系列工作次序。

在实际的应用中，有两个重要的循环或工作过程，即四冲程循环（有时又被称为奥托循环，它以首次把该循环应用于实际的德国工程师奥托的名字命名的）和二冲程循环（又被称为可勒克循环，它早期的发展很大程度上归功于 Sir Dugald Clerk）。四冲程、二冲程循环得名于一个活塞完成一次工作过程所需要的冲程数目，随着发动机的工作，这种循环不断地重复进行。

首先被提到的四冲程循环应用最广泛，小型的摩托车和汽艇发动机及大型柴油机除外。虽然四冲程循环使发动机机械结构更加复杂，但它显示出了更高的热效率，在燃油消耗方面更为经济。

图2-2以示意图的形式显示了一个四冲程发动机汽缸，该汽缸有两个蘑菇式或者称为菌状式的气门。为了方便起见，汽缸以水平放置显示。

进气门通过发动机节气门和空气滤清器相通，空气和燃油形成的可燃混合气经进气门被吸入汽缸。排气门跟消声器相通，燃烧后的废气自排气门排出，经过消声器，最终排入空气中。进、排气门由气门驱动机构控制,以合适的间隔开闭。

图 2-2a)、b)、c)、d)显示了发动机一个完整工作循环的四个冲程。

图中,汽缸的下面是发动机示功图,它显示了发动机的整个工作循环中,汽缸内气体压力的变化情况。实际上,在发动机工作时,示功图可以利用被称为示功器的专门仪器自动记录下来,示功器有很多类型。

发动机工作循环的四个冲程如下。

(a)进气冲程——排气门关闭,进气门开启。

发动机之前的工作循环、人力或发动机驱动的旋转,使飞轮具有一定的动量,该动量作用在曲轴上,使连杆拉着活塞向汽缸底部运动,汽缸内形成一定的真空度,将进气歧管中形成的混合气吸入汽缸。汽缸内气体压力低于大气压力,大小与发动机转速和节气门开度有关。

(b)压缩冲程——进、排气门均关闭。

在飞轮惯性的继续作用下,把混合气压缩到汽缸顶部的燃烧室。压力升高的程度与压缩比有关。压缩比是指活塞处于下止点时的汽缸容积与活塞处于上止点时的余隙容积之比。通常汽油机的压缩比为 8~10,在节气门全开的情况下,压缩终了的压力为 0.8~1.1MPa。

(c)燃烧或者做功冲程——进、排气门均关闭。

压缩行程即将结束时,汽缸内的可燃混合气被电火花点燃,缸内的温度和压力急剧上升。在活塞几乎没有移动的极短时间内燃烧已经完成,接着高温气体在活塞下移的过程中急剧膨胀。在气体压力的作用下活塞被推向汽缸底部,带动曲轮旋转,使汽车克服行驶时受到的外界阻力。同时,部分能量用来增加飞轮的动量,弥补其他行程中的动量损失。汽缸内的气体压力随着汽缸容积的增加而下降。

(d)排气行程——进气门关闭,排气门开启。

在飞轮惯性的作用下,活塞再次向汽缸顶部运动,将废气从排气门排出。由于排气门和消声器的阻力,排气终了时汽缸内的压力略高于大气压力。

由此可见,在每四个活塞行程或曲轴每旋转两周的过程中,只有一个行程做功,其余三个行程被看作是不做功的无效行程,尽管它们也是工作循环中必不可少的行程。这使得工程师们努力寻找能减少无效行程的工作循环方式,于是诞生了各种各样的二冲程发动机。由于二冲程发动机在单位时间内具有更多的做功行程,相同尺寸下它们的输出功率会更高。与此同时,二冲程发动机也必须承受更大的热负荷。

Lesson 3 Fuel Injection Systems of Gasoline Engine

1. Injection System Types and Layouts

Gasoline direct injection (GDI) into the cylinders is not a impossibility but it suffers, in addition to the high back-pressure, other severe disadvantages. First, because the fuel has to be injected progressively to allow time for it to be atomized and mixed thoroughly with the air before the spark occurs, it has to enter the cylinder against a rising back- pressure. Secondly, in such a short time, complete evaporation and the formation of a homogeneous mixture for maximum power output are very difficult and smoke would be emitted from the exhaust. Thirdly, since the injector nozzles are exposed to the combustion process, carbon build-up is liable to occur. Similar problems arise, though perhaps to a lesser degree with indirect injection into a swirl chamber, but the cylinder head casting would be complicated and, as in the case of the diesel engine, thermal losses higher.

Low pressure injection into the induction system has therefore been adopted virtually universally. At such low pressures, about 3 to 6 bar, as compared with 900 to 1300 bar for diesel engines, dribble is not too difficult to avoid. Moreover, if it does occur, the consequences in terms of carbon deposit formation are not even remotely so severe.

Single-point injection (SPI) into the throttle body, sometimes termed throttle body injection (TBI) or central fuel injection (CFI), is attractive on account of its simplicity, and therefore low cost, as compared with multi-point injection (MPI) into the individual valve ports. [1] All single-point systems, however, have three severe disadvantages: fuel tends to condense on the walls of the induction manifold, subsequently evaporating off in an uncontrolled manner; consequently, it is virtually impossible to obtain accurate distribution of mixture equally to each cylinder; and, thirdly a hot spot must be provided in the throttle body to facilitate evaporation and prevent icing. For these reasons, and in view of the increasing stringency of emissions regulations, single-point injection is, in all probability, obsolescent.

The alternative, multi-point injection, is almost universally employed on all but the smallest, low-cost cars. The fuel is now injected into either each of the induction manifold branch pipes leading to the inlet valves or, more commonly, directly into the ports in the cylinder head. This avoids all the previously mentioned disadvantages of throttle body injection. Accommodation of the injectors complicates manifold castings but, As regards cost, there is little to choose between port and manifold injection. Assembly on to the manifold is in some circumstances easier. Moreover, less heat will be conducted with it than from the cylinder head to the injectors. On the other hand, some heat may be desirable for assisting evaporation.

If the fuel spray is aimed directly at the hot inlet valve, not much will condense in the port. Moreover, there will be less risk of some of the charge being drawn off into an adjacent cylinder by the negative pressure pulse generated by the opening of its inlet valve. Aiming the spray at the inlet valve, Fig. 3-1 is relatively easy with port injection. Even with manifold injection it is not impossible, provided the injector nozzle can be accurately aligned in the manifold and the latter similarly aligned relative to the induction port. Incidentally, if fuel is to be injected on to the valves, care has to be taken to ensure that the material selected for the valves is corrosion resistant.

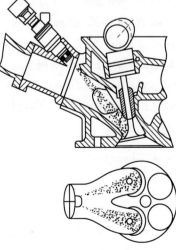

Fig. 3-1 Spray at the inlet valve

2. Injection Strategies

The simplest, and therefore potentially the least costly, of all the strategies is continuous injection. This is applicable to both single- and multi-point systems. In either case, a cloud of mixture is formed in the manifold, ready to be drawn into each cylinder when its inlet valve opens. With port injection, swirl and turbulence in the cylinder play a major role in the production of a homogeneous ignitable mixture.

With continuous flow, the air: fuel ratio can be controlled by varying the pressure of the fuel delivered to the injectors, as in the Bosch K-Jetronic and KE-Jetronic systems. Where overall electronic control is required, for example with the Bosch L-Jetronic, it is difficult to avoid an undue time lag between receipt of the signals from the control and effecting the required changes in air: fuel ratio. Therefore the fuel is maintained at constant pressure but the duration of delivery varied.

An alternative to continuous injection is timed injection, in which injection takes place over a limited period usually, though not always, once per revolution of the crankshaft. The timing of the opening of the solenoid-actuated valve in the injector is generally fixed, and control over the duration of delivery exercised by varying the timing of its closing. An example is the Bosch L-Jetronic system.

A later development was termed sequential injection, or phased injection, which, with electronic control, enables the air: fuel ratio to be regulated extremely accurately. It entails the injection of fuel into the individual ports as the relevant inlet valve opens, and therefore once every two revolutions of the crankshaft. This considerably reduces the risk of some of the mixture being drawn off into an adjacent cylinder, but is more costly than timed injection.

An advantage of both timed and phased injection is the ease with which they can be used in conjunction with electronic ignition control to avoid detonation. Either a single detonation sensor can be mounted on the cylinder head or block or there can be one for each cylinder, or pair of cylinders.[2] The sensors are generally mounted on the head. Signals from them and, of course, a crankshaft angle sensor is the basis on which the central processing unit (CPU) modifies either the ignition timing or the fuelling, or both, to stop the detonation. If more than one detonation sensor is installed, corrections can be made directly to the fuelling of individual cylinders or pairs of cylinders. Clearly, applying corrections to individual cylinders offers optimum performance as regards both fuel consumption and emissions.

New Words

atomise ['ætəmaiz] (=atomize)	vt. 使化为原子,使雾化,使粉化
evaporate [i'væpəreit]	vt. 使蒸发；通过升华使(金属等)沉淀
homogeneous [ˌhməu'di:njəs]	adj. 同种的,同类的；相似的,纯一的,均质的
combustion [kəm'bstən]	n. 燃烧(有机体内营养料的)氧化
swirl [swə:l]	n. (水、风等的)旋转；旋涡

liable [ˈlaiəbl]		adj. 有（法律）责任的,应受（罚）的；应付（税）的；应服从的
casting [ˈkɑːstiŋ]		n. 投掷；钓鱼；投掷的技巧或动作,铸造品,铸件；铸型法
dribble [ˈdribl]		vt. 使点滴流下；使淌（口水）；使逐渐落下
deposit [diˈpzit]		vt. 放下,寄存,存放储蓄,贮存,沉淀,淤积
obsolescent [ˌɔbsəˈlɛsənt]		adj. 逐渐被废弃的；废退的；萎缩的
butterfly [ˈbʌtəflai]		n. 蝴蝶；蝶式,蝶形
accommodate [əˈkmədeit]		vt. 给方便,使适应,供给……住宿,照应,招待
spray [sprei]		n. 喷雾,飞沫
		vt. 喷射,喷溅
corrosion [kəˈrəuən]		n. 腐蚀,侵蚀；(铁)锈蚀；【植】溶蚀
simultaneously [ˌsaiməlˈteiniəsli]		ad. 同时地
instantaneous [ˌinstənˈteinjəs]		adj. 即刻的,瞬间的；立刻做成的,立即发生的
phased [feizd]		adj. 定相的
consumption [kənˈsʌmpən]		n. 消费（量）；消尽；消耗
obviate [ˈbvieit]		vt. 消除；排除（障碍、危险等）；预防,避免

Phrases and Expressions

induction system	进气系统
throttle body injection	节气门体燃油喷射
butterfly valve	蝶形阀
branch pipe	歧管
sequential injection	顺序燃油喷射
timed injection	定时喷射
solenoid-actuated value	电磁阀
volumetric efficiency	容积效率,充气效率

Notes to the Text

[1] Single-point injection (SPI) into the throttle body, sometimes termed throttle body injection (TBI) or central fuel injection (CFI), is attractive on account of its simplicity, and therefore low cost, as compared with multi-point injection (MPI) into the individual valve ports.

喷入节气门体的单点喷射（SPI）,有时还被称为节气门体燃油喷射系统（TBI）或中央单点燃油喷射系统（CFI）,与多个燃油喷射器把燃料喷入进气门口的多点喷射（MPI）相比,单点喷射具有构造简单、成本低廉的优点。

[2] Either a single detonation sensor can be mounted on the cylinder head or block or there can be one for each cylinder, or pair of cylinders.

爆震传感器安装在汽缸盖或汽缸体上,可以只装一个,也可以每个汽缸一个,或每两个汽缸一个。

Review Questions

1. What are the main disadvantages of the gasoline direct injection?
2. What are the main differences between SPI and MPI?
3. Why do the manufacturer have the fuel to be directly injected at the hot inlet valve?
4. Please list the common injection strategies on gasoline engines.
5. Please state the advantages a sequential injection.

参考译文

第三课 汽油发动机燃油喷射系统

1. 喷射系统的类型和布局

汽油直接喷射(GDI)进汽缸不是不可能的事情,但是除了承受高背压外,它还受到其他恶劣条件的不利影响。第一,因为燃料必须被逐渐增多地喷射,并在火花产生之前的规定时间内雾化且完全与空气混合,它必须克服正在升高的背压进入汽缸。第二,在如此短的时间里面,燃料完全蒸发并形成与最大输出功率相匹配的均质混合气实际上是非常困难的,且会造成冒烟。第三,因为喷油器被暴露在燃烧过程中以来,易于形成积炭。类似的问题也随之产生。虽然在间接喷射进入涡流燃烧室的情况下程度会减轻,但是汽缸盖铸造将会复杂得多,这种情况与柴油机一样,会使热量损失增加。

低压喷入进气系统已经被广泛应用到实际当中。与柴油发动机90～130MPa的压力相比,0.3～0.6MPa这样的低气压下,滴漏不难避免。而且如果确实发生滴漏,积炭形成也不会很严重。

喷入节气门体的单点喷射(SPI),有时还被称为节气门体燃油喷射系统(TBI)或中央单点燃油喷射系统(CFI),与多个燃油喷射器把燃料喷入进气门口的多点喷射(MPI)相比,单点喷射具有构造简单、成本低廉的优点。然而,所有的单点喷射系统都有三个严重的缺点:首先,燃油容易凝结在进气歧管的管壁上,在不可控制的情况下蒸发;其次,混合气根本不可能精确地平均分配到每一个汽缸;第三,节气门体必须加热,以促进蒸发防止结冰。因为上述原因,鉴于日趋严格的排放法规,单点喷射趋于淘汰。

单点喷射的替代品,多点喷射系统已经被普遍应用到除极小排量、低价位车辆外的其他车辆上,现在燃料有的被喷入通向进气门的每一个进气歧管,大多数是直接喷到汽缸盖上的进气口处,这样避免了上述节气门喷射的缺点。但是,喷油器的安装,使进气管铸造结构变得复杂。关于成本,进气口喷射和进气管喷射之间无多大差别。有时安装在进气歧管上更容易些。而且,安装在进气歧管上的喷油器受的热量比装在缸盖进气口处的喷油器少。另一方面,适量的热量有助于燃油蒸发。

如果燃料被直接喷射到高温的进气门,就不会在进气口上凝结太多。而且,这样会减少混合气被毗邻汽缸因进气门开启形成真空而吸入的可能性。在进气门处喷射燃油,如图3-1所示,通过进气口喷射相对更容易一些。尽管进气歧管喷射也不是不可能,但需要让喷油器在进气歧管上精确地排列,且进气歧管排成一行,紧靠进气门。如果燃油喷射到进气门上,需注意确保气门材料具有抗腐蚀性。

2. 喷射策略

喷射策略中最简单，成本最低的是连续喷射，其既适用于单点喷射也适用于多点喷射。不论是单点连续喷射还是多点连续喷射，大量混合气预先在进气歧管形成，准备在进气门开启时进入汽缸。对于进气口喷射，涡流和湍流在形成可燃混合气的过程中起到主要的作用。

随着燃油的不停流动，空燃比可以通过改变喷油器的燃油压力进行控制，就如在 Bosch-Jetronic 和 KE-Jetronic 系统中一样。而采用全面电子控制的系统，例如 Bosch L-Jetrornic 系统，很难避免从接收控制系统信号后到实现空燃比调节有不确定的时间间隔。因此，燃油被维持在恒压状态，通过改变喷油持续时间进行空燃比控制。

连续喷射的替代方式是定时喷射。通常曲轴转一圈喷射一次，但也不是一直如此。一般情况下，喷油器电磁阀的开启时刻是固定不变的，通过改变电磁阀的关闭时刻控制供油时间长短。Bosch L-Jetronic 系统就是其中一例。

随后开发出的顺序喷射系统或者称为定相喷射系统，通过电子控制使空燃比能够精确地调整。曲轴每转两圈喷油一次，当某缸进气门开启时，燃料喷入相应的进气门，大大降低了混合气进入相邻汽缸的风险，但比定时喷射成本高。

定时喷射和顺序喷射的共同优点是易于和电子点火系统结合，避免爆燃发生。爆震传感器安装在汽缸盖或汽缸体上，可以只装一个，也可以每个汽缸一个，或每两个汽缸一个。爆震传感器通常安装在汽缸盖上。爆震传感器和曲轴位置传感器的信号是 CPU 用来修正点火时间或燃油喷射量，或者同时修正两者的基础从而阻止爆燃。如果安装多个爆震传感器，可能单独修正每个汽缸或者每两个汽缸的燃油喷射量。显然，单独修正每个汽缸可以使燃油经济性和排放达到最佳。

Lesson 4 Variable Valve Timing

Since 1880, almost 800 patents on variable valve timing have been issued in the USA alone. In general, they can be further categorized under two main heading: variable phase control (VPC), combined valve life and timing control (VLTC) systems.

Variable valve timing is generally applied in one of two ways: either the point of inlet valve closure is fixed and that of its opening varied, or both are fixed relative to each other but their timing (i.e., the inlet phase) advanced or retarded simultaneously, generally by rotating the cam relative to the shaft. The latter, termed phase change has two advantages: first, the dynamic loading of the valve gear is unchanged, and secondly, the mechanisms for varying the timing are generally considerably less complex.

1. Advantages of VVT

Because of the increasing stringency of legislation regarding emissions, including CO_2, interest in variable valve timing was intensifying by the early 1990s. By optimizing the valve timing, volumetric efficiency and therefore power and torque can be increased. During low speed operation, the valve overlap period can be reduced to increase the effective expansion ratio, improve idling stability and cold starting, and especially for naturally aspirated diesel engines, reduce emissions throughout the low-speed light load range.[1] For turbocharged engines, in particular, VVT can be utilized for recirculation of the exhaust gas. Because exhaust gas contains water vapor, sculpture and other corrosive media, the currently available EGR valves are not as reliable as might be desired. [2]

With fixed valve timing, designers mostly aim at high nominal output, with the result that because the inlet valve is still open after BDC in Fig. 4-1. Torque at the lower end of the speed range is impaired owing to back flow over a significant proportion of the operating range. By optimizing inlet valve closure over the whole range, improvements in full load torque of over 12% and in maximum torque of about 4% can be obtained.

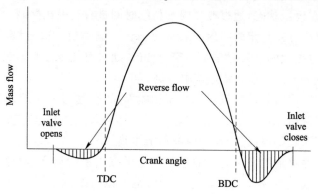

Fig. 4-1 The diagram of mass flow of air plotted against crank angle

If the inlet valve is closed very early, the flow fully into the combustion chamber occurs only when the piston speed is low. This adversely affects both the flow pattern and turbulence within the chamber, and subsequent expansion further slows both swirl and mixing. As the piston moves down to BDC, expansion can cool the gases to as low as $-15°C$, the total drop being perhaps as much as 50°C. [3] This causes re-condensation, which continues into the early part of the compression stroke. The condensation increases with decreasing load but, as the speed falls, there is more time for heat transfer from the walls of the combustion chamber, which tends at least partly to offset the increase.

With late closure, part of the charge tends to be returned into the induction manifold as the piston passes BDC. In these circumstances, the gas exchange occurs at approximately constant pressure. Consequently, only the proportion of charge trapped in the cylinder after inlet valve closure is compressed. As the throttle is opened, wherefore, closure should be progressively brought forward to the standard timing for the engine.

If the inlet valve closure is too late, the quality of combustion can be inferior. In this respect, multi point fuel injection as at a disadvantage relative to single point or carburetion unless the volumes of the primary induction pipes (branch pipes) are large enough to contain the return flow into the manifold so that there is no possibility of their being robbed, by an adjacent induction pipe, of some of the mixture they contain. [4] At light load, any maldistribution of fuel is aggravated because back-flow into the plenum can remove during some strokes most of the fuel that has been injected and in others virtually none, so running becomes unstable.

2. Some VVT Mechanisms

Variable phase control (VPC) can be affected in a number of ways. One is to advance and retard the camshaft by means of a sliding muff coupling on a divided shaft, with spiral spines on the driven and straight spines on the drive interfaces, or vice versa. This, however, suffers the disadvantage of high frictional resistance to control operation. [5] Another method is to install, in the belt or chain drive to the camshaft, a movable idler pulley in combination with a tensioned having a longer than usual stroke. Movement of the idler pulley towards or away from the drive, Fig. 4-2, rolls it around the half—speed wheel to advance or retard the timing while, at the same time, the tensioned compensates for the movement. In general, this appears to be the most practicable and least costly variable valve timing system.

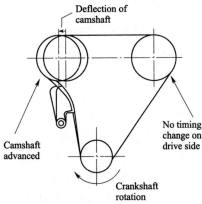

Fig. 4-2 The camshaft can be deflected horizontally

Variable phase control, Fig. 4-3, implies varying the overlap so that low-speed torque and, with it, specific fuel consumption are improved over most of the speed range. Since the duration of opening remains constant, wide-open throttle power is unaffected.

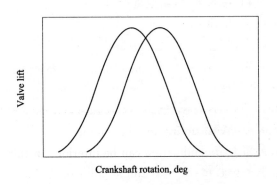
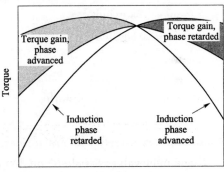

Fig. 4-3 With the variable phase control system (VPC), the inlet opening point can be retarded

A combination of lift and timing control (VLTC), Fig. 4-4, can offer further performance enhancement, but is more costly than VPC. One way of combining these two is to have axially stepped cams, the variation being effected by shifting the followers from step to step, but such a mechanism is complex. Tapered cams, such as the Fiat Tattoo system combining variable lift and event timing, are an alternative but this means virtually point contact, between cam and follower and, if the duration of opening is kept constant, the cam is extremely difficult to manufacture. Moreover, the axial loading introduced is about

10% of the force between the cam and follower, so a powerful controller is needed.

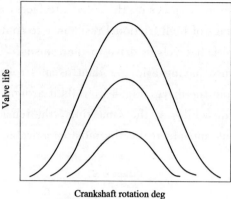

Fig. 4-4 Stepped cams provide variable lift and timing

New Words

categories [ˈkætigəraiz]	v. 加以类别，分类
simultaneous [ˌsiməlˈteinjəs]	adj. 同时发生的
inevitably [inˈevitəbli]	ad. 不可避免地
investigate [inˈvestigeit]	v. 调查，研究
stringency [ˈstrindʒənsi]	n. 迫切，银根紧
volumetric [vɔljuˈmetrik]	adj. 测定体积的
corrosive [kəˈrəusiv]	adj. 腐蚀的，腐蚀性的，蚀坏的
	n. 腐蚀物
atmospheric [ˌætməsˈferik]	adj. 大气的
scavenge [ˈskævindʒ]	v. 打扫，排除废气，到处觅食
associate [əˈsəuʃieit]	n. 同伴，伙伴
	v. 联合，联想
	adj. 副的
intermittently [intəˈmitəntli]	ad. 间歇地
subsequent [ˈsʌbsikwənt]	adj. 随后的，后来的
circumstance [ˈsəːkəmstəns]	n. 环境，状况，事件
maldistribution [ˌmældistriˈbjuːʃən]	n. 分布不均
aggravate [ˈægrəveit]	v. 使……恶化，使……更严重
gradient [ˈgreidiənt]	n. 倾斜度，坡度，升降率
	adj. 倾斜的，步行的
elimination [iˌlimiˈneiʃən]	n. 除去，消除
axially [ˈæksiəli]	ad. 轴向地
magnitude [ˈmægnitjuːd]	n. 大小，重要，光度，(地震)级数

Phrases and Expressions

VPC	可变相位控制

VLTC	气门升程和气门相位控制
valve gear	气门机构
dynamic loading	动载荷
multi point fuel injection	多点燃油喷射
volumetric power output	单位排量输出功率
expansion ratio	膨胀比
naturally aspirated diesel engines	自然进气(非增压)发动机
turbocharged engines	涡轮增压发动机
recycle of the exhaust gas	废气再循环
vice versa	反之亦然
nominal output	额定(标称)输出
induction manifold	进气歧管
tapered cam	锥形凸轮
rocker-actuated	摇臂驱动

Notes to the Text

[1] During low speed operation, the valve overlap period can be reduced to increase the effective expansion ratio, improve idling stability and cold starting and, especially for naturally aspirated diesel engines, reduce emissions throughout the low-speed light load range.

在发动机低速运转时,通过减小气门重叠角可以提高发动机有效膨胀率、怠速稳定性以及冷启动性能,尤其是对非增压式柴油机,在整个低速轻载工况内,可以减少尾气排放。

[2] Because exhaust gas contains water vapor, sculpture and other corrosive media, the currently available EGR valves are not so reliable as might be desired.

因为废气中含有水蒸气、硫化物和其他腐蚀性物质,使得目前采用的 EGR 阀不像所期望的那么可靠。

[3] As the piston moves down to BDC, expansion can cool the gases to as low as $-15℃$, the total drop being perhaps as much as $50℃$.

随着活塞向下止点运动,气体膨胀,会使混合气的温度下降 $50℃$,达到 $-15℃$ 的低温。

[4] In this respect, multi point fuel injection as at a disadvantage relative to single point or carburetion unless the volumes of the primary induction pipes (branch pipes) are large enough to contain the return flow into the manifold so that there is no possibility of their being robbed, by an adjacent induction pipe, of some of the mixture they contain.

就这种情况而言,多点喷射相对于单点喷射和化油器来说有不足,除非各进气歧管的容积足够大,能够防止混合气流回到总进气管中,使相邻进气歧管之间没有抢气现象发生。

[5] One is to advance and retard the camshaft by means of a sliding muff coupling on a divided shaft, with spiral spines on the driven and straight spines on the drive interfaces, or vice versa. This, however, suffers the disadvantage of high frictional resistance to control operation.

一种是在从动轴和主动轴的内表面上分别装配上螺旋键和普通键,在分离轴上连接滑动套管,通过移动套管提前或延迟配气相位。然而这种方式具有控制操作摩擦阻力大的缺点。

Review Questions

1. Do you know the two ways in which variable valve timing is generally applied?
2. What are the main advantages of the termed phase change?
3. Please briefly describe the advantages of the VVT.
4. What does variable phase control imply?
5. What is the common way to have lift and timing both controlled?

参考译文

第四课 可变气门正时

1880年以后,仅在美国就有约800项关于可变气门正时的专利被申请。总体来说,这些专利可进一步被分为两大类:可变相位控制(VPC)、气门升程和气门相位控制(VLTC)。

可变气门正时的应用通常分两种情况:一种是进气门关闭时刻固定不变,而开启时刻可变;另一种是气门开启持续角相对固定,而气门配气正时相对提前或者延迟(也就是进气相位),一般是通过凸轮相对于轴旋转一定的角度来实现。后者被称为"可变相位",有两点优势:首先,气门传动机构上的动载荷是不变的;其次,这种可变正时装置普遍不太复杂。

1. 可变气门正时的优点

面对日益严格的排放法规,其中包括CO_2,早在1990年,人们就加强了对可变气门正时技术的研究。最佳的配气正时,可以提高发动机的充气效率,进而增大功率和扭矩。在发动机低速运转时,通过减小气门重叠角可以提高发动机有效膨胀率、怠速稳定性以及冷启动性能,尤其是对非增压式柴油机,在整个低速轻载工况内,可以减少尾气排放。对于涡轮增压发动机来说,可变气门正时可以被用于废气再循环系统。因为废气中含有水蒸气、硫化物和其他腐蚀性物质,使得目前采用的EGR阀不像所期望的那么可靠。

对于固定配气正时来说,设计者通常旨在实现高标定功率,这里因为进气门在活塞通过下止点以后依然开着,如图4-1所示。在较低转速时有相当部分的可燃混合气倒流回进气管,使得扭矩减小。在整个工作范围内,通过选择最佳的进气门关闭时刻,可将全负荷时的扭矩提高12%,最大扭矩提高4%。

如果进气门关闭太早,只有在发动机低速时气流才会充分进入燃烧室,这对燃烧室内的气流类型和涡流的形成将会带来不利的影响。随后的膨胀进一步削弱了涡流和混合气的形成。随着活塞向下止点运动,气体膨胀,会使混合气的温度下降50℃,达到-15℃的低温。这将导致汽油的冷凝,这种现象一直持续到压缩冲程的早期。冷凝现象随着负荷的减小更加严重,但是当速度下降时,有更多的时间通过燃烧室壁进行热交换,这种现象至少可以部分抵消。

随着气门关闭时刻的推迟,当活塞经过下止点后,部分混合气有回流到进气歧管的趋势。在这种情况下,气体交换在一个接近恒定的压力下进行。这必然导致只有一定比例的新鲜气体在进气门关闭后留在汽缸内被压缩。因此,随着节气门被打开,进气门关闭时刻应逐渐靠近发动机的标准正时。

如果进气门的关闭时刻过晚,燃烧质量将会下降。就这种情况而言,多点喷射相对于单点喷射和化油器来说有不足，除非各进气歧管的容积足够大，能够防止混合气流回到总进气管中，使相邻进气歧管之间没有抢气现象发生。在小负荷时，有些喷油器喷射的燃油大部分被回流到总进气管，而另一些喷油器喷射的燃油几乎没有被回流到总进气管，这使得燃油的不均匀性加剧，发动机的运转也变得不平稳。

2. 几种可变配气正时装置

可变相位控制受多种方式影响。一种是在从动轴和主动轴的内表面上分别装配上螺旋键和普通键，在分离轴上连接滑动套管，通过移动套管提前或延迟配气相位。然而这种方式具有控制操作摩擦阻力大的缺点。另一种是在皮带或链传动中安装一个可动的惰轮和一个比一般张紧器行程大的张紧器。如图4-2所示，惰轮接近或远离传动带（或传动链）的运动使它沿半速轮滚动，以提前或延迟正时时刻，同时张紧器也在运动。一般来说，这种方式是可变正时系统中最实用，也是最便宜的。

如图4-3所示，可变相位控制（VPC）显示了多种气门重叠角，使低速扭矩和大部分转速范围内的燃油经济性得到改善。由于气门持续开启角度保持不变，大负荷时功率将不受影响。

如图4-4所示，气门升程和配气正时的联合控制可以进一步提高发动机的性能，但是这将比单纯的可变相位控制成本高。实现气门升程和配气正时同时控制的一种方式是，采用可以轴向移动的凸轮，通过推杆使凸轮一步一步轴向移动，实现气门升程和配气正时的调节。但是这种装置很复杂。像采用锥形凸轮实现可变升程和配气正时同时控制的菲亚特 Tattoo 系统可作为替代方法，但是这意味着凸轮和推杆之间实际上是点接触，如果气门的开启持续角保持恒定，那么凸轮制造非常困难。而且，轴向荷载大约是凸轮和推杆之间作用力的10%，因此要求控制器动力强劲。

Lesson 5   Transmission

1. Transmission Requirements

In passing down the drive live, the torque of the engine is modified, stage by stage, until it becomes the propulsive force, or tractive effort, at the interface between the tyres and the road. If rapid acceleration is required, either when starting from rest or in any other circumstances, for overtaking, for example that tractive effort must be increased. This is done partly by increasing the torque output of the engine but, since this alone may not be enough, the gear ratios will generally have to be changed too.

Another requirement for the transmission stems from the fact that, when the vehicle is cornering, the outer wheels must roll faster than the inner ones which will be traversing circles of smaller radii, yet their mean speed, and therefore both the rotational speed of the engine and the translational speed of the vehicle, may be required to remain constant.[1]

Then again, to reduce the transmission of vibrations to the chassis frame, the engine is universally mounted on it, while the driving wheels, attached to the frame by the road springs, also have a degree of freedom of movement relative to it.[2] Both these movements must be accommodated by the transmission.

In summary, therefore, the requirements for the transmission are as follows.

(1) To provide for disconnecting the engine from the driving wheels.

(2) When the engine is running, to enable the connection to the driving wheels to be made smoothly and without shock.

(3) To enable the leverage between the engine and driving wheels to be varied.

(4) It must reduce the driveline speed from that of the engine to that of the driving wheels in a ratio of somewhere between about 3 : 1 and 10 : 1 or more, according to the relative size of engine and weight of vehicle.

(5) Turn the drive, if necessary, through 90° or perhaps otherwise realign it.

(6) Enable the driving wheels to rotate at different speeds.

(7) Provide for relative movement between the engine and driving wheels.

There are several ways in which these requirements can be met, and transmissions fall into three categories:

(1) Mechanical;

(2) Hydraulic(hydrostatic, hydrodynamic);

(3) Electric and electromagnetic.

While the first of these is the commonest, combined mechanical and hydrodynamic transmissions are becoming increasingly popular, even on certain types of heavy commercial vehicle.

2. Transmission Arrangement

While the basic principles of transmission remain the same for virtually all classes of road vehicle, the actual arrangements vary-for instance, some may have four-wheel drive and others either front- or rear-wheel drive. Where the engine is installed at the front and the axis of its crankshaft is parallel to, or coincident with, the longitudinal axis of the vehicle, ultimately, the drive must be turned through 90° in order that it may be transmitted out to the wheels the axes of which are of course perpendicular to that longitudinal axis. [3] Such a turn, however, is not necessary if the engine is installed transversely, though other complications, such as a need for dropping the driveline to a level below that of the crankshaft while turning it through 180°, may arise. [4]

This general arrangement of mechanical transmission is shown diagrammatically in Fig. 5-1. The engine is at the front, with its crankshaft parallel to the axis of the vehicle. From the engine, the drive is transmitted through a clutch and a short shaft to the gearbox. In cars, this short shaft is almost invariably integral with the primary gear in the gearbox but, in some commercial vehicles, it is a separate component, generally with flexible or universal joints at each end and, in some instances, with a sliding joint at one end. [5] From the gearbox, a propeller shaft or cardan shaft also with a sliding joint at one end and a universal joint at both ends takes the drive to a live back axle. A live axle is one through which the drive is transmitted, while a dead axle is one that does not transmit the drive. Bevel or worm gearing within the axle turns the drive through 90°, and differential gears divide it equally between the two drive shafts, or halfshafts, which take it out to the wheels.

The functions of the components are as follows.

A clutch is used for disconnecting the engine from the driving wheels and it must also enable the driver to connect the engine, when it is running, without shock to the driving wheels. Since the clutch is kept in engagement by a spring-loading mechanism and is disengaged by pressure of the foot on a pedal, it cannot be disengaged except when the driver is in the vehicle. Therefore, when the driver wants to leave the vehicle with the engine running and preferably for starting the engine, too he has to disconnect the engine from the driving wheels by use of the gear-shift lever, which he sets in a neutral, or gears-disengaged, position.[6]

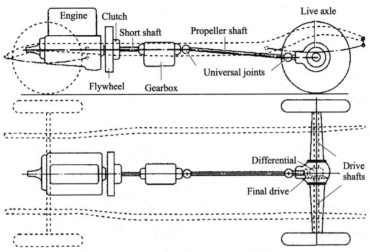

Fig. 5-1 General arrangement

The principal function of the gearbox is to enable the driver to change the leverage between the engine and driving wheels to suit the prevailing conditions gradient, load, speed required, etc.

As the propeller shaft transmits the drive on to the back axle, the universal joints at its ends allow both the engine-and-gearbox assembly and the back axle to move relative to one another, as their spring elements deflect. The sliding joint, usually integral with one of the universal joints, accommodates variations in length of the propeller shaft as its rear end rises and falls vertically with the back axle and its front end pivots about the universal joint just behind the gearbox.

Final drive turns the drive through 90° and reduces the speed in a ratio of about 4 : 1, since the driving wheels must rotate much more slowly than the engine. Within the final drive unit too is the differential gearing, which shares the driving torque equally between the two road wheels while allowing them, nevertheless, to rotate simultaneously at different speeds while the vehicle is cornering.

New Words

provision [prə'vɪʒ(ə)n]　　　　　n. 供给[应];准(预、防)备,(预防)措施;设备,装置,构造

propulsion [prə'pʌlʃən]　　　　 n. 推进(力);推进器

leverage [ˈlev(ə)rɪdʒ]		n. 杠杆作用；杠杆机构；杠杆(效)率，杠杆臂长比；扭转力矩
longitudinal [ˌlandʒɪˈtud(ə)nəl]		adj. 经度的，经线的；纵的，长度的
perpendicular [ˌpɜrpənˈdɪkjələr]		adj. (与另一线或面)成直角的，垂直的，正交的(to)；直立的
vibration [vaɪˈbreɪʃ(ə)n]		n. 震(颤、振)动；摆动；振荡；(思想情绪的)激动；摇摆；犹豫
hydrostatic [ˌhaɪdrəˈstætɪk]		adj. 流体静力学的；流体静压力的
hydrodynamic [ˌhaɪdroʊdaɪˈnæmɪk]		adj. 水力的；水压的，液力的；流体动力学的
electromagnetic [ɪˌlektroʊmægˈnetɪk]		adj. 电磁的；电磁学的
engagement [ɪnˈgeɪdʒmənt]		n. 接合，咬合
prevailing [prɪˈveɪlɪŋ]		adj. 流行的；通行的，普遍的；占优势的；主要的；有力的
gradient [ˈgreɪdiənt]		adj. 倾斜的 n. 梯度，倾斜度，坡度
vertical [ˈvɜrtɪk(ə)l]		adj. 垂直的，直立的，顶点的，[解]头顶的 n. 垂直线，垂直面，竖向
neatness		n. 整洁，干净
accessibility [əkˌsesəˈbɪləti]		n. 易接近，可到达的
obviate [ˈɑbviˌeɪt]		vt. 消除，排除(危险、障碍等)，回避，预防，避免
whirl [hwɜrl]		v. (使)旋转，急动，急走 n. 旋转，一连串快速的活动
epicyclic [ˌepɪˈsaɪklɪk]		adj. [数]周转圆的，[天]本轮的

Phrases and Expressions

cardan shaft	万向轴，(汽车的)中间轴，推进轴
live axle	活络轴；有效轴；主动轴，传动轴
fluid coupling	液力耦合器

Notes to the Text

[1] Another requirement for the transmission stems from the fact that, when the vehicle is cornering, the outer wheels must roll faster than the inner ones which will be traversing circles of smaller radii, yet their mean speed, and therefore both the rotational speed of the engine and the translational speed of the vehicle, may be required to remain constant.

传动系统的另一功用源自一个实际的问题。当汽车转弯时，外侧车轮旋转速度比内侧车轮快，内侧车轮划过一个半径较小的圆弧，而内外车轮的平均速度、发动机转速及汽车运行速度要求基本恒定。

[2] Then again, to reduce the transmission of vibrations to the chassis frame, the engine is universally mounted on it, while the driving wheels, attached to the frame by the road

springs, also have a degree of freedom of movement relative to it.

再者,为了减少振动向车架的传播,发动机普遍被固定在车架上,驱动轮通过弹性元件与车架连接,并且能相对车架做一定的运动。

[3]Where the engine is installed at the front and the axis of its crankshaft is parallel to, or coincident with, the longitudinal axis of the vehicle, ultimately, the drive must be turned through 90° in order that it may be transmitted out to the wheels the axes of which are of course perpendicular to that longitudinal axis.

对于发动机前置,曲轴轴线与汽车纵向轴线平行或重合,而车轮旋转轴线与汽车纵向轴线垂直,为了最终将动力传输到车轮,必须将传动方向转90°。

[4]Such a turn, however, is not necessary if the engine is installed transversely, though other complications, such as a need for dropping the driveline to a level below that of the crankshaft while turning it through 180°, may arise.

若发动机横置,虽然可能出现别的复杂问题,如需将传动部分布置在曲轴下面、方向转180°,但是避免了上述传动方向改变90°的问题。

[5]In cars, this short shaft is almost invariably integral with the primary gear in the gear-box but, in some commercial vehicles, it is a separate component, generally with flexible or universal joints at each end and, in some instances, with a sliding joint at one end.

在乘用车上,短轴几乎总是与变速器的输入齿轮为一体;但在一些商用车上,它是一个独立部件,两端都有万向节,有时一端还有滑动接头。

[6]Therefore, when the driver wants to leave the vehicle with the engine running and preferably for starting the engine, too he has to disconnect the engine from the driving wheels by use of the gear-shift lever, which he sets in a neutral, or gears-disengaged, position.

所以,驾驶员想离开车辆又要保持发动机运转时,或更好地起动发动机时,他必须应用换挡机构,将变速杆置于"空档"或齿轮分离位置,以断开发动机和驱动轮之间的动力传递。

Review Questions

1. What are the main functions of the transmission?
2. According to the functions of the transmission, what are the requirements for the transmission?
3. Please list the main categories of the transmission.
4. What is the general arrangement of mechanical transmission?
5. What are the main components that make up an automatic transmission?

参考译文

第五课 传动系统

1. 对传动系统的要求

在输出动力时,发动机转矩经过一步步调整,最后在轮胎和地面的接触面间形成推动力或牵引力使用。如果要求汽车迅速加速,如汽车原地起步或其他工况(例如过载),则牵引力必须随之增加。靠增加发动机的输出转矩能部分实现这一目标,但仅靠这一方法可能是不够的,通常还需改变传动比。

传动系统的另一功用源自一个实际的问题。当汽车转弯时,外侧车轮旋转速度比内侧车轮快,内侧车轮划过一个半径较小的圆弧,而内外车轮的平均速度、发动机转速及汽车运行速度要求基本恒定。

再者,为了减少振动向车架的传播,发动机普遍被固定在车架上,驱动轮通过弹性元件与车架连接,并且能相对车架做一定的运动。这些运动要求都需要传动系统来实现。

总之,对传动系统的要求如下:
(1)能切断发动机与驱动轮间的动力传输;
(2)当发动机运转时,保证其与驱动轮平顺接合,没有冲击;
(3)确保发动机与驱动轮间转矩可以变化;
(4)可根据发动机的规格和汽车质量,调节传动系传动比,使其能在3∶1和10∶1或更大传动比之间变化,从而降低发动机与驱动轮间的传动速度;
(5)根据需要,改变转矩的传递方向,使其转过90°或重新调整;
(6)保证左右车轮能以不同转速旋转;
(7)能够保证驱动轮相对于发动机的运动。

能够满足以上要求的传动方案较多,分为以下三种类型:
(1)机械式传动系统;
(2)液力式传动系统(静液式传动系统,动液式传动系统);
(3)电力式或电磁式传动系统。

第一种方案最普遍,但综合运用液力式传动和机械式传动的传动系统越来越流行,甚至已经在一些重型商用车上应用。

2. 传动系统的布置

各种类型的道路车辆,其传动系统的基本原理是相同的,只是实际布置不同,比如有些汽车是四轮驱动而有些汽车是前轮或后轮驱动。对于发动机前置,曲轴轴线与汽车纵向轴线平行或重合,而车轮旋转轴线与汽车纵向轴线垂直,为了最终将动力传输到车轮,必须将传动方向转90°。若发动机横置,虽然可能出现别的复杂问题,如需要将传动部分布置在曲轴下面、方向转180°,但是避免了上述传动方向改变90°的问题。

最常用的机械式传动系统布置方案如图5-1所示。发动机前置,曲轴轴线与汽车纵向轴线平行。动力由发动机输出,经离合器和一根短轴传到变速器。在乘用车上,短轴几乎总是与变速器的输入齿轮为一体;但在一些商用车上,它是一个独立部件,两端都有万向节,有时一端还有滑动接头。动力从变速器输出后,经传动轴或中间轴传到后面的驱动桥。传动轴的一端有滑动接头,两端都有万向节。驱动桥能传输动力而支撑桥则不能。驱动桥内的锥齿轮或蜗轮将转矩的传递方向改变90°,差速器将转矩平均分配给两个驱动轴或半轴,半轴再传给车轮。

系统中各组成部件作用如下所述。

离合器用来切断发动机与驱动轮间的动力传输并且确保发动机运转时与驱动车轮平稳接合。因为离合器靠弹性元件的机械作用保持接合,靠离合器踏板的作用分离。可见,除非驾驶员在车内,否则,无法使离合器分离。所以,驾驶员想离开车辆又要保持发动机运转时,或更好地起动发动机时,他必须应用换挡机构,将变速杆置于"空档"或齿轮分离位置,以断开发动机和驱动轮之间的动力传递。

变速器的基本功用是使驾驶员能改变发动机与驱动轮间的转矩比,以适应多变的行驶条件,如上下坡、起步、加减速等。

传动轴将动力传到后桥,两端的万向节能保证在弹性元件变形时后桥和发动机—变速器总成的相对运动。滑动接头通常与一端的万向节一体,以满足传动轴后端随后桥上下运动引起传动轴长度变化的要求,同时满足传动轴前端相对于变速器后面万向节摆动的要求。

因为驱动轮的旋转速度要比发动机的转速慢得多,所以主降速器能将转矩方向转过90°,并以大约 4:1 的传动比降低速度。差速器也在主降速器总成内,用来将驱动转矩平分给驱动轮,另外,在汽车转弯时,允许车轮以不同转速运转。

Lesson 6　Brakes

The operation performed in braking is the reverse of that carried out in accelerating. In the latter the heat energy of the fuel is converted into the kinetic energy of the car, whereas in the former the kinetic energy of the car is converted into heat. Again, just as when driving the car the torque of the engine produces a tractive effort at the peripheries of the driving wheels, so, when the brakes are applied the braking torque introduced at the brake drums produces a negative tractive effort or retarding effort at the peripheries of the braking wheels. As the acceleration possible is limited by the adhesion available between the driving wheels and the ground, so the deceleration possible is also limited. Even so, when braking from high speed to a halt, the rate of retardation is considerably greater than that of full-throttle acceleration. Consequently, the power dissipated by the brakes, and therefore the heat generated, is correspondingly large.[1]

The decelerations possible with modern braking systems are, however, high enough to make the braking of all the road wheels desirable and this is a legal requirement in most countries.

1. Two Functions of Brakes

Two distinct demands are made upon the brakes of motor vehicles. First, in emergencies they must bring the vehicle to rest in the shortest possible distance, and secondly, they must enable control of the vehicle to be retained when descending long hills. The first demand calls for brakes which can apply large braking torques to the brake drums, while the second calls for brakes that can dissipate large quantities of heat without large temperature rises. It may be pointed out that the same amount of energy has to be dissipated as heat when a car descends only 400 yards of a 1:30 incline, as when the same car is brought to rest from a speed of 35 mph. Thus heat dissipation hardly enters into the braking question when emergency stops are considered, but when descending long hills the problem is almost entirely one of heat dissipation.[2]

2. Braking Systems

A driving wheel can be braked in two ways: directly, by means of brakes acting on a drum attached to it; or indirectly, through the transmission by a brake acting on a drum on the main shaft of the gearbox, or on the bevel pinion, or worm, shaft of the final drive. [3] A brake in either of the latter positions, being geared down to the road wheels, can exert a larger braking torque on them than if it acted directly on them. If the final drive ratio is 4 : 1, then the braking torque exerted on each road wheel is twice the braking torque exerted on the brake drum by the brake, that is, the total braking torque is four times the torque on the brake drum. Thus, brakes acting on the engine side of the final drive are much more powerful than those acting on the wheels directly. A transmission brake, however, gives only a single drum to dissipate the heat generated, whereas when acting directly on the road wheels there are two or more drums. Also in many vehicles a transmission brake would be badly placed as regards heat dissipation, but in commercial vehicles it can sometimes be better in this respect than wheel brakes since the latter are generally situated inside the wheels and away from any flow of air. [4] The transmission brake has the advantage that the braking is divided equally between the road wheels by the differential but the torques have to be transmitted through the universal joints and teeth of the final drive and these parts may have to be increased in size if they are not to be over loaded. The transmission brake at the back of the gearbox is fixed relatively to the frame so that its actuation is not affected by movements of the axle due to uneven road surfaces or to changes in the load carried by the vehicle. [5] In vehicles using the de Dion drive or an equivalent, the brakes are sometimes placed at the inner ends of the drive shafts and here again the torques have to be transmitted through universal joints and also through sliding splines which may cause trouble.

In present-day vehicles the wheel brakes are usually operated by a foot pedal and are the ones used on most occasions; they are sometimes referred to as the service brakes. The brakes on the rear wheels can generally be operated also by a hand lever and are used chiefly for holding the vehicle when it is parked and are consequently called parking brakes but as they can, of course, be used in emergencies they are sometimes called emergency brakes. [6]

3. Methods of Actuating the Brakes
Considering manually-operated brakes, the brake pedal or lever may be connected to the actual brake either mechanically, by means of rods or wires, or hydraulically, by means of a fluid in a pipe.

4. Types of Brake
Brakes may be classified into three groups as follows:(1)friction brakes;(2)fluid brakes;(3)electric brakes.

The last two types are, in practice, confined to heavy vehicles and are not used in cars. The principle of the fluid brakes is that a chamber has an impeller inside it that is rotated by the motion of the road wheels so that if the chamber is filled with fluid, usually water, a churning action occurs and kinetic energy is converted into heat thereby providing a braking effort. [7] To dissipate the heat the water may be circulated through a radiator.

The construction is somewhat similar to that of a fluid flywheel and the unit is generally placed between the gearbox and the front end of the propeller shaft but it can be incorporated with the gearbox. The chief drawbacks of this type are that it is difficult to control the braking effort precisely and that while it can provide large braking efforts at high vehicle speeds it can supply very little at low speeds and none at all when the road wheels are not rotating. Thus, it is can be used only to supplement a friction brake and so such devices are often called retarders rather than brakes.

The electric brake is, in effect, an electric generator which being driven by the road wheels, converts kinetic energy into an electric current and thence, by passing the current through a resistance, into heat.

New Words

periphery [pə'rifəri]	n. 周边(边缘,圆周,圆柱体表面)
retardation [.ri:ta:'deiən]	n. 智力迟钝,精神发育迟缓
proportional [prə'pɔ:ʃənl]	adj. 成比例的,相称的
	n. [数]比例项
inertia [i'nə:jə]	n. 惯性,惰性
perpendicular [.pə:pən'dikjulə]	n. 垂直线,垂直的位置
	adj. 垂直的,直立的
adhesion [əd'hi:ən]	n. 附着,粘着,固定
neutralise ['nju:trəlaiz]	vt. 中和(使……中立,使……失效)
magnitude ['mægnitju:d]	n. 大小,重要,光度,(地震)级数
resistance [ri'zistəns]	n. 抵抗力,反抗,反抗行动;阻力,电阻;反对

Notes to the Text

[1] Consequently, the power dissipated by the brakes, and therefore the heat generated, is correspondingly large.

所以,制动系的耗散功率及产生的热量相当大。

[2] Thus heat dissipation hardly enters into the braking question when emergency stops are considered, but when descending long hills the problem is almost entirely one of heat dissipation.

所以分析紧急制动时几乎不考虑热量散失问题,但当下长坡行驶时,制动问题几乎就是散热问题。

[3] A driving wheel can be braked in two ways: directly, by means of brakes acting on a drum attached to it; or indirectly, through the transmission by a brake acting on a drum on the main shaft of the gearbox, or on the bevel pinion, or worm, shaft of the final drive.

旋转的车轮可以通过以下两种方式制动:制动器通过作用于与车轮相连的制动鼓直接进行制动;或者通过作用于变速器主轴上的制动鼓间接进行制动,或通过作用于主降速器轴、锥齿轮或蜗轮上的制动鼓间接进行制动。

[4] Also in many vehicles a transmission brake would be badly placed as regards heat dissipation, but in commercial vehicles it can sometimes be better in this respect than wheel brakes since the latter are generally situated inside the wheels and away from any flow

of air.

从制动器的散热考虑,许多车辆传动系中安装制动器并不理想;但在商用车辆上,由于轮式制动器一般装在车轮内侧,远离气流,传动系制动器在散热方面有时比轮式制动器更好。

[5] The transmission brake at the back of the gearbox is fixed relatively to the frame so that its actuation is not affected by movements of the axle due to uneven road surfaces or to changes in the load carried by the vehicle.

位于变速器后面的传动系制动装置与车架相对固定,从而可以避免由于路面不平或车辆载荷变化引起的车轴运动影响它工作。

[6] The brakes on the rear wheels can generally be operated also by a hand lever and are used chiefly for holding the vehicle when it is parked and are consequently called parking brakes but as they can, of course, be used in emergencies they are sometimes called emergency brakes.

一般后轮制动器还可以通过手拉杆操纵,主要在汽车停车时保持车辆原地不动,所以被称为驻车制动器;但是,由于它们也可用于紧急制动,有时又被称为紧急制动器。

[7] The principle of the fluid brakes is that a chamber has an impeller inside it that is rotated by the motion of the road wheels so that if the chamber is filled with fluid, usually water, a churning action occurs and kinetic energy is converted into heat thereby providing a braking effort.

液力制动器的原理为:将一个被车轮带动旋转的叶轮置于贮液腔内,如果贮液腔内充满液体,通常为水,叶轮搅拌液体,动能转化为热能,从而产生制动作用。

Review Questions

1. Why we say that the operation performed in braking is the reverse of that carried out in accelerating?
2. What are the main functions of a motor vehicle brakes?
3. Do you know the ways in which a driving wheel can be braked?
4. What are the advantages and disadvantages of the transmission brake?
5. Please list the groups of brakes.

参考译文

第六课 制 动 系

制动工作过程与驱动加速过程正相反,后者是燃料的热能被转化为汽车的动能,而前者是汽车的动能被转化为热能。再者,当驱动汽车时,发动机输出的转矩在驱动轮的轮缘产生一个驱动力,而当制动器起作用时,制动鼓处的制动力矩在制动轮的轮缘作用一个反驱动力或者制动力。正如加速能力受限于驱动轮与地面之间的附着力一样,减速能力也同样受到限制。即便如此,当汽车从高速减速至静止时,减速度仍比节气门全开时的加速度大得多。所以,制动系的耗散功率及产生的相应热量相当大。

无论如何,现代制动系统的制动能力足可以满足不同路况下制动需要,这也是绝大多数国家的法规所要求的。

1. 制动系统的两个作用

对机动车的制动系统有两个根本的要求。首先,在紧急情况下,制动系统必须在尽可能短的距离内使车辆静止;其次,在下长坡时制动系统必须能控制车辆等速行驶。第一个要求需要制动系统在制动鼓上作用大的制动力矩,而第二个要求制动器可以散发大量的热量,而不至于温度升高太多。需要指出的是,一辆车沿坡度为 1:30 的斜坡下坡行驶 400 码 (356.6m)时,以热的形式所耗散的能量与该车由 35mile/h(56km/h)的速度降至停止时所散发的热量相同。所以分析紧急制动时几乎不考虑热量散失问题,但当下长坡行驶时,制动问题几乎就是散热问题。

2. 制动系统

运转的车轮可以通过以下两种方式制动:制动器通过作用于与车轮相连的制动鼓直接进行制动;或者通过作用于变速器主轴上的制动鼓间接进行制动,或通过作用于主降速器轴、锥齿轮或蜗轮上的制动鼓间接进行制动。在后者的诸多种类中制动力矩经传动到达车轮,作用于车轮上的制动力矩比直接对车轮制动时的大。如果主减速器的速比为 4:1,则作用于每个车轮的制动力矩为作用于制动鼓力矩的 2 倍,即总的制动力矩为作用于制动鼓力矩的 4 倍。所以作用于发动机一侧的主减速器上的制动比直接作用于车轮上的制动更加有力,但是传动系制动只有一个制动鼓来散发所产生的热量,而直接作用于车轮上的制动器有两个或多个制动鼓。从制动器的散热考虑,许多车辆传动系中安装制动器并不理想;但在商用车辆上,由于轮式制动器一般装在车轮内侧,远离气流,传动系制动器在散热方面有时比轮式制动器更好。传动系制动器的优点是制动力矩经差速器可在各车轮之间平分,但是制动力矩需经万向节和主减速器齿轮传动,所以这些部件需增大尺寸来避免超载。位于变速器后面的传动系制动装置与车架相对固定,从而可以避免由于路面不平或车辆载荷变化引起的车轴运动影响它工作。在使用了 de Dion 式传动或类似装置的汽车中,制动器有时被安装在半轴的内端,转矩仍需经过万向节和滑动花键传动,可能引起滑动花键故障。

在现代车辆上,车轮制动器经常通过脚踏板来操纵,而且应用机会最多,它们有时被称为行车制动器。一般后轮制动器还可以通过手拉杆操纵,主要在汽车停车时保持车辆原地不动,所以被称为驻车制动器;但是,由于它们也可用于紧急制动,有时又被称为紧急制动器。

3. 实施制动的方式

就制动器的人工控制而言,借助制动踏板或制动拉杆,可以通过杆件或缆绳对制动器进行机械控制,也可以通过管道中的液体对制动器进行液力控制。

4. 制动器的种类

制动器可分为以下三类:(1)摩擦式制动器;(2)液力制动器;(3)电力制动器。

后两种制动器在实际应用中仅限于重型车辆,而不用于轿车。液力制动器的原理为:将一个被车轮带动旋转的叶轮置于贮液腔内,如果贮液腔内充满液体,通常为水,叶轮搅拌液体,动能转化为热能,从而产生制动作用。为了散失这些热量,水可能经散热器循环。

液力制动器的构造与液力耦合器有些相似,该总成一般安装在变速器和传动轴前端之间。但它可以与变速器合为一体,该类型的主要缺点是难于精确控制制动力,且车速较高时可产生大的制动力,车速较低时仅能提供较小的制动力,车轮不旋转时不能提供制动力。所以它常被用作摩擦式制动器的辅助设备,因此这类装置常被称为缓速器而非制动器。

电力制动器实际上就是被车轮驱动的发电机,将动能转化为电流,电流通过电阻,转化为热能。

Unit 2 Inspecting and Maintenance of Automobile

Lesson7 Automobile System Diagnosis

With computerized engine-control systems, a service manual that applies specifically to the vehicle being serviced is a must. Such a manual will provide you with accurate information on the following: location of engine and emission control parts; system wiring and block diagrams; description of the various components; operation of the various subsystems for fuel, spark, and emission control; safety precautions and recommended service procedures; specifications for sensors and actuators; accessing of self-diagnosis codes; interpretation of diagnostic trouble codes; tools and instruments necessary for diagnosis and repair.

Almost every automobile manufacturer uses some type of Assembly Line Communication Link (ALCL) or Assembly Line Data Link (ALDL) to test the system's operation as it leaves the assembly line.[1] Special automotive diagnostic scanners are available for accessing information from computerized vehicles through connections to this serial data link. Information on inputs and outputs to the computer, such as fault codes, coolant temperature, RPM, timing retard/advance, vacuum, manifold absolute pressure, and oxygen sensor output can be retrieved using these devices. This information can be displayed on a screen, shown as a digital readout, or printed on a piece of paper and used for troubleshooting the system.

A diagnostic breakout box as shown in Fig. 7-1 can be connected to provide an easy way to access all electrical circuit connections to the engine computer. When used with a digital multimeter, resistance and voltage measurements are easily accessible from all circuits of the computer through the remotely located box. The data from the tests are compared with available diagnostic and voltage charts to indicate the problem.[2] These are the same tests you would be performing without a breakout box, only now the tests are easy to do.

In some cases, diagnosis of the fuel injection system

Fig. 7-1 A diagnostic breakout box

may lead you to suspect that there is something wrong with the fuel injectors. For example, if the engine misses or lacks power, it could mean that one or more of the fuel injectors has become clogged with a tarlike residue. [3] Generally, this condition is resulted from the use of fuel that does not have sufficient detergent additives or from frequent city driving. Most diagnostic trouble codes relate to the computer input voltages or signals and must exist for a specific period of time to be recognized as a hard fault.

Before beginning to troubleshoot a system, take time to discuss the problem with the driver. The driver can be an excellent source of information on problems, especially intermittent ones. It is important to understand the symptoms fully and know what conditions occur that cause the driver to complain.

When diagnosing engine performance, the sensitivity of electronic control systems makes organized troubleshooting a must. [4] The following troubleshooting plan will give you a logical approach for diagnosing any problem.

(1) Verify the complaint. Ask the driver then check the vehicle. Make sure the problem actually occurs by using an operational check. For example, if the complaint is hard starting, check the starting performance.

(2) Determine related symptoms. Know how the problem system should work. Related symptoms are identified by operation checks on circuits or components connected to the problem circuit. For example, a rough idle could be caused by an electrical or a vacuum problem.

(3) Analyze the symptoms. Think! What did the driver say? What did the operational checks show? Consider the symptoms and their possible causes. Positive symptoms (things working as they should) rule out certain causes, whereas negative symptoms (things not working as they should) indicate certain causes.

(4) Isolate the trouble. Be logical and systematic. Start with knowing the system. Then, test from the general to the specific. The split-half method of testing can save a lot of time. The trouble lies between a positive symptom and negative symptom. Start halfway between. If a positive result is obtained, split the next half, going toward the problem. If a negative result is found, split the other half, going back toward the area where the positive symptom was found. [5]

(5) Correct the trouble. Repair wiring problems, replace faulty components, and service of adjust parts if necessary.

(6) Check for proper operation. Make sure that, the problem is fixed. Is the specific complaint corrected? Has the cause of the problem been identified and corrected? What may cause the problem to happen again? Are all the symptoms now positive? Have any new problems shown up in other circuits?

In diagnosing a problem on a computerized engine-control system, it is helpful first to pinpoint the problem as being related to the fuel system, the ignition system, a mechanical problem, or a problem with the components of the electronic control system. [6] All fuel injection systems consist basically of a fuel pump, supply lines, fuel filter, injector(s), pressure regulator, and return line. Basic checks include proper fuel pressure, delivery of fuel by the injector, and the amount of injector ON time. Common fuel related problems include blocked fuel line or filter; inoperative fuel pump; incorrect system fuel pressure; defective, dirty, or sticking injectors; and contaminated fuel.

A computer-controlled ignition system consists basically of a pickup sensor and the device it is sensing, engine computer-timing circuitry, an electronic ignition-control module, ignition coil(s), and connective wiring. The first thing to check in the ignition system is whether spark is coming out of the plug wirer then work back from this point. Common ignition-related problems include fouled or faulty spark plugs, defective distributor cap or rotor, open or shorted ignition coil(s), defective high-voltage cables, faulty pickup sensor, defective electronic ignition-control module, and bad connections.

The mechanical system includes such nonelectrical components as vacuum hoses, intake air system, exhaust system, engine head and block, belts, oil pump, camshaft, crankshaft, timing chain or belt, nuts, and bolts. Mechanical problems can often be spotted by a good visual inspection. In fact, a visual inspection should always be the first step in troubleshooting any system. A seemingly unrelated mechanical problem such as a cracked or disconnected vacuum hose can have a direct impact on the performance of the system.

The electronic control system consists basically of the computer or electronic control module, engine wiring harness, input sensors, and output actuators. The electronic troubleshooting principles used are similar to those used on other automotive electrical and/or electronic systems. If a check engine or service engine soon light is ON, then deal with it immediately. Each vehicle manufacturer has its own way of retrieving diagnostic codes from computer memory and also its own system of code numbers.

The presence of trouble codes dose not always mean the computer is defective, and usually these codes indicate that a specific input to the computer is missing or incorrect.[7] Some technicians overlook this fact and are tempted to replace the computer first. Similarly, at times, some problems may occur in the system even when there has been no check engine light or trouble code signal. Remember that most trouble codes relate mainly to inputs, few outputs are monitored. Even if the input does not deviate from the normal reading long enough to be recognized as a problem, this does not completely eliminate it as a source of the problem.

It is important when troubleshooting to understand how the different inputs and outputs react with the computer to achieve the desired engine control. Each vehicle manufacturer has its own control process or way of retrieving sensor information and issuing commands to various solenoids and relays.

New Words

component [kəm'pounənt]　　　　　　　n. 部件，构件
procedure [prə'sidʒər]　　　　　　　　n. 程序，工序

sensor ['sensər]	n. 传感器
actuator ['æktʃʊˌeɪtə]	n. 促动器
retrieve [rɪ'triv]	n. 检索
troubleshooting ['trʌb(ə)l.ʃutɪŋ]	n. 故障诊断
multimeter ['mʌltimi:tə]	n. 万用表
tarlike [tɑrlaɪk]	adj. 像炭一样的
residue ['rezɪdu]	n. 残余，残渣
fault [fɔlt]	n. 故障
diagnose ['daɪəg.noʊz]	vt. 诊断
pinpoint ['pɪnˌpɔɪnt]	vt. 为……正确定位
module ['mɑdʒʊl]	n. 模块
deviate ['diviət]	v. 偏差

Phrases and Expressions

apply to	将……应用于
service manual	维修手册
provide with	给……提供
emission control	排放控制
block diagram	框图
self-diagnosis code	自诊断故障码
diagnostic trouble code	诊断故障码
Assembly Line Communication Link (ALCL)	集线通信连接
Assembly Line Data Link (ALDL)	集线数据连接
fault code	故障码
timing retard/advance	正时延迟/正时提前
digital readout	数字读出器
diagnostic breakout box	诊断断接盒
digital multimeter	数字万用表
be compared with	可与……相比
clog with	阻塞
result from	起因于
detergent additive	清洁添加剂
relate to	涉及
hard fault	永久性故障
make sure	确保
start with	从……开始
show up	出现，显露出来
consist of	由……组成
come out of	出自，生自
electronic ignition-control module	电子点火控制组件

have an impact on	对……有影响
be similar to	与……相似，类似于
deal with	处理
at times	有时，偶尔
deviate from	脱离

Notes to the Text

[1] Almost every automobile manufacturer uses some type of Assembly Line Communication Link (ALCL) or Assembly Line Data Link (ALDL) to test the system's operation as it leaves the assembly line

当一辆汽车驶下流水线的时候，几乎每个汽车制造厂都会使用集线通信连接（ALCL）或集线数据连接（ALDL）来测试系统的工作情况。

[2] The data from the tests are compared with available diagnostic and voltage charts to indicate the problem.

将测试的数据与诊断数据和电压图表相比较，以分析故障所在。

[3] For example, if the engine misses or lacks power, it could mean that one or more of the fuel injectors has become clogged with a tarlike residue.

例如发动机缺缸或缺乏动力，它可能意味着一个或多个喷油器由于积炭而阻塞。

[4] When diagnosing engine performance, the sensitivity of electronic control systems makes organized troubleshooting a must.

当诊断发动机状态的时候，通过电子控制系统的灵敏度实现故障检查。

[5] If a negative result is found, split the other half, going back toward the area where the positive symptom was found.

如果发现结果不正常，回到现象正常的测点去将另外一半分开。

[6] In diagnosing a problem on a computerized engine-control system, it is helpful first to pinpoint the problem as being related to the fuel system, the ignition system, a mechanical problem, or a problem with the components of the electronic control system.

在诊断一个计算机控制的发动机故障时，首先确定故障是与燃料系统、点火系统、机械故障有关，还是电子控制系统部件的问题，这是非常有用的。

[7] The presence of trouble codes dose not always mean the computer is defective, and usually these codes indicate that a specific input to the computer is missing or incorrect.

出现故障码并非总是意味着计算机出现问题，这些故障码通常表明计算机的某些特定输入数据丢失或异常。

Review Questions

1. What information will a service manual provide you with?

2. What is the use of a special automotive diagnostic device?

3. What problems in the fuel system may result in misfire or power shortage of the engine?

4. What is a logical approach for diagnosing an automobile problem?

5. What are the common problems in the ignition system?

参考译文

第二单元　汽车检测与维修

第七课　汽车系统诊断

　　随着计算机在发动机控制系统中的应用,一本专门用于汽车维修的服务手册是必需的。这本手册将会准确提供下列各项信息:发动机和排放控制部分的位置,系统线路图和框图,各种不同组成部分的描述,燃油、点火和排放控制的各子系统的工作原理,安全预防知识和推荐的维修程序,传感器和执行器的规格,故障码的存取,故障码的解释以及诊断与修理必需的工具和仪器。

　　当一辆汽车驶下流水线的时候,几乎每个汽车制造厂都会使用集线通信连接(ALCL)或集线数据连接(ALDL)来测试系统的工作情况。通过接头把专用的汽车诊断扫描仪连接到串行数据连线上,以存取来自计算机控制的汽车上的数据。输入或者输出计算机的数据,比如故障码、冷却水温度、转速、正时延迟/提前、真空度、进气歧管绝对压力,以及氧传感器的输出都能用这些装置读取。这些数据可以用数字显示在荧屏上或打印出来,用来诊断系统故障。

　　连接一个图 7-1 所示的诊断用的断接盒可以很容易地进入发动机电脑连接的任何电路中。使用数字式万用表,通过这一远程接线盒就能轻而易举地测得所有与计算机相连线路的电阻和电压。将测试的数据与诊断数据和电压图表相比较,以分析故障所在。也可以不用断接盒来完成这些相同的测试,只不过,现在这么做容易一些。

　　在某些情况下,燃油喷射系统的诊断可能使你怀疑喷油器有故障。例如发动机缺缸或缺乏动力,它可能意味着一个或多个喷油器由于积炭而阻塞。通常,这种情况是由于使用的燃料中没有加入足够的清洁添加剂或经常在城市中驾驶。绝大多数的诊断故障码与计算机的输入电压或信号有关,其必须持续一定时间才作为一种硬故障。

　　在开始查找一个系统的故障之前,需要与驾驶员交流。驾驶员很了解故障信息,尤其是一些间歇性的故障。充分了解驾驶员反映的故障现象以及引起驾驶员抱怨的情况,对查找故障很重要。

　　当诊断发动机状态的时候,通过电子控制系统的灵敏度来实现故障检查。下列查找故障的步骤会为你诊断故障提供合理的方法。

　　(1)核实故障。询问驾驶员,然后再检查汽车。通过运行检查确定实际出现的问题。例如,如果驾驶员说起动困难,就检查发动机的起动性能。

　　(2)确定故障现象。了解故障系统应该如何工作。通过检查,判断相关故障现象是由线路还是与故障线路连接的部件所引起的。例如,怠速不稳可能是由电气或真空问题造成的。

　　(3)分析故障现象。想一想! 驾驶员说了些什么? 检查的过程中表现出什么? 分析故障现象和可能引起该故障的原因。若正常(如它们所应该的那样),就可以排除某些因素,若不正常(与它们所应该的不一样),就可以确定某些因素。

　　(4)隔离故障。这一步要合乎逻辑,有系统性。先了解该系统。然后,从一般到具体进行测试。一分为二的测试方法能节省许多时间。故障就在现象正常和现象不正常的两个测点之间，从中间一分为二。如果获得的结果正常，往现象不正常的测点去，再分下一半。如果发现结果不正常，回到现象正常的测点去将另外一半分开。

(5) 修复故障。修理线路，更换故障部件，必要时对可调整的部分进行维护。

(6) 对维修情况进行检查，确定故障已经被修复。客户所述的故障现象消失了吗？故障的原因找到并修理好了吗？还有什么原因可能会再次引起故障？现在所有的现象都正常吗？在其他线路中是否出现新的故障？

在诊断一个计算机控制的发动机故障时，首先确定故障是与燃料系统、点火系统、机械故障有关，还是电子控制系统部件的问题，这是非常有用的。所有的燃油喷射系统主要由燃油泵、输油管、燃油滤清器、喷油器、油压调节器和回油管组成。基本检查包括燃油压力是否合适、喷油器喷射是否正常以及喷油脉宽是否适当。通常遇到的问题有输油管或燃油滤清器阻塞、燃油泵不工作、系统燃油压力不正常、喷油器损坏、脏污或胶结以及燃油污染。

计算机控制的点火系统主要由含有转换元件和敏感元件的传感器、发动机计算机正时电路、电子点火控制模块、点火线圈和连接的配线组成。点火系统检查的第一件事是火花塞是否有火花，然后再从这儿往回检查。通常，与点火相关的故障包括火花塞脏污或损坏、分电器盖或分火头损坏、点火线圈断路或短路、高压导线损坏、传感器转换元件损坏、电子点火控制模块损坏和电路连接不良。

机械系统包括那些非电的部分，比如真空管路、进气系统、排气系统、发动机舱盖和缸体、皮带、机油泵、凸轮轴、曲轴、正时链或正时皮带、螺钉和螺栓。机械的问题通常能通过外观检查很容易被发现。事实上，在查找系统故障时外观检查应该总是首先进行。表面上无关的机械问题，比如一条破裂的或断开的真空管可能直接影响系统的性能。

电子控制系统主要由计算机或电子控制模块、发动机线束、传感器和执行器组成。电子部分的故障诊断原理，与其他汽车电器设备及电子系统类似。如果"检查发动机"指示灯或"发动机维护"指示灯是点亮的，那么就应该立刻对此进行处理。各汽车制造厂商有自己的方法读取计算机存储的故障代码，同时系统代码也不一样。

出现故障码并非总是意味着ECU存在问题，这些故障码通常表明ECU的某些特定输入数据丢失或异常。有些技术人员会忽略这一点，而是首先想更换ECU。同样，有时有些故障可能在系统中已经产生，但"检查发动机"指示灯未点亮或故障码信号并没有被显示。记住，多数故障码主要与输入数据有关，输出数据很少检测。即使输入数据异常的时间还不足以被认定为故障，也不能完全排除它是故障的原因。

查找故障的时候，了解各传感器和执行器通过计算机对发动机正常工作的影响是很重要的。各汽车制造厂在读取传感器数据和传送各种电磁阀和继电器指令方面都有自己的控制程序或方法。

Lesson 8 Automobile Maintenance

Maintenance is something most of us ignore, until our vehicle stops functioning, and then we wonder what went wrong, where. [1] Maintenance is one of the most serious aspects of ownership. It determines the longevity, performance and reliability of whichever vehicle you drive. Looking after your vehicle involves more than taking care of its external coat of paint and keeping it clean and shiny.

Maintenance means taking care of all the parts, even those that are inside the bonnet. These are the ones that directly concern the performance of the vehicle. Besides taking it to the service station at regular periods, it is a good idea to go through the owner's manual that will give a fair idea about its routine maintenance. [2]

Air filter. Check it every month. Replace it when it becomes dirty or as part of a tune-up. It is easy to reach, right under the big metal "lid", in a carbureted engine; or in a rectangular box at the forward end of the air in a duct hose assembly.

Battery. Extreme caution should be taken while handling a battery since it can produce explosive gases. [3] It is advisable not to smoke, create a spark or light a match near a battery. Always wear protective glasses and gloves.

Belts. Inspect belts and hoses smoothly. Replace glazed, worn or frayed belts. Replace bulging, rotten or brittle hoses and tighten clamps. If a hose looks bad, or feels too soft or too hard, it should be replaced.

Brake fluid. Check the brake fluid monthly. First wipe dirt from the brake master cylinder reservoir lid. Pry off the retainer clip and remove the lid or unscrew the plastic lid, depending on which type your vehicle has. If you need fluid, add the improved type and check for possible leaks throughout the system. Do not overfill.

Engine oil. Check the oil after every filling up. Remove the dipstick, wipe it clean and insert it fully. If it is low, add oil. To maintain peak performance, the oil should be changed every 3000 kilometers or 3 months, whichever comes first. Replace the oil filter with every oil change.

Exhaust. Look underneath for loose or broken exhaust clamps and supports. Check for holes in muffler or pipes. Replace the rusted or damaged parts. Have the emission checked at once per year for compliance with local laws.

Lights. Make sure that all your lights are clean and working, including the brake lights, turn signals and emergency flashers. Keep spare bulbs and fuses in your vehicle.

Power steering fluid. Check the power steering fluid level once per month. Check it by removing the reservoir dipstick. If the level is down, add fluid and inspect the pump and hoses for leaks.

Shock absorbers. Look for signs of oil seepage on shock absorbers, and test shock action by bouncing the car up and down. The car should stop bouncing when you step back. Worn or leaking shocks should be replaced. Always replace shock absorbers in pairs.

Tyres. Keep tyres inflated to recommended pressure. Check for cuts, bulges and excessive tread wear. Uneven wear indicates tyres are misaligned or out of balance.

Transmission fluid. Check transmission fluid monthly with engine warm and running, and the parking brake on. Shift to drive, then to park. Remove dipstick, wipe dry, insert it and remove it again. Add the approved type fluid, if needed. Never overfill.

Washer fluid. Keep the windshield washer fluid reservoir full. Use some of it to clean off the wiper blades.

Wiper blades. Inspect the windscreen wiper blades whenever you clean your windshield. Do not wait until the rubber is worn or brittle to replace them. They should be replaced at least once per year, and more often if smearing occurs.

Car parts need regular care.

Engine. For the protection of the engine, change its oil regularly. Follow the manufacturer's recommendations on oil and filter changes. Engine oil, transmission fluid and fuel are systems that need to be checked and replaced periodically.

Brakes. At times you may notice that brakes tend to become unresponsive, wobbly and act slowly. [4] It is time to check and top-up the brake fluid reservoir.

Battery. For the prevention of corrosion, it is imperative that you clean the battery terminals regularly and apply a light coating of grease. Also, check the level of distilled water in the battery and ensure that the plates are covered at all times. If the level of water is very low, the acid becomes concentrated and the plates get corroded.

Interior. The interior of the cars must always be spotlessly clean. Regular vacuum of the interior will prevent the deposition of any kind of sand, dust, grime or salt from damaging the floor surface. [5] Wipe the dash, seats, instrument panel and the rear parcel shelf. Use special car cleaners and not household stuff for cleaning.

Exterior. A well maintained exterior is a sign of good maintenance and goes a long way in jacking up its resale value. [6] This is especially important in coastal cities where salt air corrodes unprotected metal surfaces. Wash regularly to keep rust at bay.

Wash windscreens with soap and water. Follow it up with clean water. Then use chamois leather to wipe all the spots dry. When the car is dry, use a rag dipped in mentholated spirit and water solution to polish the glass.

Lights. It is important for the lights to be properly focused, for your own and for the oncoming vehicle's safety. Travel on low beam so that it does not obstruct your view instead of helping you along.

Tyres. They wear out unevenly. For them to last longer, keep rotating the position of the tyres and balance them at intervals of around 10 000 km. Under-inflated tyres also increase your fuel consumption by 10%. A periodic check for stone and gravel enmeshed in the tyres is also a must.

Tyre pressure. The required amount of air pressure needs to be strictly maintained if the car is to get the right mileage and pick-up. [7]

Water. If the engine uses water for cooling, take care to ensure that it is regularly changed. Water can also be used for cleaning the windshield.

New Words

maintenance ['meɪntənəns]	n. 维修；维护
longevity [lɒnˈdʒevəti]	n. 使用寿命，耐久性
reliability [rɪˌlaɪəˈbɪləti]	n. 可靠性
bonnet ['bɒnət]	n. 发动机罩
tune-up ['tunˌʌp, 'tjun-]	n. 维护

glazed [gleɪzd]	adj. 磨光的
frayed [freɪd]	adj. 磨破的
brittle ['brɪt(ə)l]	adj. 易碎的，老化的
clamp [klæmp]	n. 夹子，夹钳
dipstick ['dɪp.stɪk]	n. 机油尺
muffler ['mʌflər]	n. 消声器，消音器
seepage ['sipɪdʒ]	n. 渗透
inflate [ɪn'fleɪt]	v. 充气
bulge [bʌldʒ]	n. 凸出部分，膨胀
tread [tred]	n. 轮胎花纹，轮胎胎面
misalign ['misəlain]	vt. 不对正
tyre ['taɪr]	n. 轮胎
overfill [ˌovɚ'fɪl]	vt. 装得过满
unresponsive [ˌʌnrɪ'spansɪv]	adj. 无反应的
wobbly ['wɑbli]	adj. 摆动的
top-up ['tɒpʌp]	vt. 加注，注满
deposition [ˌdɪpə'zɪʃ(ə)n]	n. 沉积物
grime [graɪm]	n. 尘垢，污点
rag [ræg]	n. 抹布
mentholated ['menθəleɪtɪd]	adj. 含薄荷醇的
gravel ['græv(ə)l]	n. 砂砾
enmesh [ɪn'meʃ]	vt. 使陷入
mileage ['maɪlɪdʒ]	n. 英里数

Phrases and Expressions

take care of	照料，注意
routine maintenance	例行维护，例行维修
air filter	空气滤清器
duct hose assembly	通气管总成
brake fluid	制动液，制动油
pry off	撬开
fill up	装满
oil filter	机油滤清器
make sure	确保
brake light	制动灯
turn signal	转向灯
emergency flasher	应急指示灯
power steering	动力转向
shock absorber	减振器
windscreen wiper	风窗玻璃刮水器

instrument panel	仪表板
jack up	提高,抬高
chamois leather	麂皮
at intervals of	相隔,每隔
periodic check	定期检查
air pressure	气压

Notes to the Text

[1] Maintenance is something most of us ignore, until our vehicle stops functioning, and then we wonder what went wrong, and where.

汽车的维护总是被我们大多数人忽视,直到汽车不能运转,我们才想知道出了什么故障。

[2] Besides taking it to the service station at regular periods, it is a good idea to go through the owner's manual that will give a fair idea about its routine maintenance.

除了要将汽车定期地送到维修站去,通读汽车的用户手册也很有益,它给出了汽车常规维护建议。

[3] Extreme caution should be taken while handling a battery since it can produce explosive gases.

当装卸蓄电池时要特别小心,因为它会产生爆炸性气体。

[4] At times you may notice that brakes tend to become unresponsive, wobbly and act slowly. It is time to check and top-up the brake fluid reservoir.

有时你可能会注意到制动器反应迟钝和动作迟缓。此时,则应该检查和加注制动液了。

[5] Regular vacuum of the interior will prevent the deposition of any kind of sand, dust, grime or salt from damaging the floor surface.

车的内部必须保持清洁。定期对机体内部进行吸尘器吸尘可防止各种沙粒、灰尘、污垢或盐分损坏汽车底部。

[6] A well maintained exterior is a sign of good maintenance and goes a long way in jacking up its resale value.

良好的外观是车子得到妥善维护的标志,而且可以大大提高转售价格。

[7] The required amount of air pressure needs to be strictly maintained if the car is to get the right mileage and pick-up.

为了使汽车达到应有的行驶里程和加速性能,必须严格保持所规定的气压值。

Review Questions

1. What is the meaning of the maintenance?
2. What should we do if we want to maintain the peak performance?
3. How often do we have the emission checked?
4. What should we do for the prevention of battery corrosion?
5. What should we do if we want to get a longer life of the tyre?

参考译文

第八课 汽车维护

汽车的维护总是被我们大多数人忽视，直到汽车不能运转，我们才想知道出了什么故障。维护是对汽车拥有者最重要的一个方面。它决定了你所驾车辆的寿命、性能及可靠性。汽车维护不止包括（车身）外漆维护和保证车身外表清洁及亮丽。

汽车维护指汽车所有零件的维护，甚至那些发动机罩下面的零件。这些部分是指直接影响汽车性能的零件。除了要将汽车定期地送到维修站去，通读汽车的用户手册也很有益，它给出了汽车常规维护建议。

空气滤清器。每月检查一次。当发动机变污或需被调整时，应及时更换。这是很容易做到的，因为它刚好在化油器式发动机罩的下方，或者在进气管前方末端的一个长方形的盒子里。

蓄电池。当装卸蓄电池时要特别小心，因为它会产生爆炸性气体。不要在靠近蓄电池的地方吸烟、制造出火星或点燃火柴。靠近蓄电池时要带上保护眼镜和手套。

传动带。仔细检查传动带和塑料软管。更换那些磨光的、用坏了的及绽开口的传动带。更换那些已膨胀的、腐烂的及老化的软管和紧固管夹。如果一条软管看起来已损坏，或过软、过硬，那么就应该被更换。

制动液。每月检查制动液。首先擦掉制动总泵盖上的污垢。撬起保持器的夹子，然后拿开盖子或拧开塑料盖，这主要决定于车辆的类型。根据需要补充制动液，然后检查系统有无泄漏，注意不要过多添加。

机油。每次装满机油后都要进行一次检查。取下量油尺，把它擦干净完全插入。如果油位太低，则补充。为了保证汽车最佳的工作性能，机油需要每 3 000km 或每 3 个月（先到为准）更换一次。每次换油时都需更换机油滤清器。

排气管。从车的底部检查排气管卡有无松散或损坏。检查消音器或者管道有无穿孔。更换已经腐蚀或损坏的零件。根据当地法规，每年排放检测。

车灯。确保所有的车灯清洁，且工作正常，包括制动灯、转向灯及应急指示灯。在车里储备一些备用的灯泡和保险丝。

动力转向液。每月检测一次动力转向系统的液面高低。通过取下储液箱中的量油尺来检测。如果液面有所降低，则补充动力转向液，同时检查动力转向泵及胶管是否泄漏。

减振器。检查减振器有无渗油，通过使车上下振动来检查减振效果。当停止对施加振动后，车辆应该很快停止跳动。更换磨旧或渗漏的减振器。减振器都是成双地更换。

轮胎。保证轮胎的充气压力至推荐标准。检查是否有破口、凸起及过度磨损。轮胎磨损不均衡说明车轮定位失准或轮胎不平衡。

变速器油。每月检测变速器油，检测时，发动机要处于预热后运转状态，且拉紧驻车制动。将变速器挂入前进挡，然后再换到驻车挡。取下量油尺，擦干，然后插入，再取出。如果需要，添加规定型号的变速器油。不要过量填充。

清洗液。保证风窗玻璃清洗液足够，用清洗液擦刮水器刮片。

刮水器刮片。每当清洗风窗玻璃时就要检查刮水器刮片，不要等到那橡胶制的刮水器刮片坏掉或者碎掉再更换。刮水器刮片至少每年更换一次，如果沾染了油污还要更频繁地更换。

需要定期维护的汽车零部件。

发动机。为了保护好发动机,需要定期更换机油。按照汽车制造商建议更换机油和滤油器。机油、变速器油及燃油需要定期检查和更换。

制动器。有时你可能会注意到制动器反应迟钝和动作迟缓。此时,则应该检查和加注制动液了。

蓄电池。为了阻止蓄电池的腐蚀,定期清洁蓄电池接线柱且清洁后在其表面涂少许油脂是非常必要的。还要检查蓄电池中蒸馏水的液面位置,同时确保蓄电池极板完全浸入电解液中。如果蓄电池液面过低,酸性增强,蓄电池极板就容易被腐蚀。

内部。车辆内部必须保持清洁。定期对机体内部进行吸尘器吸尘可防止各种沙粒、灰尘、污垢或盐分损坏汽车底部。擦拭座椅、仪表板及后面的车架。要使用专用的而不是家用的洗涤液进行清洗。

外部。良好的外观是车子得到妥善维护的标志,而且可以大大提高转售价格。这在海滨城市显得尤为重要,因为含有盐分的空气会腐蚀没有保护的金属外壳。定期清洗以防锈蚀。

先用肥皂水清洗风窗玻璃。然后再用清水清洗。接着用麂皮革擦干所有的污迹。当车辆晾干后,用蘸有薄荷溶液的抹布抛光玻璃。

车灯。车灯合适的配光性对自己和迎面开来的车辆的安全很重要。在近光下行驶,并不会妨碍你的视野,相反还会帮助行车安全。

轮胎。它们通常是磨损不均匀的。为了延长其寿命,大约每 10 000 km 对轮胎进行换位和平衡。充气不足的轮胎会增加 10% 的燃油消耗。定期剔除陷入轮胎中的沙砾是必要的。

轮胎压力。为了使汽车达到应有的行驶里程和加速性能,必须严格保持所规定的气压值。

水。如果发动机用水进行冷却,注意要定期更换。水也能用于清洗风窗玻璃。

Lesson 9　Engine Maintenance

A sound engine should develop full power, run steadily under full-load and no-load conditions, without overheating, smoking, oil or coolant leakage. [1] Some troubles can be identified by their symptoms without disassembling the engine.

The symptoms indicative of some troubles with the crank gear include foreign noise and knocks, loss of power, excessive oil and fuel consumption, smoky exhaust. [2]

Noise and knocks in the engine are caused by the wear of its basic parts leading to excessive clearance between its mating parts.

If the piston and cylinder are worn and the clearance between them is excessive, a clear metallic knocking appears, which is most vivid when the engine runs cold. [3] If the knocking grows when the engine is sharply throttled up, the main or crankpin bearing shells are worn, the duller knocks symptomizing the wear of the main bearings. Sharp continuous knocking in the engine accompanied by the oil pressure drop is an evidence of melting out of bearings. [4] The engine knocks can be listened to with the use of stethoscope.

Loss of engine power stems from the drop of compression which may occur when the cylinder block head nuts are tightened nonuniformly or insufficiently, or the head gasket is damaged, the piston rings are stuck in the grooves owing to carbon or lacquer deposit; the rings are worn, broken or lost their resilience; the cylinders are worn. [5]

The compression can be checked with a compression gauge. To check the compression with a compression gauge, warm up the engine, drive out the spark plugs, fully open the throttle valves. [6] Install a rubber nipple of the compression gauge into the plug hole, turn the crankshaft 8 or 10 times and check the gauge reading. After the crankshaft is turned, the pressure in the good cylinder should be 0.8~0.9MPa. This procedure should be used to check the compression consecutively in all the cylinders of the engine.

Excessive fuel and oil consumption and smoky gray exhaust (the oil level in the crankcase being normal) are usually attributed to the sticking or wear of the piston rings. [7] Sticking can be remedied without disassembling the engine; for this purpose, mix equal parts of denatured alcohol and kerosene and pour 20g of the mixture into each cylinder through the spark plug hole, leaving it there overnight. In the morning start the engine, run it for 10 to 15 minutes, shut down and change the oil.

Cracks in the walls of the cylinder block and head may result from freezing of water or filling cold water into a hot engine.

The main troubles characteristic of the valve gear are improper seating or incomplete opening of the valves.

Improper seating is symptomized by poor compression, popping in the inlet and exhaust manifolds, loss of power. [8] Improper seating may be caused by carbon deposit on the valves in the guides, absence of clearance between the valve stem and the rocker.

Incomplete opening of the valves is characterized by knocking in the engine and loss of power. This derangement stems from excessive clearance between the valve stem and the rocker.

The valve gear troubles also include wear of the crankshaft gears, tappets, guides, excessive end play of the camshaft, wear of rocker bushings and fulcrums. [9]

To adjust the clearance between the valve stem and the rocker, remove the valve cover, first detaching all the parts mounted on it; shift the piston to TDC on the compression stroke so that the valves are closed; check the clearance and adjust it, if necessary, as follows: undo the lock-nut on the rocker adjusting screw, set the required clearance by rotating the adjusting screw, tighten the lock-nut holding the screw with the screwdriver and recheck the clearance. [10]

The engine that has not been maintained well looks like that the engine oil has not been changed for a long time. This engine has relatively low mileage and already needs serious and costly repair. As to the engine that has been maintained well, after 310 000 km (192 000 miles) it is still in a very good condition, and needs no repair at all.

So, what is most important to keep engine in a good shape?

—Change oil regularly.

—Avoid overheating the engine.

—Changing spark plugs, air filter, timing belt and other items from maintenance schedule may save you from costly repairs.

—Fix any small problem right away before it causes a serious damage.

Engine oil has limited life—after a certain point it starts losing lubricating qualities and carbonizes. Once it happens, the engine gets contaminated with carbon deposits (sludge) that significantly shorten engine's life.

While checking the oil level, look at its condition. If the oil is black, change it. Always use only appropriate engine oil type (usually you can find it on oil cap or in the owners manual). Use synthetic oil under heavy conditions (high temperature, excessive load, long trips without oil change, etc.). The advantage of synthetic oil is that it can withstand higher temperature and can work longer without losing its lubricating qualities. But it is not worth to use synthetic oil on high-mileage or very old engines—thicker mineral oil will be OK.

Over a period of time, rust and scale accumulate in the radiator and engine water jackets; the rust and scale restrict the circulation of water, and the engine tends to overheat.

If there is any problems with your engine, such as irregular noise or smell, or performance problems, leaks or smoke, or "check engine" light is on, etc., have car inspected with a mechanic.[11] It is always better to fix any small problem right away before they can cause engine damage.

New words

sound [saʊnd]	adj. 可靠的，正常的
leakage ['liːkɪdʒ]	n. 泄漏，渗漏
symptoms ['sɪmptəm]	n. 症状；表现
indicative [ɪn'dɪkətɪv]	adj. 指示的
knock [nɑk]	v. 敲打，敲击
	n. 敲缸
wear [wer]	v. 磨损
indicate ['ɪndɪ.keɪt]	vt. 指出，显示
stethoscope ['steθə.skoʊp]	n. 听诊器
nonuniformly [nɒn'juːnɪfɔːmlɪ]	ad. 不一致地，不均匀地
resilience [rɪ'zɪljəns]	n. 恢复力
nipple ['nɪp(ə)l]	n. 接头
drain [dreɪn]	vi. 排水
symptomize ['sɪmptəmaɪz]	vt. 表明
tappet ['tæpɪt]	n. （气门）推杆
fulcrum ['fʊlkrəm]	n. 支点

undo [ʌn'du]	vt.	解开，松开
schedule ['skedʒəl]	n.	计划表，日程表
carbonize ['kɑ:bənaɪz]	vt.	碳化
contaminate [kən'tæmɪ.neɪt]	v.	污染
dipstick ['dɪp.stɪk]	n.	量油计，机油尺
lubricate ['lubrɪ.keɪt]	vt.	润滑

Phrases and Expressions

full-load	全负荷
fuel consumption	燃油消耗
throttled up	加油（节气门增大）
lacquer deposit	釉质沉积
warm up	暖机
foreign noise	异响
eposition of carbon	积炭
valve stem	气门杆
TDC	上止点
lock-nut	防松螺母
in a good shape	保持良好状态
synthetic oil	合成润滑油
mineral oil	矿物油
water jackets	冷却水套

Notes to the Text

［1］A sound engine should develop full power, run steadily under full-load and no-load conditions, without overheating, smoking, oil or coolant leakage.

　　一台正常的发动机应该能够发出全功率，在满载和无负荷条件下运转平稳，无发动机过热、冒黑烟、机油或冷却液泄漏现象。

［2］The symptoms indicative of some troubles with the crank gear include foreign noise and knocks, loss of power, excessive oil and fuel consumption, smoky exhaust.

　　反映曲柄连杆机构故障现象包括异响和敲击、功率不足、机油和燃料消耗过快、排气冒烟。

［3］If the piston and cylinder are worn and the clearance between them is excessive, a clear metallic knocking appears, which is most vivid when the engine runs cold.

　　如果活塞和汽缸磨损，使缸壁间隙过大，就会出现清脆的金属敲缸声，且发动机低温运转时最明显。

［4］Sharp continuous knocking in the engine accompanied by the oil pressure drop is an evidence of melting out of bearings.

　　伴随着油压降低的连续的尖锐敲击说明轴承熔化。

［5］Loss of engine power stems from the drop of compression which may occur when the cylinder block head nuts are tightened nonuniformly or insufficiently, or the head gasket is damaged, the piston rings are stuck in the grooves owing to carbon or lacquer deposit; the rings are worn, broken or lost their resilience; the cylinders are worn.

发动机功率不足源于压缩压力的降低,这可能由于缸盖紧固不紧或不均匀或缸垫损坏,活塞环由于积炭或釉质沉积在槽中被粘接;活塞环磨损、断裂或失去弹性;汽缸磨损。

[6]To check the compression with a compression gauge, warm up the engine, drive out the spark plugs, fully open the throttle and choke valves.

要用压力表检查压缩压力时,先暖机,取出火花塞,完全打开节气门。

[7]Excessive fuel and oil consumption and smoky gray exhaust (the oil level in the crankcase being normal) are usually attributed to the sticking or wear of the piston rings.

燃油和机油过度消耗和排气冒黑烟(曲轴箱中机油油位正常)通常是活塞环粘着或磨损所致。

[8]Improper seating is symptomized by poor compression, popping in the inlet and exhaust manifolds, loss of power.

压缩压力不足是气门密封不良的表现,进气和排气歧管漏气,造成功率下降。

[9]The valve gear troubles also include wear of the crankshaft gears, tappets, guides, excessive end play of the camshaft, wear of rocker bushings and fulcrums.

配气机构故障还包括曲轴齿轮、挺杆、导杆的磨损、凸轮轴游隙过大、摇臂衬套和支点磨损。

[10]To adjust the clearance between the valve stem and the rocker, remove the valve cover, first detaching all the parts mounted on it; shift the piston to TDC on the compression stroke so that the valves are closed; check the clearance and adjust it, if necessary, as follows: undo the lock-nut on the rocker adjusting screw, set the required clearance by rotating the adjusting screw, tighten the lock-nut holding the screw with the screwdriver and recheck the clearance.

为了要调整气门杆和摇臂之间的间隙,首先卸下气门室盖上的所有零部件;把活塞移到压缩冲程上止点,以便关闭气门;检查并调整气门间隙,如果需要,参照下列各项进行:松开摇臂调整螺钉上的锁紧螺母,通过旋转调整螺钉设定气门间隙,用旋具固定调整螺钉的同时拧紧锁紧螺母,再检查气门间隙。

[11]If there is any problems with your engine, such as irregular noise or smell, or performance problems, leaks or smoke, or "check engine" light is on, etc., have car inspected with a mechanic.

如果有不规律的噪声或异味、性能问题、漏油或者冒烟、"发动机检测"灯闪亮等发动机问题时,找技师检查车辆。

Review Questions

1. What is the reason of the noise and knocks in the engine?
2. How to check the compression with a compression gauge?
3. What is the reason of the excessive fuel and oil consumption and smoky gray exhaust?

4. How to remove the carbon deposit?
5. What is the reason of the improper seating?

参考译文

第九课　发动机维修

　　一台正常的发动机应该能够发出全功率,在满载和无负荷条件下运转平稳,无发动机过热、冒黑烟、机油或冷却液泄漏现象。有些故障现象在不解体发动机的情况下可以根据现象识别。

　　反映曲柄连杆机构故障现象包括异响和敲击、功率不足、机油和燃料消耗过快、排气冒烟。

　　发动机的异响和敲击是由于基础零部件之间磨损导致的配合件之间的间隙过大引起的。

　　如果活塞和汽缸磨损,使缸壁间隙过大,就会出现清脆的金属敲缸声,且发动机低温运转时最明显。金属敲击声随发动机节气门快速打开而增大表明主轴颈或连杆轴颈轴瓦磨损,如果声音较低沉表示曲轴主轴颈轴承磨损。伴随着油压降低的连续的尖锐敲击说明轴承熔化。发动机敲击可以通过听诊器来诊断。

　　发动机功率不足源于压缩压力的降低,这可能由于缸盖紧固不紧或不均匀或缸垫损坏、活塞环由于积炭或釉质沉积在槽中被粘接;活塞环磨损、断裂或失去弹性;汽缸磨损。

　　压缩压力可以用压力表检查。要用压力表检查压缩压力时,先暖机,取出火花塞,完全打开节气门。把压力表的橡皮接头插到火花塞孔,转动曲轴 8 或 10 次,检查压力表读数。曲轴转动后,良好的汽缸压力应该是 0.8~0.9MPa。应对发动机所有汽缸连续地进行压缩压力检查。

　　燃油和机油过度消耗和排气冒黑烟(曲轴箱中机油油位正常)通常是活塞环粘着或磨损所致。活塞环粘着可以不解体发动机进行修复;等量混合的工业酒精和煤油,经火花塞孔向每个汽缸倒入 20g,放置一夜。次日早晨起动发动机,运行 10~15 分钟,停机,更换机油。

　　汽缸壁和缸盖裂痕可能是冷却液冻结或向热的发动机加冷水所致。

　　配气机构故障是气门密封不良或开度不够。

　　压缩压力不足是气门密封不良的表现,进气和排气歧管漏气,造成功率下降。气门密封不良可能是气门密封锥面积炭、气门和摇臂间隙过小所致。

　　气门开度不够将导致发动机异响和功率下降,这种故障是由气门和摇臂之间间隙过大引起的。

　　配气机构故障还包括曲轴齿轮、挺杆、导杆的磨损,凸轮轴游隙过大,摇臂衬套和支点磨损。

　　为了要调整气门杆和摇臂之间的间隙,首先卸下气门室盖上的所有零部件;把活塞移到压缩冲程上止点,以便关闭气门;检查并调整气门间隙,如果需要,参照下列各项进行:松开摇臂调整螺钉上的锁紧螺母,通过旋转调整螺钉设定气门间隙,用旋具固定调整螺钉的同时拧紧锁紧螺母,再检查气门间隙。

　　没有很好维护的发动机看起来像机油很长时间没有换一样。这样的发动机相对费油,需要彻底昂贵的修理。维护得好的发动机,在经过 310 000km(192 000 英里)之后,技术状况仍然很好,根本不需要修理。

因此,保持发动机良好状况最重要的有哪些?

——定期更换机油。

——避免发动机过热。

——依据维护程序更换火花塞、空气过滤器、正时皮带和其他可能帮你省下昂贵修理费用的项目。

——在造成严重损坏之前,及时修理任何的小问题。

机油寿命有限——在一个特定的阶段后,机油性质开始加速下降,碳化加快。一经出现,发动机机油由于积炭(泥渣)污染而严重地短缩发动机的寿命。

当检查机油油位的时候,检查它的状况。如果机油是黑色的就需要更换。使用规定类型的机油(通常能在机油加注口盖或在车主手册上看到类型要求)。在重负荷条件(高温、过载、长距离旅行而没有更换机油等)之下使用合成油。合成油的优势是能抵抗较高的温度,能工作更久而且不损失油性。但是在总里程数较高或非常旧的发动机上使用合成油并不值得——较稀的矿物油就很好。

一段时间后,锈和水垢在散热器和发动机水套中聚集;锈和水垢会限制水的循环,而且发动机容易过热。

如果有不规律的噪声或异味、性能问题、漏油或者冒烟、"发动机检测"灯闪亮等发动机问题时,找技师检查车辆。最好在造成发动机损伤之前,处理任何一个小问题。

Lesson 10 The Check Engine Light

This lesson tried to get a basic idea about what is behind the "check engine" light, rather than the directions for a repair. Quality repair is only possible by a skilled mechanic. Do not try to repair anything by yourself if you are not sure what to do—a car could be unsafe if repaired improperly. Take your car to a dealer or a service shop.

1. Why My Check Engine Light Comes On

All modern vehicles have a computer or ECM (Electronic Control Module) that controls the engine operation. The main purpose of this is to keep the engine running at top efficiency with the lowest possible emissions. With today's strictest emission regulations it is not very easy to achieve-the engine needs to be constantly and precisely adjusted according to various conditions such as speed, load, engine temperature, gasoline quality, ambient air temperature, road conditions, etc.[1]

2. How It Basically Works

There is number of sensors that provide the ECM with all necessary inputs such as the engine temperature, ambient temperature, vehicle speed, load, etc. According to these inputs, the ECM makes initial adjustments adding or subtracting fuel, advancing or retarding the ignition timing, increasing or decreasing idle speed, etc.[2] There is a primary (upstream) oxygen sensor installed in the exhaust before catalytic converter that monitors the quality of combustion in the cylinders. Based on the feedback from this oxygen sensor the ECM makes fine adjustment to the air-fuel mixture to further reduce emissions.

There is another, secondary (downstream) oxygen sensor installed after catalytic converter in the exhaust that monitors catalytic converter's efficiency.

Besides, there are few additional emission control related vehicle systems. For example, there is an Evaporative system (EVAP), designed to prevent gasoline vapors from the gas tank from being released into the atmosphere. It also contains number of sensors and actuators controlled by the ECM.

The ECM has self-diagnostic capability and constantly tests operation of sensors and other components. When any of the sensor signals is missing or out of normal range, the ECM sets a fault and illuminates the "Check Engine" or "Service Engine Soon" light also called MIL (Malfunction Indication Light) storing the corresponding Diagnostic Trouble Code (DTC) in the ECM memory.[3] The same will happen if a mechanical component of controlled system fails. For example, if the EGR valve fails, this will also cause the "check engine" light to come on. Even a loose gas cap will cause the "check engine" to come on.

The stored trouble code can be retrieved with the special scan tool by the technician at your local dealer. The code itself does not tell exactly what part to replace, it only gives a direction where to look for-the technician has to perform certain tests specific for each code to find the exact cause of the problem.[4]

When the "check engine" light is on the simplest way is to visit your local dealer for proper diagnostic. They have all the equipment and information needed to correct the problem. The problem might be even covered by the manufacturers warranty and repaired free of charge.

Whether it is safe to drive if my check engine light is on or not really depends what code is stored and what caused it. In worst cases driving with check engine light may cause more damage to the vehicle. A car may even stall while driving. If your check engine light came on, I would certainly recommend visiting your dealer or a mechanic as soon as possible, just to be on a safe side.

Disconnecting the battery might reset the check engine light on some cars. However, instead of doing so, I recommend bringing your car to a dealer for a proper diagnostic, and here is why:

(1) not all cars will clear the code after disconnecting the battery;

(2) often, the problem may be actually covered by the warranty and repaired free of charge by your dealer. For example, if you have the code P0420—Catalyst System Efficiency Below Threshold, it is very possible that your catalytic converter is still covered by the original emission warranty and may be replaced free of charge (would cost you close to $1000 otherwise).[5]

—Some problems, if not repaired in time may cause a serious damage and more costly repair.

—Disconnecting the battery will cause many other basic settings of the vehicle's computer to be erased (e.g., idle settings, fuel trim settings, transmission shift points, etc.).

—The radio, if code-protected, may be locked after disconnecting the battery, and the "check engine" light will come back anyway if the problem still exist.

3. Self-Diagnosis Systems

Most computerized automotive control systems are equipped with built-in self-diagnostic systems that conduct a multitude of tests of the system. The basic microcomputer self-diagnosis system is designed to monitor the input and output signals of the sensors and actuators and to store any malfunctions in its memory as a trouble code.[6] In general, checks are made for open and short circuits and illogical sensor readings. The number of codes stored and the meaning of the code numbers varies from one manufacturer to another. The Tab. 10-1 below illustrates a typical trouble-code decoding chart.

A typical trouble-code decoding chart   Tab. 10-1

Trouble code identification			
Flash code	Trouble code	Fault location	Probable cause
1	PO151	Heated oxygen sensor(HO_2S)-LH front-circuit/voltage low	Wiring short circuit, HO_2S, Fuel system, ECM
2	PO152	Healed oxygen sensor(HO_2S)-LH front-circuit/voltage high	Wiring open circuit, HO_2S, ECM
3	PO131	Heated oxygen sensor(HO_2S)-RH front-circuit/voltage low	Wiring short circuit, HO_2S, Fuel system, ECM
4	PO132	Heated oxygen sensor(HO_2S)-RH front-circuit/voltage high	Wiring open circuit, HO_2S, ECM
5	PO1071	Manifold absolute pressure (MAP) sensor-circuit/voltage low	Wiring MAP sensor, ECM

The method used to activate the self-diagnosis mode varies with each manufacturer. For example, on the General Motors computer command control (CCC) system, when a malfunction is detected, the check engine or service engine soon light illuminates on the instrument panel. If, for example, the engine-temperature sensor is supplying illogical readings, the light will come ON and the computer will substitute a fixed value from its programmed memory so the car can be driven. The light turning ON also means a trouble-code number has been stored in the ECM memory to record the detected failure. The service technician can, at a later time, ground a test terminal under the dash and retrieve the trouble code, or codes, stored in memory.[7] The stored codes are displayed in a series of flashes of the check engine light.

If the problem is intermittent, the check engine light will go out, but the trouble code will remain stored. After all service is completed, any trouble codes stored in memory should be cleared by removing the ECM fuse for 10s. [8] This will ensure that the trouble code does not remain stored in memory even though repairs have been made.

New Words

quality [ˈkwɑləti]	n. 品质，性质	
mechanic [məˈkænɪk]	n. 机修工，机械师	
module [ˈmɑdʒul]	n. 模数，模块	
regulations [ˌreɡjəˈleɪʃ(ə)n]	n. 规章，法规	
initial [ɪˈnɪʃ(ə)l]	adj. 最初的，初始的	
upstream [ʌpˈstrim]	ad. 上游	
evaporative [iˈvæpərətɪv]	adj. 蒸发的	
diagnostic [ˌdaɪəɡˈnɑstɪk]	adj. 诊断的	
retrieve [rɪˈtriv]	vt. 读取	
technician [tekˈnɪʃ(ə)n]	n. 技术员，技师	
specific [spəˈsɪfɪk]	adj. 详细而精确的，明确的，特殊的	
warranty [ˈwɔrənti]	n. 授权，担保	
stall [stɔl]	v. (使)停转，(使)停止	
charge [tʃɑrdʒ]	n. 费用，充电	
threshold [ˈθreʃˌhoʊld]	n. 限值	
multitude [ˈmʌltɪˌtud]	n. 大量，多倍	
illogical [ɪˈlɑdʒɪk(ə)l]	adj. 异常的，不合理的	
manufacturer [ˌmænjəˈfæktʃərər]	n. 制造商	
identification [aɪˌdentɪfɪˈkeɪʃ(ə)n]	n. 鉴定，证明	
wiring [ˈwaɪrɪŋ]	n. 配线，接线	
illuminate [ɪˈlumɪˌneɪt]	vt. 照亮，说明	
ground [ɡraʊnd]	vt. 使……接地(搭铁)	
intermittent [ˌɪntərˈmɪt(ə)nt]	adj. 间歇性的	

Phrases and Expressions

check engine light	检测发动机指示灯
comes on	点亮
ambient air temperature	环境空气温度
catalytic converter	催化转换器
free of charge	免费
built-in	内置的
service technician	服务技师
EGR(exhaust gas recirculation)	废气再循环
service shop	维修车间

Notes to the Text

[1] With today's strictest emission regulations it is not very easy to achieve—the engine needs to be constantly and precisely adjusted according to various conditions such as speed, load, engine temperature, gasoline quality, ambient air temperature, road conditions, etc.

按照现在最严格的排放法规,这并不容易做到—发动机需要根据各种不同的条件,如速度、负荷、发动机温度、汽油品质、环境空气温度、道路条件等进行连续、精确地调整。

[2] According to these inputs, the ECM makes initial adjustments adding or subtracting fuel, advancing or retarding the ignition timing, increasing or decreasing idle speed, etc.

根据这些输入信息,ECM做出最初的调节:增加或减少燃料、提前或推迟点火正时、提高或降低怠速转速。

[3] When any of the sensor signals is missing or out of normal range, the ECM sets a fault and illuminates the "Check Engine" or "Service Engine Soon" light also called MIL (Malfunction Indication Light) storing the corresponding Diagnostic Trouble Code (DTC) in the ECM memory.

任何一个传感器信号消失或超出正常范围时,ECM就认定有故障并且点亮"检测发动机"指示灯或者"尽快检修"指示灯(也称作故障指示灯),并将对应的诊断故障码(DTC)储存在有记忆功能的ECM存储器中。

[4] The code itself does not tell exactly what part to replace, it only gives a direction where to look for—the technician has to perform certain tests specific for each code to find the exact cause of the problem.

故障码本身不能确切地告诉你什么零件需要更换,它只提供检查方向,要确定故障码对应的确切故障原因—技术人员必须根据每个码进行特定的测试。

[5] For example, if you have the code P0420—Catalyst System Efficiency Below Threshold it is very possible that your catalytic converter is still covered by the original emission warranty and may be replaced free of charge (would cost you close to $1 000 otherwise).

例如,如果故障码为P0420—催化效率在限值以下,那么很有可能你的催化转换器仍然属于初始排放担保范围,可以免费更换(否则可能会花费你接近$1 000)。

[6] The basic microcomputer self-diagnosis system is designed to monitor the input and output signals of the sensors and actuators and to store any malfunctions in its memory as a trouble code.

基本的微机自诊断系统被设计用来检测传感器和执行器的输入、输出信号,并以故障码的形式将故障存储在它的储存器里。

[7] The service technician can, at a later time, ground a test terminal under the dash and retrieve the trouble code, or codes, stored in memory.

稍后,修理人员可以通过将位于仪表板下的测试端读取故障码或储存在存储器内的编码。

[8] After all service is completed, any trouble codes stored in memory should be cleared by disconnecting the battery power supply or by removing the ECM fuse for 10s.

在所有的维修服务完成后,储存在存储器中的任何故障码都应通过取去 ECM 熔断丝并保持断开 10s 以上的方法来清除。

Review Questions

1. What is the main purpose of ECM?
2. What is the main purpose of the Evaporative (EVAP) system?
3. What will happen when any of the sensor signals is missing or out of normal range?
4. What to do if my "check engine" light is on?
5. What is the main purpose of the self-diagnosis system?

参考译文

第十课 检测发动机指示灯

本课只是试图说明"检测发动机"指示灯后面隐含的基本含义,而非修理指南。高质量的修理只可能由维修熟练的技师完成。如果你不能确定该做什么,不要试图独自修理故障——不当的修理,可能会影响车辆安全。把你的车送到经销商或服务商处(维修)。

1. 检测发动机灯为什么会亮

所有的现代车辆都有一个计算机或者 ECM(电子控制模块)控制发动机运转。其主要目的是使发动机保持最高效率、尽可能低的排放运转。按照现在最严格的排放法规,这并不容易做到——发动机需要根据各种不同的条件,如速度、负荷、发动机温度、汽油品质、环境空气温度、道路条件等进行连续、精确地调整。

2. 检测发动机指示灯的基本原理

有许多传感器用来给 ECM 提供所有必需的输入信息,如发动机温度、环境温度、车辆速度、负荷等。根据这些输入信息,ECM 做出最初的调节:增加或减少燃料、提前或推迟点火正时、提高或降低怠速转速。用来监控汽缸内燃烧质量的主(上游)氧传感器安装在排气装置中催化转换器之前。基于来自氧传感器的反馈信息,ECM 对空气-燃料混合气进行微调以便进一步减少排放。

另一个辅助(下游)氧传感器安装在排气装置中催化转换器之后,用来检测催化转换器的催化效率。

此外,还有其他的汽车排放辅助控制系统。例如,蒸发系统(EVAP),用来阻止来自燃油箱的汽油蒸汽被释放到大气之内。它同样含有传感器和被 ECM 控制的执行器。

ECM 具有自诊断能力,不停地测试传感器和其他元件的工作情况。任何一个传感器信号消失或超出正常范围时,ECM 就认定有故障并且点亮"检测发动机"指示灯或者"尽快检修"指示灯(也称作故障指示灯),并将对应的诊断故障码(DTC)储存在有记忆功能的 ECM 存储器中。如果受控制的机械系统元件失效,将会出现同样的情况。例如,如果 EGR 阀失效,将会导致"检测发动机"指示灯点亮,甚至加油口盖松动也会导致"检测发动机"指示灯点亮。

被储存的故障码可以在当地经销商那里由技术人员用专用诊断仪读取。故障码本身不能确切地告诉你什么零件需要更换,它只提供检查方向,要确定故障码对应的确切故障原因—技术人员必须根据每个码进行特定的测试。

当"检测发动机"指示灯亮后,最简单的方法是找当地经销商来做适当的诊断。他们有解决问题的所有的设备和信息。有些问题甚至可能属于制造商担保范围而可以免费修理。

至于"检测发动机"指示灯亮后操纵是否安全取决于被储存的故障码及其造成原因。在最坏的情况下,驾驶"检测发动机"指示灯亮的车辆可能对车辆造成更多损害,甚至使汽车停止运转。如果你的"检测发动机"指示灯亮了,为确保安全建议你尽快拜访你的经销商或者维修技师。

断开蓄电池连接可能在一些车上会重新设定"检测发动机"指示灯。然而,不建议这种做法,而是建议把车开到经销商处进行恰当的诊断,原因是:

(1)不是所有的车在断开蓄电池之后都会清除故障码;

(2)所发生的问题实际上通常属于制造商担保范围而由经销商免费修理。例如,如果故障码为 P0420—催化效率在限值以下,那么很有可能你的催化转换器仍然属于初始排放担保范围,可以免费更换(否则可能会花费你接近 $1 000)。

——些故障如果不及时修理可能会造成更严重的损坏和更昂贵的修理。

—断开蓄电池将会引起车辆计算机的许多其他基本设定信息被擦除(例如怠速转速设定、燃油微调设定、变速器换挡点等。)

—如果收音机有密码保护的话,断开蓄电池之后可能被锁住,如果故障仍然存在,无论如何"发动机检测"灯依旧会亮。

3. 自诊断系统

大部分汽车计算机控制系统都装备内置的可以进行大量系统测试的自诊断系统。基本的微机自诊断系统被设计用来检测传感器和执行器的输入、输出信号,并以故障码的形式将故障存储在它的储存器里。通常用于检测断路、短路和不合逻辑的传感器信息。不同的制造商,其储存的故障码数目和故障码的含义不同。表 10-1 举例说明了一个典型的故障码译码表。

典型故障码的译码表 表 10-1

故障码定义			
闪码	故障码	故障位置	可能的原因
1	PO151	热氧传感器(HO$_2$S)-左前电路/电压低	接线短路,HO$_2$S,燃油系,ECM
2	PO152	热氧传感器(HO$_2$S)-左前电路/电压高	接线断路,HO$_2$S,ECM
3	PO131	热氧传感器(HO$_2$S)-右前电路/电压低	接线短路,HO$_2$S,燃油系,ECM
4	PO132	热氧传感器(HO$_2$S)-右前电路/电压高	接线断路,HO$_2$S,ECM
5	PO1071	歧管绝对压力(MAP)传感器电路/电压低	歧管绝对压力传感器接线,ECM

不同制造商的自诊断模式的激发方法不同。例如,通用汽车公司计算机指令控制(CCC)系统,当一个故障被发现时,在仪表板上的检测发动机指示灯或者尽快检修指示灯点亮。举例来说,如果发动机冷却液温度传感器提供的信息异常,检测发动机指示灯将会点

亮,而且计算机将会以预置的数值替换来自它的错误值,维持车辆运行。检测发动机指示灯的点亮也意味着一个故障码已经被储存在 ECM 中,以记录被发现的故障。稍后,修理人员可以通过将位于仪表板下的测试端读取故障码或储存在存储器内的编码。被储存的故障码通过发动机检测指示灯一系列的闪烁加以显示。

如果故障是间歇性的,检测发动机指示灯将会熄灭,但是故障码将会依然储存在存储器中。在所有的维修服务完成后,储存在存储器中的任何故障码都应通过取去 ECM 熔断丝并保持断开 10s 以上的方法来清除。这将会确保修理后,故障码不再储存于存储器中。

Lesson 11　Safety and Performance Testers

There are many types of safety and performance testers for vehicle. The style and design depend on the test items, the vehicle style, the year of the tester, and the manufacturer. Diagnostic test lanes for passenger cars are described in this paper. It is integrated fully automatic testing lanes for passenger cars and light utility vehicles up to a GVW of 3500 kg. The test lane consists of an electronic console and three mechanical units which mounted in the floor, are: a side slip tester, a suspension tester and a roller brake tester. [1]

The software, that controls the measurements, is designed for fully automatic testing. The operator can perform all tests one after the other without any need to interfere with the system. All the operator has to do is to drive the car and to watch the results on the screen. After each test, the measuring result of the particular test is shown. After completion of all tests, a summary report is shown on the screen.

1. The Side Slip Tester

The side slip tester is a steel plate that can roll sideways on bearings. When the operator drives a wheel of a car over the plate, the tire may move the plate sideways. These forces arise among others, when the toe setting of an axle is out of specification. The side slip tester measures the distance in meters over which a wheel of an axle is dragged sideways, when the other wheel of that axle runs straight for 1km. [2]

The main influencing factor of the measurement is the total toe adjustment of the axle. The alignment is set to have all wheels run straight forward at cruising speed. The wheels should also run parallel to the car centre line. The side slip reading will correspond to a toe adjustment between the dynamic toe value and the static toe value. The operator must always drive over the side slip tester at walking speed. He should avoid that the car body moves up and down, as this causes bump steer.

When the side slip tester measures more than 7 m/km effective toe-in or toe-out, the operator must cheek the wheel alignment. [3] When the measurement is between 4 and 7 m/km effective toe-in or toe-out, the operator is advised to check the wheel alignment.

2. The Suspension Tester

The suspension tester measures the spring system of a vehicle. The quantities, related to vehicle parts, that influence the measurement, are from top to bottom: body mass, body spring, shock absorber, wheel mass and tire stiffness. [4] Also the stabilizer bar can influence the measurement. Each wheel is sequentially brought into vibration with a fixed amplitude and with frequencies from 0 to 25 Hertz. During this vibration the variation of the vertical wheel load are measured. [5] After the measurement the measured data is analyzed according to different methods.

The suspension tester consists of two measuring plates that sequentially vibrate sinusoidally with a variable frequency and a constant amplitude. The tester measures the dynamic vertical force that the wheel exerts on the measuring plate. After the measurement of the two wheels of an axle, the measured data are processed and the results are presented on the screen.

The available measurement method is Eusama which has the Damping method and the Altus Speed method.

1) Eusama

The Eusama value is an internationally recognized measure for the road holding safety of a vehicle. It shows how well the suspension parts can keep the tire in contact with the road under worst case conditions. It is a measure for how well the suspension can transmit the braking forces during an emergency stop. The computer compares the measured adhesion value with rejection limits that are stored in memory: 0% to 20% Dangerous, 21% to 40% Fair, 41% to 60% Good, more than 61% Excellent. [6] A difference Left/Right that exceeds 20% should be investigated. The Eusama value is sensitive to the tire stiffness and to the weight of the vehicle. Please note that the Eusama value is measured at the relatively high frequencies between 12 and 24 Hertz and so the Ensama value does not necessarily correlate with what the drivers feels when he enters a corner with the vehicle. [7]

2) Damping

With this method the Wheel Damping Factor of the suspension system is calculated. This value indicates how well the wheel bounce resonance is controlled by the shock absorber. For most cars the damping factor is between 0.2 and 0.4. A difference Left/Right which exceeds 0.05 should be investigated. The damping factor is not dependent on the weight (and the load) of the vehicle, but depends on the ratio sprung to unsprung weight and the damping force of the shock absorber.

3) Altus Speed

With this method, the speed is calculated at which the car under test can safely travel over the Altus Test Track. This imaginary test track is composed of surface irregularities that cause the suspension to vibrate. The Altus speed can then be compared to the legal speed limits in a country or with the design speed of the vehicle. [8] A difference in Altus speed Left/Right on one axle that exceeds 25% should be investigated. Be sure to enter the correct tire speed index as this influences the speed value. The weight (and the load) of the vehicle also influences the results.

3. The Roller Brake Tester

1) General

The roller brake tester is a well known method to analyze and judge the efficiency of the braking system of a vehicle. The system consists of a pair of rollers for each wheel. The roller pair is driven by an electric motor. The brake forces induce reaction forces on the electric motor. These reaction forces are measured by an electronic transducer with strain gauges. The roller diameter is sufficiently large to keep the tire flexing to a minimum.

2) Testing Brakes on a Roller Tester

A good testing procedure is the following. Each step in this process should take about 5s, so the total process takes about 30 s.

(1) Stabilize the vehicle.

(2) During the first 5 s the operator should not touch the brake pedal in order to measure the wiling resistance. An arrow is visible on the screen. It indicates the desired magnitude (higher or lower) of the pedal force that the operator should apply.

(3) Slowly increase the pedal force until the brake forces (in N) are about equal to the weight of the car (in kg) and quickly release the brake pedal. [9] Check that the left and the right brake forces increase simultaneously and that not one of them lags.

(4) Hold the pedal force at a constant value to check the ovality (out-of-roundness) of both sides.

(5) Slowly increase the pedal force until the brake forces are about twice the weight of the car and quickly release the brake pedal. Check that the left and right brake force simultaneously returns to the value of the rolling resistance and that not one of them lags or remain at a higher value.

(6) Slowly increase the pedal force until slip occurs and the tester stops. After 5s the rollers will start again to assist you in driving out of the rollers. If you do not drive out within 2s, the software will assume that you want to repeat this measurement and the first test will be overwritten.

New Words

item ['aɪtəm]	n. 项目
console ['kɑn.soʊl]	n. 控制台
adherence [əd'hɪrəns]	n. 粘着[附，结];粘着(力)
specification [ˌspesɪfɪ'keɪʃ(ə)n]	n. 规格,规范
alignment [ə'laɪnmənt]	n. 调正,定位
dynamic [daɪ'næmɪk]	adj. 动力的,动态的
static ['stætɪk]	adj. 静态的,静力的
amplitude ['æmplɪ.tud]	n. 振幅
sequentially [sɪ'kwenʃəli]	ad. 继续地;顺序地
exert [ɪg'zɜrt]	v. 竭尽全力
investigate [ɪn'vestɪ.geɪt]	v. 调查,研究
sprung [sprʌŋ]	adj. spring 的过去式及过去分词;支在弹簧上的
unsprung [ˌʌn'sprʌŋ]	adj. (车、椅等)不支承在弹簧上的
altus ['æltəs]	adj. 高的

imaginary [ɪˈmædʒɪ.nerɪ]	adj.	假想的
simultaneously [ˌsaɪməlˈteɪnjəslɪ]	ad.	同时地
ovality [əʊˈvælɪtɪ]	n.	椭圆度,椭圆形

Phrases and Expressions

diagnostic test lane	诊断检测线
GVW　Gross Vehicle Weight	车辆总重
light utility vehicle	轻型多用途车
roller brake tester	滚筒制动试验台
interfere with	妨碍
toe-in	前束
toe-out	负前束
brake pedal	制动踏板
tire stiffness	轮胎刚度
shock absorber	减振器
Eusama	欧洲减振器制造协会(EUSAMA)推荐的测试标准,按接地力分为四级：80%以上为优秀；60%～79%为良好；40%～59%为合格；0～39%为不足。
Wheel Damping Factor	车轮阻尼因数

Notes to the Text

[1] The test lane consists of an electronic console and three mechanical units which mounted in the floor, are: a side slip tester, a suspension tester and a roller brake tester.

检测线由电子仪表控制台和安装在地板中的三个机械单元组成,三个机械单元分别是：侧滑量测试仪、悬架测试仪和滚筒制动试验台。

[2] The side slip tester measures the distance in meters over which a wheel of an axle is dragged sideways, when the other wheel of that axle runs straight for 1km.

侧滑量测试仪以米为单位测出当车桥直线行驶1km时该轴车轮被外拖的距离。

[3] When the side slip tester measures more than 7 m/km effective toe-in or toe-out, the operator must cheek the wheel alignment.

当侧滑量测试仪测得的前束或负前束超过7m/km时,一定要检查前轮定位。

[4] The quantities, related to vehicle parts, that influence the measurement, are from top to bottom: body mass, body spring, shock absorber, wheel mass and tire stiffness.

对应于影响测试的相关车辆零配件,测试量从上到下有：车身质量、悬架弹簧、减振器、轮胎质量和刚度。

[5] Each wheel is sequentially brought into vibration with a fixed amplitude and with frequencies from 0 to 25 Hertz. During this vibration the variation of the vertical wheel load are measured.

每个车轮依次进行0～25Hz频率的固定振幅的振动。测出振动期间车轮上垂直动载荷的变化。

[6] The computer compares the measured adhesion value with rejection limits that are

stored in memory: 0 to 20% Dangerous, 21 to 40% Fair, 41 to 60% Good, more than 61% Excellent.

计算机将测得的附着系数值与储存在存储器内的限值作比较:0%~20%为危险,21%~40%为合格,41%~60%为好,大于61%为优良。

[7] Please note that the Eusama value is measured at the relatively high frequencies between 12 and 24 Hertz and so the Ensama value does not necessarily correlate with what the drivers feels when he enters a corner with the vehicle.

请注意,Eusama 评价值是在 12~24Hz 之间的相对高频测试的,因此该值不需要考虑当车辆进入一个弯道时驾驶员的感觉。

[8] The Altus speed can then be compared to the legal speed limits in a country or with the design speed of the vehicle.

Altus 速度可以与国家的法规限制车速或车辆的设计速度相比较。

[9] Slowly increase the pedal force until the brake forces (in N) are about equal to the weight of the car (in kg) and quickly release the brake pedal.

慢慢地增大制动踏板上的力(单位 N)直到制动力与车重(单位 kg)相等,然后迅速释放制动踏板。

Review Questions

1. What is the function of the engine analyzer?
2. How do side slip tester work?.
3. What is the main influencing factor of the side slip tester measurement?
4. What is the Eusama value ?
5. What is the function of the roller brake tester?

参考译文

第十一课 安全性能测试仪

市场上有许多类型的车辆用安全性能测试仪。型号和设计取决于测试项目、车辆型号、测试仪的制造年份和制造商。本文将介绍乘用车诊断检测线。它综合了总重不超过 3500kg 的乘用车和轻型多用途汽车的综合检测线。检测线由电子仪表控制台和安装在地板中的三个机械单元组成,三个机械单元分别是:侧滑量测试仪、悬架测试仪和滚筒制动试验台。

控制测量的软件为全自动测试而设计。操作者无须任何参与,系统连续地进行所有的测试。操作者所做的仅仅是驾驶车辆并在屏幕上看结果。每个测试之后,详细的测试结果都可被显示。所有的测试完成之后,屏幕将显示一个简要的报告。

1. 侧滑量测试仪

侧滑量测试仪是一个能在轴承上侧向滑动的钢盘。当操作者驾车驶过钢盘时,轮胎可以使钢盘侧向移动。当车轴的前束定位超出范围时,轮胎和钢盘之间的作用力增加。侧滑量测试仪以米为单位测出当车桥直线行驶 1km 时该轴车轮被外拖的距离。

该测量的主要影响因素是车桥总前束。车轮定位的目的是使汽车在滑行中所有的车轮都直行。车轮应该平行于车的中心线。前束调整使侧滑量示数在相应的动态前束值和静态前束之间。操作者应当保持车辆以步行速度在侧滑量测试仪上行驶,应该避免车身上下运动,以免引起转动。

当侧滑量测试仪测得的前束或负前束超过 7m/km 时,一定要检查前轮定位。当侧滑量测试仪测得的前束或负前束在 4~7m/km 时建议检查前轮定位。

2. 悬架测试仪

悬架测试仪测量车辆的弹簧系统。对应于影响测试的相关车辆零配件,测试量从上到下有:车身质量、悬架弹簧、减振器、轮胎质量和刚度。稳定杆对测量也有影响。每个车轮依次进行 0~25Hz 频率的固定振幅的振动。测出振动期间车轮上垂直动载荷的变化。测试结束后,测试数据依照不同的方法进行分析。

悬架测试仪有两个测试板,以可变连续频率、振幅不变的正弦曲线振动。测试仪测量车轮垂直施加在测试板上的力。测量完后车轴的两个车轮,处理测得的数据,结果显示在屏幕上。

现用的测量方法是欧洲减振器制造协会试验法(Eusama),包括阻尼模式和 Altus 模式。这些方法在下面解释。

1) Eusama

Eusama 评价指标是一个国际公认的车辆行驶安全尺度。它表示悬挂零配件在最坏的情况下轮胎与道路接触情况。它是在紧急制动时,悬架可以传递的制动力的度量。计算机将测得的附着系数值与储存在存储器内的限值作比较:0%~20% 为危险,21%~40% 为合格,41%~60% 为好,大于 61% 为优良。左右轮之间的差值超过 20% 需要检查。Eusama 评价值对轮胎刚度和车辆的质量敏感。请注意,Eusama 评价值是在 12~24Hz 之间的相对高频测试的,因此该值不需要考虑当车辆进入一个弯道时驾驶员的感觉。

2) 阻尼模式

通过这一模式,来计算悬架车轮阻尼因数。该测量值表示减振器车轮跳动谐振的情况。大部分悬架车轮阻尼因数在 0.2 和 0.4 间。左右轮之差超过 0.05 需要检查。阻尼因数并不取决于车辆的质量(和负载),而是取决于簧载质量与非簧载质量的比值和减振器的阻尼力。

3) Altus 模式

通过这一模式,测试车辆在 Altus 车道上保持安全行驶的速度。这个模拟的测试道由导致悬挂振动的不规则路面组成。Altus 车速可以与国家的法规限制车速或车辆的设计速度相比较。一轴左右轮之间的 Altus 模式差值超过 25% 时,需要检查车桥。当轮胎速度系数影响试验结果时,一定要确保轮胎速度系数输入正确。车辆的质量(和负载)也影响结果。

3. 滚筒制动试验台

1) 简介

滚筒制动试验台是用来分析、判断车辆制动效能的一个广为人知的方法。该系统对应每个车轮有一对滚筒。这对滚筒由电机驱动。制动力产生的反力作用在电机上。这些反力由一个应变计式电子传感器测量。滚筒直径应当足够大以使轮胎变形处于最小。

2) 在滚筒制动试验机上测试制动器

良好的测试过程如下。过程中每个步骤应该持续大约 5s,整个进程大约为 30s。

(1)固定车辆。

(2)最初 5s 期间,操作者不应该碰触制动踏板以测量阻滞力。屏幕上可以看到一个箭头。它提示操作者施加到制动踏板上的力的大小(更高或者更低)。

(3)慢慢地增大制动踏板上的力(单位 N)直到制动力与车重(单位 kg)相等,然后迅速释放制动踏板。同时检查左右边的制动力的增加量,确保任何一边没有延迟。

(4)保持制动踏板上的力不变来检查两侧车轮的椭圆度(圆度)。

(5)慢慢地增加制动踏板上的力,直到制动力达到两倍车重,然后迅速释放制动踏板。检查左右的制动器力应同时地回到滚动阻力值,而不是其中之一落后或保持在较高的力。

(6)慢慢地增加制动踏板上的力直到打滑,测试停止。5s 之后滚筒重新运转协助车辆驾驶出滚筒。如果车辆 2s 之内不驶出滚筒,软件将会认为想要重复测量,第一个测试结果将会被重写。

Unit 3　Sell Automobile

Lesson 12　The 5W's of World Class Customer Service Training

The interaction anyone has at any level with your employees, including you, gives a customer-whether current, potential, internal or external—an opportunity to make a judgment about you and your company.

I am not just talking about call centers here. All technical support or help desk personnel are included as well, as a matter of fact, anyone who is in the customer service business period.

With continued focus on customer satisfaction, customer retention, and lifetime value of the customer, it is no surprise that contact center operations continue to increase in importance as the primary hub of a customer's experience. For the customer, the person on the other end of the phone is the company. The contact center is still the most common way that customers get in touch with businesses. In fact, Gartner reports that 92% of all contact is through the center. And it is been reported that 70% to 90% of what happens with customers is driven by human nature, having nothing to do with technology.

People often talk about taking customer service and "kicking it up a notch". In the food industry, the word "lagniappe" is often used. Its definition is "a small present given to a customer with a purchase". For example, when you go to the bakery and buy a dozen donuts or bagels, you oftentimes get a "free" one. That is what customer service should be about—giving the customer more than they expected! Let us bring lagniappe into the contact center industry.

If we are going to speak about world class customer service, let us have a working definition it so we are all on the same page. Customer service is those activities provided by a company's employees that enhance the ability of a customer to realize the full potential value of a product or service before and after the sale is made, thereby leading to satisfaction and repurchase.

1. The ♯1 W: Why(Why Should be Trained?)

The state of customer service today is not good, be it over the phone or self service. Because 92% of people feel their call experience is important in shaping the image of a company, this reinforces the importance of centers in branding the image of their companies.

In a Mobius Management Systems Survey, here is what happened because of poor customer service:

60% cancelled accounts with banks;
36% changed insurance providers;
40% changed telephone companies;
35% changed credit card providers;
37% changed Internet service providers.

Are you one of these statistics? I certainly am.

In a study done by Purdue University and BenchmarkPortal.com, in answer to (1) how did agents satisfy your needs and handle the call, and (2) based on any negative experience, would you stop using this company in the future? The findings reveal a strong correlation between the participant's age and the tendency to stop using the company after a bad experience.

What does this mean? Younger participants were less tolerant and more likely to move to the competition. People over 65 were found to be more demanding than those in middle age.

What can you do? Give younger callers a "wow" experience--maintain their loyalty. People over 36 probably have more of an "emotional bank account" with the company they are dealing with—maybe had some good experience and therefore are more willing to "forgive."

Strategies for success for world class service should include:
(1) respond promptly;
(2) handle requests through the customers' choice of medium;
(3) be brief and clear;
(4) reduce back and forth communications (especially in writing, i.e., email, kick it up to a phone call if it goes beyond two);
(5) personalized service;
(6) delight the customer;
(7) inform and educate them;
(8) establish your expertise and professionalism;
(9) offer options;
(10) diffuse upset, anger, when and if necessary;
(11) escalate, if required;
(12) take ownership of the call.

Remember we are still on the first W-the Why. Today's pressures on agents are different than in the past. They are asked to handle more customer, more volume, more complex and/or complicated calls. After all if the customer could handle their issues with self service, the customer probably would not call. But if the customer tried self service and it did not work, now customer is upset and it is an escalated call from the get go.

2. The ♯2 W: Who(Who Should be Trained?)

We suggest front line agents/representatives, supervisors, team leaders, managers, assistant managers, internal customers and other departments—anyone who is a touch point so that they can learn to speak the same language, and more importantly, not be in an adversarial position, but rather, together they are serving the external customer or end user.

3. The ♯3 W: Where(Where Should the Training Take Place?)

Offsite vs. onsite, and there are advantages and disadvantages for both.

Certainly it is most effective to have training on site. However, distractions are rampant as is the participant's availability to a person or problem.[1]

Offsite is more costly. However, there are no distractions and the participants are unavailable to their managers, other departments, or any issues. I believe there is psychic value in taking people away from their work stations and off site to acknowledge the touch jobs they have.

4. The ♯4 W: What(What Should be Included in Any Training?)

The following modules provide a robust, powerful, and succinct training curriculum: Quality Customer Service; Rapport Building; Customer Expectations; Perception Shifting; Conflict Resolution; Language Skills; Anger Management; E-Mail Protocol; Stress Reduction; Empathetic Responsiveness; Change Management; Communication/Listening Skills; Interaction/Role Play Service with a Smile.

The more professionally are employees treated, the more professionally they will treat your customers.

5. The ♯5 W: When(When Should the Trainning Take Place?)

We say for new hires, monthly, ongoing, consistently, whenever change occurs, when stressors increase, and as needed.[2]

For example, it is suggested that each employee get a minimum of 24 hours per year of ongoing training, spread out over time for the most absorption. It can be divided that our trainings into two-four hour sessions per day and deliver 6 days per employee. Therefore, 30 people can participate in the training per day. If there has been no ongoing training, conduct the train four days once a month for four months and then a session three months later, and then another three months later. In this manner, training is customized, in real time, and can address whatever challenges are presented when they occur.

New Words

interaction [ˌɪntərˈækʃən]	n. 相互作用,相互影响
retention [rɪˈtenʃən]	n. 保存(保持力,包装牢固,记忆力,保留物)
customer retention	n. 客户维系,客户保留,客户营销,培养客户忠诚度
endeavor [ɪnˈdevə]	n. 努力,尽力
	v. 努力,尽力

lagniappe [læn'jæp]		n. 小赠品
bagel ['beigəl]		n. 百吉饼(一种点心)
reinforce [ˌriːin'fɔːs]		n. 加固物
		vi. 增援,加强
		vt. 加强,增援
statistics [stə'tistiks]		n. 统计;统计数字;统计学
reveal [ri'viːl]		v. 显示,透露
correlation [ˌkɔri'leiʃən]		n. 相互关系,相关,关联
tolerant ['tɔlərənt]		adj. 宽容的,容忍的
demanding [di'mɑːndiŋ; (US) di'mændiŋ]		adj. 要求多的,吃力的
wow [wau]		n. 巨大的成功
		int. 哇
loyalty ['lɔiəlti]		n. 忠诚,忠心
seminar ['seminaː]		n. (大学的)研究班,研讨会
profitable ['prɔfitəbəl]		adj. 有益的,有用的
medium ['miːdjəm]		n. 媒体,方法,媒介
		adj. 适中的,中等的
diffuse [di'fjuːz]		v. 散播
escalate ['eskəleit]		v. 扩大,升高,增强
rampant ['ræmpənt]		adj. 猖獗的,蔓延的,奔放的
psychic ['saikik]		adj. 灵魂的,精神的,心灵的,对超自然力敏感的;通灵的
		n. 巫师,灵媒,心灵研究
robust [rə'bʌst]		adj. 强壮的,强健的
succinct [sək'siŋkt]		adj. 简洁的
rapport [ræ'pɔːt]		n. 关系,同意,一致
empathetic [ˌempə'θetik]		adj. (=empathic)移情作用的,感情移入的
absorption [əb'sɔːpʃnə]		n. 吸收

Phrases and Expressions

get in touch with	与……保持联系
state of the art technology	最新的技术
kick it up a notch	提升到一定程度(量)
top notch	最出众的人或其他东西,大腕
on the same page	大家关注/讨论同一个问题
negative experience	不愉快的经历
using this company	使用公司产品,引申为:光顾这个公司
emotional bank account	感情账户(意思为用户对企业的感情因素)
back and forth communications	反复沟通

Notes to the Text

[1] However, distractions are rampant as is the participant's availability to a person or problem.

然而,参与者的注意力很容易被其他的人或者问题所分散。

[2] We say for new hires, monthly, ongoing, consistently, whenever change occurs, when stressors increase, and as needed.

我们鼓励各种培训,包括对新雇工进行的、按月进行的、正在进行的、常年计划的以及根据情况变化需要的、压力增加及其他需要时的培训。

Review Questions

1. Do you think what kind of training is the best for salesman?
2. What is the 5 W's of world class customer service training?
3. As a employee working at the customer service of one auto manufacture, what he should study?
4. Please talk about the project in a company you know.
5. How many people changed Internet service providers because of poor customer service?

参考译文

第三单元 汽车销售

第十二课 客服培训的五"W"宝典

客户(无论是现有客户、潜在客户、内部客户或者外部客户)可以通过包括你在内的任何人与雇员之间的沟通,来判断你和你的公司。

这里说的并不仅仅是呼叫中心。其也包括所有的技术支持或者服务台,事实上,包括所有从事客户服务工作的人。

随着对客户的满意度、客户忠诚度以及客户价值关注的增加,客户联络中心作为主要的客户体验信息中心,变得越来越重要。对于客户而言,电话的另一端代表的是公司。客户联络中心仍然是与客户进行商业沟通的最普遍的方式。事实上,Gartner 的报告显示,92%的业务联系都要通过客户联络中心。据说70%到90%客户的行为都源于人类本性的驱动,与技术没有任何关系。

人们经常谈到客户服务问题,并上升到一定高度来认识。在食品工业领域,"赠品"这个词很常见。它的意思就是"赠送给产生购买的消费者的一个小礼物"。比如,你去面包店买一打甜甜圈或者百吉饼,面包店老板经常会再免费送你一个。这就是客户服务的宗旨—给予超乎客户想象的服务!我们应该把这种"增值"服务借鉴到客户联络中心中去。

如果谈到世界级的客户服务,为了便于讨论,首先我们应该对客户服务有一个明确的定义。客户服务是指在销售前后由公司的员工提供的一些活动,通过这些活动可以提高消费者全面了解一种产品的潜力价值或者服务的能力,从而使客户满意,并且再次购买本公司的产品或服务。

1. 第一个 W(Why):(为什么接受培训)?

客户服务的现状并不是很好,电话服务或者自助服务除外。因为92%的人认为他们的电话交流对于树立公司形象是至关重要的,这就加强了电话服务中心在树立企业品牌中的重要性。

Mobius公司一项管理系统调查的资料显示,缺乏良好的客户服务造成以下后果:

60%的储户取消银行账户;

36%投保人更换了保险公司;

40%的用户更改了电话公司;

35%的用户更换了信用卡提供商;

37%的用户更换了网络服务提供商。

你是否也曾是这些数据中的一员呢?我就是其中一个。

在一项由普渡大学和BenchmarkPortal.com组织的调查中研究了以下问题:(1)这些机构是如何满足您的需要和处理您的电话的?(2)如果有一些不愉快的经历,今后你还会光顾这个公司吗?结果发现在经历了不良的服务后,参与调查者的年龄与不再使用该种产品的趋向程度之间有着重要的关系。

这说明一个什么问题呢?越年轻的消费者越相对缺乏耐性,更有可能转向去购买其竞争对手的产品或服务。65岁以上的人比中年人的要求更为苛刻。

那公司应该怎样做呢?给予年轻客户一些惊喜的体验,以维持他们的忠诚度。36岁以上的人可能对曾经有过美好经历的公司带有更多的感情因素,因此更能包容该公司的一些不足。

世界级客服的服务策略应该包括以下几个方面:

(1)反应迅速;

(2)根据客户选择的方式处理客户的要求;

(3)简单明确;

(4)减少反复沟通(尤其是书面形式,比如,电子邮件,如果超过两次,最好进行电话沟通);

(5)个性化服务;

(6)让客户感到轻松愉快;

(7)组织培训客户;

(8)建立你的专业知识和技术;

(9)提供多种选择;

(10)必要时表达烦恼和愤怒的情绪;

(11)如果有需要,也可以将这种情绪提升;

(12)掌握电话的主动权。

记住我们现在还在讨论第一个"W"——为什么。现在企业面对的压力跟与往不同。他们需要面对更多的客户,和更多更复杂的客户电话。毕竟如果通过自助服务能解决问题的话,客户可能不会打电话。但是如果客户尝试了自助服务,没有解决问题,他们将很不耐烦,就会拨打电话。

2. 第二个 W(Who):谁(谁应该接受培训?)

我们建议那些第一线的代理商/代表、主管人员、团队领导者、管理人员、助理人员、内部客户和其他部门等所有与外界打交道的人,都应统一服务用语。更重要的是,这些人不要处在对立的状态,而是要团结一致为外部客户或最终用户服务。

3. 第三个 W(Where):哪里(应该在哪里进行培训?)

非现场培训与现场培训,这两种培训方式皆有利弊。

当然最有效的方法就是现场培训。然而,参与者的注意力很容易被其他的人或者问题所分散。

非现场培训比较昂贵。可是参与人员的注意力容易集中,参与者不受其经理、其他部门或者任何问题的影响。我认为这种方式有一定的价值,它可以让人们远离工作状态,去认识自己从事的工作。

4. 第四个 W(What):什么(培训什么内容?)

一个完善的、丰富的、精炼的培训应包括以下内容:客户服务质量;建立良好的客户关系;客户期望;观念改变;客户异议处理;语言技巧;缓解愤怒;电子邮件协议;减压方法;移情回应;变动管理;沟通/倾听技巧;互动/角色扮演微笑服务。

总之,员工培训得越专业,他们就会越专业地对待客户。

5. 第五个 W(When):时间(应什么时候进行培训?)

我们鼓励各种培训,包括对新雇工进行的、按月进行的、正在进行的、常年计划的以及根据情况变化需要的、压力增加及其他需要时的培训。

例如,建议每个员工每年最少接受 24 小时的培训,可以根据员工消化知识的情况分别进行培训。培训可分成每天 2 个阶段,每个阶段 4 小时,每个员工培训 6 天。这样,每天可以有 30 人接受培训。如果没有正在进行的培训,进行为期 4 个月的培训,每个月培训 4 天,3 个月后还会开设一个培训阶段,再隔 3 个月又进行下一阶段的培训。通过这种形式,可以根据实际情况安排用户化的培训,并且能够应对随时出现的各种问题。

Lesson 13 Leader of Heavy Truck

As a corporation which has a longest history in China for manufacturing heavy duty trucks, relying on its unparalleled research and development strength, applying globally key leading technology of heavy duty trucks, China National Heavy Duty Truck Group Co., Ltd.(SINOTRUK) has developed a new generation heavy duty truck with independent brand and China topping technology and grade—HOWO Heavy Truck 7 Series.

HOWO 7 series heavy duty trucks are designed with the concept of "maximizing the customer's value" through long-time and multi-angle cooperation and study with most famous heavy duty truck experts in the world. Compared with other truck models, HOWO 7 series super powerful strong working ability, pleasurable interior and exterior decoration, safety, comfortableness, easy operation and economy from fuel consumption to maintenance make customers who choose them have a sense of pride of "the best choice of product whose value is higher than price". HOWO 7 series heavy duty trucks are the integration of characteristics of worldwide advanced technologies. Advanced key assemblies are adopted and reasonable technical connections are done for these product. The whole truck shows a good layout, in which main assemblies are in harmonious, integrated, reliable and sensitive, making the product have perfect features aspects of the duration, power, reliability, economy and friendly environment among China's heavy duty trucks.

HOWO series heavy duty trucks have deluxe and grand appearance with both fortitude and streamline and both magnificence and grace, showing the unique qualities of a leader. [1] Especially in respect of humanization, such as comfort, safety and operation, HOWO 7 series heavy duty trucks have reached the level of international heavy duty truck with full scale.

HOWO heavy duty trucks fully embody SINOTRUK's corporate business concept "Scientific Design, Rational Management, Meticulous Operation, Optimal Effect" and concentrate SINOTRUK's corporate operative idea of the ceaseless pursuit of maximizing customer value.

1. Safety

Strict standard for safety guarantees thorough protection to drivers and passengers. All-steel forward control cab of HOWO 7 series heavy duty trucks adopts integrated steel structure, which makes its safety meet requirements of Swedish safety regulations, and thus protects safety of drivers and passengers in an all-round way. It really embodies the corporate management philosophy of SINOTRUCK for human orientation and untiring pursuit of maximization of user's interests.

(1) The main body with integrated steel construction is solid and tough, it has high strength to resist collision and stress of external force.

(2) The cab shell is welded on full-automatic robot production line with fully program controlled operation that is designed jointly with foreign experts. The production line has reached world wide advanced level.

(3) The cab transverse stabilizer is fitted.

(4) The powerful protecting grille is installed against front collision.

(5) The cured windshield provides a wide visual field.

(6) Double-locking mechanism is adopted for driver's safety belt, so safety coefficient is greatly in creased.

2. Comfort

Comfortable and humanized design has already integrated with European heavy duty trucks, which makes HOWO 7 series heavy duty trucks become a qualified mobile "home" and a honorable "office". According to evaluation by experts in the industry, HOWO 7 series heavy duty trucks have reached the highest level nationwide and international level at present in terms of comfortableness and indexes for physical-tiredness resistance.

(1) For driver's cab of on-road trucks, worldwide top-ranking shock absorber system with four-point full-floating air suspension is adopted, which can achieve the best effect of shock absorption under any road conditions. It is as steady and comfortable as a yacht "playing" on waters. [2]

(2) Improved steering wheel is made from flexible plastic material for cars with better hand touch. It can be adjusted in height of 25mm and angle of 5 degrees forward and backward.

(3) Trucks with engine output above 290 horsepower (around 216 kW) are equipped with air conditioner for heating and cooling, which can be operated by power and the temperature can be controlled automatically. The configuration reaches the level for luxury cars.

(4) Berth with a width of 600mm is designed as per body size of occidentals. The aluminum alloy framework has features of light weight, good rigidity and built-in netted structure of steel wire, which can ease fatigue more effectively than bunk mattress of other products.

(5) The upper folding berth can be secured at any position.

(6) The unique design for ventilating system of cab is a domestic originality:

①ventilating outlets can keep the air inside cab clean effectively under fully closed condition of cab;

②warm air ducts accessing to doors can rapidly defrost and defog glasses of both sides;

③good air circulation can remove dust and peculiar smell effectively.

(7) Luxurious storage trunk inside cab provide big storage space, its standard configuration includes a truck-mounted refrigerator.

(8) The effect of silence system has already reached the level of world top-grade heavy duty trucks. The noise is reduced obviously and makes drivers and passengers have a happier mood.

3. Humanization

Humanized design is orientated according to internationally accepted level at present.

(1) Design of artificial intelligence is the most important form of representation to embody competitive strength of product technology and maintain interests of customers.[3] HOWO heavy duty trucks possess domestically original technology of artificial intelligence, which has already been close to and reached the world level. It represents as follows.

①Controlling the temperatures of engine coolant and oil, engine oil consumption and combustion.

②Controlling the oil amount and oil passage system and etc. All control points can be displayed with different symbols on the liquid crystal display (instrumental panel).

③Automatic fault inspection.

④Automatic storage of important operating data.

(2) The latest design of seat embodies characteristics of SINOTRUK's patented technology. The design not only conforms with beautiful visual effect of HOWO heavy duty trucks on appearance, but also fully adopts principles of human engineering.

①Electric heating devices are fitted in seat cushion and backrest.

②Air bag is fitted at waist of high backrest, which can provides an effective support to the driver's waist.

③Top part of high backrest can be adjusted, which can ease fatigue of driver at shoulder and neck effectively.

(3) Mirror are designed with reference to the most advanced vehicle model abroad, power mirror and electric defrosting as options. Rear mirrors, right road-surface mirror and front down-view mirror offer a wide vision to grasp the driving environment in an all-round way.

(4) Unique door opening and closing mechanism with 90°door opening angle, handles on two side doors and two footsteps with stainless steel anti-slip board make door opening and getting-safer, more convenient and more humanized.

(5) A folding footstep is fitted at middle part of the front bumper in order to clean the windshield conveniently.

(6) Reading lamp with mild luminance brightness offers great convenience handing official business in truck.

New Words

decoration [dekə'reiʃən]	n. 装饰, 装饰品
integration [inti'greiʃən]	n. 整合, 集成
assembly [ə'sembli]	n. 集合, 集会, 装配
integrate ['intigreit]	v. 整合, 使……成整体; 真诚的
meticulous [mi'tikjuləs]	adj. 一丝不苟的, 精确的
tipper ['tipə]	n. 自(动倾)卸车, 翻斗车, 倾卸装置
duration [djuə'reiʃən]	n. 持续; 持久; 持续时间; 延续性; 期限[间]; 存在时间; 波期; 宽度
fortitude ['fɔːtitjuːd]	n. 坚强意志, 坚忍, 刚毅
embody [im'bɔdi]	vt. 包括, 包含, 收录, 概括; 使具体化, 使形象化, 体现; 配备, 连接, 接合, 补充
meticulous [m'tkjuləs]	adj. 细心的; 小心翼翼的; 注意细节的
collision [kə'liʒən]	n. (车、船的)碰[互]撞, (利益, 意见的)冲突, 抵触, (政党派系之间的)倾轧; 振动, 跳跃, 颠簸; 打[冲]击, 截击(空中目标)
transverse ['trænzvəːs]	n. 横向[截]; 横梁[材, 骨]; 横墙; 横放物
grille [gril]	n. (银行, 邮局柜台上的)铁栅
windshield ['wndʃiːld]	n. (汽车)风窗玻璃
coefficient [kəui'fiʃənt]	n. 系数
index ['indeks]	n. 索引, 指针, 指数 v. 编入索引中, 指出
suspension [səs'penʃən]	n. 悬挂, 未决, 中止
berth [bəːθ]	n. (船与灯塔, 沙滩等之间留出的)安全距离; (船、车、飞机等的)座[铺]位 卧铺; 停泊

	地，锚[泊]位；船台；（轮船上的）住舱
occidental [ˌɔksi'dentl]	*adj.* 欧美人的，西方人的；欧美的，西方国家的；西方人，欧美人
rigidity [ri'dʒiditi]	*n.* 硬，劲直，硬度
secure [si'kjuə]	*adj.* 无虑的，安心的，安全的
	v. 固定，获得，使……安全
ventilate ['ventileit]	*v.* 使……空气流通
duct [dʌkt]	*n.* 管，输送管，排泄管
	vt. 通过管道输送
luminance ['lju:minəns]	*n.* 亮度
combustion [kəm'bʌstʃən]	*n.* 燃烧；（有机体内营养料的）氧化
bumper ['bʌmpə]	*n.* 防撞物，缓冲器，减振器；防撞器；（汽车前后部的）保险杠；消音器，阻尼器
chassis ['ʃæsi]	*n.* 底盘，底架，底板[座]；机架[壳，箱]，框[车，炮，起落]架

Phrases and Expressions

maximizing customer value	客户价值最大化
human orientation	以人为本
safety coefficient	安全系数
in terms of	根据，按照，用……的话，在……方面
indexes for physical-tiredness resistance	人体抗疲劳指标
four-point full-floating air suspension	四点全浮式空气悬架
ventilating system	通风系统
liquid crystal display	液晶显示屏
artificial intelligence	人工智能
desert air cleaner	沙漠空滤器

Notes to the Text

[1] HOWO series heavy duty trucks have deluxe and grand appearance with both fortitude and streamline and both magnificence and grace, showing the unique qualities of a leader.

HOWO 重卡外观豪华、大气，刚毅与流畅并存，雄壮与优美齐现，尽显其独特的领袖气质。

[2] It is as steady and comfortable as a yacht "playing" on waters.

如同游艇在水面"嬉戏"，稳定而舒适。

[3] Design of artificial intelligence is the most important form of representation to embody competitive strength of product technology and maintain interests of customers.

人工智能化设计是体现产品技术竞争实力和维护客户利益的最重要表现形式。

Review Questions

1. Please give a presentation of the character of HOWO in Humanization.
2. What is the meaning of four-point full-floating air suspension?
3. Should we how to understand the idea of the ceaseless pursuit of maximizing customer value?
4. What is the cab transverse stabilizer?
5. How can the driver adjust the steering wheel in HOWO truck?

参考译文

第十三课 重卡领袖

作为中国重型汽车生产历史最为悠久的企业,中国重型汽车集团有限公司依靠国内业界首屈一指的重型汽车(简称重卡)研发实力,应用世界重卡关键先进技术,面向中国市场,自主开发出了达到当代国际水平,具有自主品牌的,国内最先进、最高档的新一代重型汽车——HOWO重卡7系列。

HOWO7系列汽车是通过与国际重卡专家经长时间、多角度的研究、合作,按"客户价值最大化"的设计理念而设计的。与其他车型相比,HOWO7系列具有超强作业功能、令人愉悦的内外装饰、良好的安全性、舒适性、易操作性、从油耗到维护的良好经济性,使用户有一种"物超所值、最佳选择"的自豪感。HOWO7系列重卡融合了国际先进技术的特色,采用了关键的先进总成,并进行了合理的技术连接。整车布置合理,各大总成协调、统一、可靠、灵便,使其在国内重卡中,具有完美的持续性、动力性、可靠性、经济性以及环境友好性。

HOWO重卡外观豪华、大气,刚毅与流畅并存,雄壮与优美齐现,尽显其独特的领袖气质。尤其是在舒适性、安全性和方便性等人性化方面,HOWO重卡完全达到了世界级重卡水平。

HOWO重卡的推出,充分体现了中国重汽"科学策划、理性经营、精心操作、最佳效果"的企业经营理念,集中体现了中国重汽不懈追求客户价值最大化的企业经营思想。

1. 安全

严格的安全标准,对驾乘人员的保护周全。主体采用整体钢架结构的HOWO7系列重卡驾驶室安全性达到瑞典安全法规要求,全面保护驾乘人员安全。其真正体现了中国重汽以人为本和不懈追求用户利益最大化的企业经营理念。

(1)主体为整体钢架结构,坚实、牢固,抗撞击和抗外力压迫能力极强。

(2)车身是在与国外专家共同设计的控制操作全部程序的全自动机器人生产线上焊装的。其生产线达到世界先进水平。

(3)增加了驾驶室横向稳定装置。

(4)安装了强力的正面碰撞保护架。

(5)大曲面前风窗玻璃使视野开阔。

(6)驾驶员安全带采用双锁止结构,保险系数大大增加。

2. 舒适

已与欧洲重卡接轨的舒适化、人性化设计,使HOWO7系列重卡成为一个名副其实的流动的"家",一个体面"办公室"。HOWO7系列重卡舒适性和人体抗疲劳指标被业内专家评价为已达到目前国内最高水平和国际水准。

(1)公路用车驾驶室采用世界顶级的四点全浮式空气悬架减振装置,可在任何路况下,达到最佳减振效果。如同游艇在水面"嬉戏",稳定而舒适。

(2)转向盘改进为乘用车型柔性塑胶材料制作,手感好。可上下25mm、前后5°调节。

(3)290马力(约216kW)以上车型全部配置冷暖空调,可电动操纵,自动控制温度。其配置高档轿车水平。

(4)HOWO重卡卧铺按欧美人的体形设计,宽度达600mm。铝合金骨架质量轻、刚性好,内置钢丝网状结构,较国内其他产品的铺垫能更有效地缓解疲劳状态。

(5)上层卧铺可抬高至任意角度停置。

(6)驾驶室通风系统的独特设计为国内首创:

①设置有通风窗口,在驾驶室全封闭状态下,仍能有效地保持驾驶室内空气清洁;

②暖风通道此至两侧车门,可迅速对两侧玻璃除霜除雾;

③空气循环状态好,可有效除尘、除异味。

(7)驾驶室内配置豪华储物箱,储物空间大,其基本配置包括车用冰箱。

(8)消声系统的消声效果已达到国际顶级重卡的水准。明显降低了噪声,使驾乘人员的心情更加舒畅。

3. 人性化

人性化设计是按目前国际通用水准来定位的。

(1)人工智能化设计是体现产品技术竞争实力和维护客户利益的最重要表现形式。HOWO重卡具备国内独创的人工智能化技术,已接近和达到了国际水平。其表现如下。

①对发动机水温和油温的控制,对机油消耗和燃烧的控制。

②对油量及油路系统控制等。各控制节点可全部在液晶显示器(仪表盘)上以不同符号显示。

③自动故障检测。

④自动储存重要运行数据。

(2)最新座椅设计体现了中国重汽专利技术特色。该设计不仅在外观上与HOWO重卡视觉上的美观效果相一致,而且充分采用了人体工程学原理。

①座椅座垫、靠背设有电加热装置。

②高靠背腰部配置气囊,可对腰部给予有效支撑。

③高靠背上部可做调节,能有效缓解驾驶员肩部和颈部的疲劳。

(3)以根据国外最先进车型为参考设计反光镜,可选装电控操作、电动除霜。后视镜、右侧路面镜和前部下视镜为驾驶提供开阔的视野,使驾驶员全面掌握驾驶环境。

(4)独特的车门开启和关闭机构、90°的最大车门开角、两个侧门把手以及两级不锈钢防滑踏板,使开门和上下车更加安全、方便,更加人性化。

(5)保险杠中部设置有可翻转踏脚板,方便擦拭玻璃。

(6)驾驶室阅读灯光亮度柔和,为随车办公提供了极大便利。

Lesson14   The Character of CROWN

The TOYOTA CROWN(CROWN for short) is a brand of mid-size luxury sedan by TOYOTA. Introduced in 1955, it has been at a distinct advantage with technologies updating.

Safety: world-class high level safety performance originates from unremitting pursuit of people- oriented spirit.

In the field of passenger car passivity safety, let us take GOA (Global Outstanding Assessment) as an example, it is vehicle body structure designed and adopted not only for mutual survival in full consideration of coming into collision with vehicle of different body structure and weight, but also for pursuit of world-class high-level safety performance conceived of coming into collision with SUV which has relative advantages in body structure and weight. Meanwhile, for the safety of foot passengers, energy-absorbing design has been adopted for engine cowling and fender to ease up the impact on the other party in case of collision with foot passengers. [1] The four front and rear seats are equipped with pre-tensioning & force-limiting safety belts (whole seat ELR 3-point safety belt) with amplitude limiter and with capacity of adjusting occupant carrying capacity and improving straining effect. The front seat is equipped with warning light and alarm buzzer with automatic cueing function in the case of safety belt is unworn. More than that ,8-place inside the car has been equipped with SRS air bags to improve safety protection effect and take precautions against accident.

In the field of passenger car active safety, new CROWN adopts advanced brake technology and different excellent driving accessories. TRC (Traction Control System) and VSC(Vehicle Stability Control System) can guarantee that vehicle wheels have optimum road behavior under different road conditions, in this way, outstanding operating and controlling effectiveness can be realized. When the Hill Assist-Downhill Control System (HAC) has been started on abrupt slope and slippery slope, slow brake will be applied automatically as soon as the car sliding backwards as to decelerate the sternward velocity. The high-intensity xenon headlights HID (High Intensity Discharge) similar to color of sunshine are adopted to support driving and enhance nighttime visibility, which lightens visual burden of nighttime driving effectively. [2]

GOA safe vehicle body is solely possessed by TOYOTA , which was researched and developed independently by TOYOTA according to basic safety standards of most countries in the world and combining with actual automobile accidents occurring situations. The energy-absorbing car body and high-strength driver cabin are capable of absorbing collision energy and scattering it onto different body skeletons as well as minimizing deformation of driver cabin to assure cabin spaces.

Comfortable: up-to-date arrangement of rear row of seats, reflecting elaborate and considerate service fully.

Letting the person seating on the back-row seat feel peaceful and agreeable best embodies the considerate design. In order to give the driver a sensation of gallop, new CROWN integrates pleasant sensation of operation and control, pleasure of traveling and blissful happiness of seating harmoniously. If you want to prove this you can feel it immediately as long as you rely on the back-row seat. If you operate every switch on adjustment and control panel on central armrest of back-row seat: stereophonic-sound acoustics and rear air conditioner become easy to access and have everything under your perfect control. The position of backrest of power adjustable back-row seat and heater unit can also be adjusted as you like. If you selected model of car equipped with rear air conditioner, then you can enjoy the cool beverage in car-mounted refrigerator. It has been also designed foot rest which can be set level backwards at assistant driving seat, which provide spacious extensible space for the personnel seating on back-row seat. The reading light can stimulate pleasure in reading at night to enjoy precious time in car. The opening angle of vehicle door is a right angle approximately, which ensure your secure getting on and down from the car; meanwhile, both welcoming illuminating lamps for feet set at seats and vehicle door can automatically light.

The quietness both inside and outside of the car make people exclaim with admiration.

The greatly well-rounded car body of new CROWN is also water-like quiet car body. While the driver freely enjoying the pleasure in driving on front seat, the person seating on rear seat can take a rest sweetly, which is better illustration of comfortable space provided by new CROWN. The vibration and noise produced in car are analyzed through computer and eliminated one by one during the research and development process, the construction car body reaches the lightness and effective-restraining vibration and noise effect. In similar manner, the air performance has been greatly improved through computer analysis and adjustment, wind resistance coefficient down to not only benefit to reduce fuel consumption, but also ensure excellent traveling stability and secure operationality through reducing the front and rear suspending sense. Low wind resistance coefficient can also free the car from external windage noise when running at high speed so as to achieve quietness when car is traveling. The reasonable configuration of different light-weight noise-controlling materials and vibration-restraining materials present you with widely accepted and incomparable quietness of new CROWN in more laconic form.

Excellent equipment: intelligent logging in and starting. Moved, does without any form.

Affecting overture begins with the moment of approaching to new CROWN. As long as you close to the vehicle door with intelligent key in the evening, the welcoming illumination hidden in rear-view mirror will illuminate for you automatically. At the same time, the illumination in car will switch on. If you touch the handle of vehicle door slightly, the vehicle door will unblock automatically. When you relying on advanced genuine leather seat with dulcet tactility, if you press start button slightly, the V6 engine will start quietly and insensibly. Only with one intelligent key, all these can be completed momentarily, easily and elegantly. In addition, the color-background inductive display screen for backing is convenient and practical, which not only can display the view behind the car, but also mark the cue line for a driver as distance measuring reference. The inconvenience in backing car can be readily solved due to the cue of angle of turning.

The driving sensation and unforgettable sensation of space beyond your imagination consist in driving seat.

If you want experience new CROWN further, please find your most comfortable seating posture firstly. Just like customize according to actual circumstances of each driver, the driving seat is equipped with 8-direction power adjusting seat which can front and rear, up and down and the other angle of inclination, and etc. in the manner of power adjustment. The waist support can also be adjusted in the manner of power adjustment. You will feel that you have been integrated with car body. New CROWN adopts optimum position memory of driving seat and automatic adjustment system, which can record optimum driving positions and positions of steering wheel of 3 persons simultaneously. Nothing remains but to touch memory key, the seat will automatically adjust to the angle which driver feel most comfortable. In addition, the assistant driving seat is also equipped with 4-directional power adjustable seat which can be slid and reclined.

New Words

unremitting ['ʌnri'mitiŋ]		adj. 不歇的,不断的,坚忍的
mutual ['mju:tjuəl, 'mju:tʃuəl]		adj. 共同的,相互的
conceive [kən'si:v]		v. 构思,以为,怀孕
cowling ['kauliŋ]		n. 发动机罩
fender ['fendə]		n. 防御者,防御物,防撞者;火炉围栏;炉格子;(车辆的)挡泥板;[英](电车、机车等的)缓冲装置,救护装置;碰垫,叶子板,翼子板;护舷木
amplitude ['æmplitju:d]		n. 广阔,广大;充足,丰富;(思想的)广度;(天体)出没(磁)方位角;(交变电流的)幅度,(无线电波的)波幅;调幅;(音波场中空气压力的)振幅,(钟摆持的)摆幅
optimum ['ɔptiməm]		n. 最适宜
		adj. 最适宜的
sternward ['stə:nwəd]		adj 船尾的,后面的
		ad. 在船尾
scatter ['skætə]		n. 散播之物,散布
		v. 散开,散布,散播
deformation [ˌdi:fɔ:'meiʃn]		n. 变形,变态,形变,畸变;在绘画中由于明暗、色调不准而歪曲了原来的形象
gallop ['gæləp]		n. (马等的)疾驰,飞奔;骑马,奔跑,快步;用最大速度跑

blissful ['blisful]	adj. 有福的,极乐的
armrest ['ɑːmrest]	n. 椅子扶手
acoustics [ə'kuːstks]	n. 声学;音响效果
stimulate ['stimjuleit]	vt. 刺激,激励,鼓舞
illuminate [i'ljuːmineit]	v. 照明,阐释,说明
intently [in'tentli]	ad. 一心一意地,心无旁物地,专心地
vibration [vai'breiʃən]	n. 震动,颤动
beverage ['bevəridʒ]	n. 饮料(如茶、酒、牛奶、汽水、低度汽水等);[英方]餐费,酒费
coefficient [kəʊ'fʃənt]	n. 系数;率
wind resistance coefficient	风阻系数
laconic [lə'kɔnik]	adj. 简洁的
overture ['əʊvətjuə]	n. [常用复]建议;提议,提案;开端,序幕;【音】序曲;前奏曲;序诗
inductive [in'dktiv]	adj. 引入的;诱进的;吸入的;感应的;电感的;入门的,绪论的;诱人的,动人的,感人的
dulcet ['dʌlsit]	adj. 优美的,美妙的,美味的
tactility [tæk-'tiləti]	n. 触知性,触感

Phrases and Expressions

well-rounded	丰满的,匀称的
people-oriented spirit	以人为本的精神
pre-tensioning & force-limiting safety belts	预紧限力式安全带
ELR (Emergency Locking Retractor)	安全带的一种方式
SRS (Supplemental Restraint System)	辅助约束(防护)系统(一般译为安全气囊,实际上它包括座椅安全带收紧机构和安全气囊两部分)

Notes to the Text

[1] Meanwhile, for the safety of foot passengers, energy-absorbing design has been adopted for engine cowling and fender to ease up the impact on the other party in case of collision with foot passengers.

同时,为了顾及行人安全,还在发动机舱盖及翼子板上采用了冲撞吸能式设计,以缓和与行人相撞时给对方带来的冲击。

[2] When the Hill Assist—Downhill Control System (HAC) has been started on abrupt slope and slippery slope, slow brake will be applied automatically as soon as the car sliding backwards as to decelerate the sternward velocity. The high-intensity xenon headlights HID (High Intensity Discharge) similar to color of sunshine are adopted to support driving and enhance nighttime visibility, which lightens visual burden of nighttime driving effectively.

在陡坡及易滑坡道启动上下坡辅助控制系统后,一旦车辆向后方滑行,会自动加以缓慢刹车,减缓后退速度。为支持驾驶,提高夜间可视性,采用了接近阳光色调的高强度氙气前照灯 HID(高压钠灯),有效地减轻了夜间驾驶的视觉负担。

Review Questions

1. Please demonstrate some characters of CROWN for example.
2. How to use pre-tensioning and force-limiting safety belts?
3. What is the ELR?
4. What's the meaning of GOA? What does it have any characters?
5. What is the meaning of intelligent key?

参考译文

第十四课 皇冠产品特征

丰田皇冠(简称皇冠)是丰田旗下一款中型豪华轿车品牌。其始于1995年,随着技术的更新换代,已具有显著的优势。

安全性:世界级高水准的安全性能,源于对以人为本精神的不懈追求。

在被动安全方面,以 GOA(全球顶级水平的安全设计)为例,这种设计不仅是在全面考虑到与车身、车重相异的车辆相撞的情况下,以共存为目标而采用的车身构造;更是在设想了与车身、车重相对占优势的 SUV 相撞的情况下,追求世界级高水准的安全性能。同时,为了顾及行人安全,还在发动机舱盖及翼子板上采用了冲撞吸能式设计,以缓和与行人相撞时给对方带来的冲击。前后4座分别设有调整乘员负荷量、提高拉紧效果的带限幅器的预紧限力式安全带(全座 ELR 三点式安全带)。前席安装了未使用安全带时自动提示的警告灯和报警器。不仅如此,为了提高保护安全效果,还在车内8处配置了 SRS 空气囊,预防事故于未然。

在主动安全方面,新 CROWN(皇冠)采用了先进的制动技术及各项优异的驾驶辅助装备。TRC(牵引力控制系统)和 VSC(车身稳定性控制系统)确保车轮在各种路况下始终保持最佳抓地性,实现了出色的操控有效性。在陡坡及易滑坡道启动上下坡辅助控制系统(HAC)后,一旦车辆向后方滑行,会自动加以缓慢制动,减缓后退速度。为支持驾驶,提高夜间可视性,采用了接近阳光色调的高强度氙气前照灯 HID(高压钠灯),有效地减轻了夜间驾驶的视觉负担。

TOYOTA 独有的 GOA 安全车身是根据世界多数国家的安全标准,结合实际事故的发生状况,独立研究开发的。吸收碰撞能量的车身和高强度驾驶室能够在碰撞发生时有效吸收碰撞能量,并将其分散至车身各部位骨架,将驾驶室变形控制在最小限度,确保座舱空间。

舒适性:后排座椅的最新配置,尽显细心周到。

给坐在后排座椅上的乘客以安静惬意的乘坐感受,是周到设计的最好体现。为了给驾驶者以驰骋的动感,新皇冠将操控的快感、行驶的快乐、乘坐的快意和谐地融为一体。要证明这点,只要倚身在后排座椅上,马上就可以感觉到。操作后排座椅中央扶手调控面板上的每一个开关:立体声音响、后部空调,皆触手可及,操控得心应手。电动可调式后排座椅的靠背位置、加热装置,也随个人偏好调节。如果选择的是配备后部空调的车型,就可享受车载冰箱中的冰凉饮料。副驾驶席座椅靠背处还设计了可以向后放平的脚枕,为后排成员提供了宽敞的可伸展空间,以便于在路途中舒展双腿。晚上阅读灯增添阅读乐趣,从而享受宝贵的车中时光。为了保证上下车安全,车门打开角度可以近乎直角,同时,座椅和车门处设置的两处脚部迎宾照明会自动点亮。

车内车外,静谧性皆为人叹服。

新皇冠的车身激情奔放,又沉静如水。驾驶者在前席畅享驾驶乐趣的同时,乘坐者在后座静享一段甜美的小憩,是新皇冠所提供舒适空间的更好例证。在研发过程中,通过计算机分析车内产生的振动和噪音,逐一解决,最终使车身构造达到了既轻盈又有效抑制振动和噪音的效果。同样,通过计算机分析调节,空气动力性能也得以大大提高,较低的风阻系数不仅利于降低燃料消耗,通过削减前后部的悬浮感,还保证了卓越的行驶稳定性和可靠的操控性。低风阻系数还让车辆从高速行驶时的外部风阻噪音中解放出来,实现了行车时的静谧性。车身各部分轻量防噪材料和抑振材料的合理配置,将新皇冠公认的无与伦比的静谧性,以更加精练的形式呈献予您。

精良配备:智能登录,智能启动。感动,无需形式。

令人感动的序曲,从接近新皇冠那一刻就已经开始。晚间,只要携带智能钥匙靠近车门,藏于后视镜内的迎宾照明会自动为您照明。同时,车内照明也会开启。轻触车门把手,车门就会自动解锁。倚身在触感美妙的高级真皮座椅上,轻按一键启动按钮,V6发动机就会安静起动。只要一把智能钥匙,这一切就都可在一瞬间轻松优雅地完成。此外,彩色背景倒车感应式显示屏方便、实用,不仅可显示车后画面,而且还为驾驶者标出了作为倒车测距参考的提示线。倒车的不便,也会因为转向角度的提示迎刃而解。

超乎想象的驾驭感动与流连忘返的空间感受,就在驾驶席。

想更深入地体验新皇冠,首先一定要找到最舒服的乘坐姿势。就像为每位驾驶者量身定做的一样,驾驶席标准配备了电动调节前后、上下、任意倾斜角度等八向电动调节座椅。缓解腰部疲劳的腰部支撑也可以电动调节。身处新皇冠的座椅中,会感觉到自己与车仿佛已融为一体。新皇冠采用驾驶席最佳位置记忆及自动调节系统,能同时记录3个人的最佳驾驶位置、转向盘位置。只需轻触记忆按键,座椅即会自动调节到驾驶者最舒服的角度。此外,副驾驶席也标准配备了四向电动可调节座椅,可进行前后和倾斜调整。

Lesson15　The Sample of Export Trade Contracts Text

Contract No:_____　　Date:_____
Place:_____
The Buyer:_____　　The Seller:_____
ADD:_____　　ADD:_____
TEL:_____　　TEL:_____
FAX:_____　　FAX:_____

The Contract is made, in Chinese and English, both version being equally authentic, by and between the Seller and the Buyer whereby the Seller agrees to sell and the Buyer agrees to buy the under mentioned commodity subject to terms and conditions set forth hereinafter as follows.

1. Name of Commodity and specification (the commodity technical articles are integral to this contract)

2. Manufacturer & Country of Origin: _____

3. Unit Price(packing charges included): _____

4. Quantity: _____

5. Total Value: _____

6. Packing: _____

7. Shipping Marks: _____

8. Time of Shipment

　　_____ Partial Shipment

　　_____ Transshipment

9. Port of Loading: _____

10. Port of Destination: _____

11. Terms of Payment: _____

　　The Seller's Bank Name: _____

　　The Seller's Account No. _____

　　The Seller's Company: _____

　　The Seller's ADD: _____

11.1 By T/T, or irrevocable letter of credit, payable at sight.

The Buyer shall open an irrevocable credit with the first class national or international bank in favor of the Seller for the total value of shipment.[1] The letter of credit shall be available against Seller's draft(s), drawn at sight on the issuing bank for 100% invoice value accompanied by the shipping documents. The payment shall be effected by the issuing bank against presentation to them of the aforesaid draft(s) and documents. The letter of credit shall be valid until 15 days after shipments is effected.

11.2 All the bank fees incurred in China should be paid by the Seller, and all the bank fees incurred outside China should be paid by the Buyer.

12. Terms of Shipment(All terms should be in line with INCOTERMS 2000, unless otherwise agreed upon): _____.

13. Price Terms(All terms should be in line with INCOTERMS 2000, unless otherwise agreed upon): _____.

14. Goods Inspection Terms.

14.1 The goods' quality tallies with this contract and the Technical Terms of the manufacturer.

14.2 If the buyer has any dissidence of the quality or quantity of the goods, the buyer may put forward an application, within 30 days after receiving the goods, to the Commodity Inspection Bureau of China about this dissidence, and claim for compensation from the seller with the testimonial provided by the commodity inspection bureau of China.[2] The insurance agent, transportation institution or mail delivery institution will answer for any dissidence raised by the buyer about the goods or packing damaged or lost during the shipping. The Seller will not answer for any of it. If no dissidence is raised by the buyer within in the regulated time, it would be regarded as the Seller's goods tally with the contract.

15. Indemnity.

15.1 With the exception of late delivery or non-delivery due to "Force Majeure" causes, if the Seller fails to make delivery of the goods in accordance with the terms and conditions, jointly or severally, of this contract, the Seller shall be liable to indemnify the Buyer for all direct losses.

15.2 Force Majeure.

Either the Seller or the Buyer shall not be held responsible for late delivery or non-delivery owing to generally recognized "Force Majeure" causes. However in such a case, the Seller shall immediately advise by fax the Buyer of the accident and airmail to the Buyer, within 15 days after the accident, a certificate of the accident issued by the competent government authority or the chamber of commerce which is located at the place where the accident occurs as evidence thereof. If the said "Force Majeure" cause lasts over 60 days, the Buyer shall have the right to cancel the whole or the undelivered part of the order for the goods as stipulated in contract.

16. Notice.

All notices should be written in English, and sent to the other party according to the given address. If any changes in the address, the party should notice the other party in 15 days.

17. All terms should be in line with INCOTERMS 2000, unless otherwise agreed upon.

18. Arbitration.

Both parties agree to attempt to resolve all disputes between the parties with respect to the application or interpretation of any term herein, through amicable negotiation. If a dispute cannot be resolved in this manner to the satisfaction of the Seller and the Buyer within a reasonable period of time, maximum not exceeding 90 days after the date of the notification of such dispute, the case under dispute shall be submitted to arbitration. Unless otherwise agreed upon by both parties, such arbitration shall be held in Beijing, China, and shall be governed by the Foreign Trade Arbitration Commission of the China Council for the Promotion of International Trade according to the rules and procedures of arbitration. The arbitration shall be conducted in Chinese with the reference of English. The award by such arbitration shall be accepted as final and binding upon both parties. The arbitration fees shall be borne by the losing party unless otherwise awarded.

19. This contract is governed by the laws of People's Republic of China.

20. This contract comes into force on the date of _____. This contract has 4 signed copies, and each party holds 2 copies. Each copy is equal in force.

Seller:_____ Company

For and on behalf of:

Buyer:_____ Company

For and on behalf of:

New Words

authentic [ɔːˈθentik]	adj. 可靠的,可信的,真的,真正的
hereinafter [hərnˈɑːftə(r)]	ad. 在下文,以下
specification [ˌspesifiˈkeiʃən]	n. 规格,详述,详细说明书
integral [ˈintigrəl]	adj. 构成整体所必需的,组成的,主要的,必备的;完整的,整体的;综合的;【数】整的;积分的;累积的;全悬挂的
transshipment [træsˈʃipmənt]	n. 转运
irrevocable [iˈrevəkəbl]	adj. 不能取消的,不能撤回的;不能改变的;不能挽回的
invoice [ˈinvɔis]	n.【商】发票,发货单;货单托运物品
aforesaid [əˈfɔːsed]	adj. 上述的
dissidence [ˈdisidəns]	n. (意见等的)不同,不一致,异议
testimonial [ˌtestiˈməunjəl, -niəl]	n. (品格、行为、资格等的)证明书;推荐书;奖状[品、金],感谢信,纪念品
indemnify [inˈdemnifai]	vt. 保护[障,险](against, from);赔偿,偿付,付还(for);使安全;使免受伤害
severally [ˈsevərəli]	ad. 各自地,各个地,各别地
majeure [mæˈʒɜː]	n. 压倒的力量(不可抗力)
competent [ˈkɔmpitənt]	adj. 有能力的,胜任的,足够的
chamber [ˈtʃeimbə]	n. 室,房间,会所,枪膛
	v. 放在枪膛内,关在室内
certificate [səˈtifikit]	n. 证(明)书,执照
	vt. 批准
thereof [ðeərˈɔv, -ˈɔf]	ad. 关于……,将它,它的
stipulate [ˈstipjulet]	vt. 要求以……为条件;规定,约定
arbitration [ˌɑːbiˈtreiʃən]	n. 仲裁,公断;(国际法)调停;鉴定,检验;判优法
dispute [disˈpjuːt]	n. 争论
	v. 争论
interpretation [inˌtəːpriˈteiʃən]	n. 解释,演出,翻译,互动
amicable [ˈæmikəbəl]	adj. 友好的,和睦的
borne [bɔːn]	v. 生,负荷

Phrases and Expressions

Port of Destination	目的地港口
By T/T	付款方式 T/T 是电汇(Telegraphic Transfer, T/T),是国际贸易中的一种付款方式,业务上分为前 T/T(预付货款)和后 T/T(装船后或收货后付款)

INCOTERMS 2000	《国际贸易术语解释通则2000》
tally with	与……相符合；与……一致
force majeure	不可抗力，不可抗拒的力量
amicable negotiation	友好协商

Notes to the Text

[1] The Buyer shall open an irrevocable credit with the first class national or international bank in favor of the Seller for the total value of shipment.

买方应当在本国一流银行或国际一流银行开具以卖方为受益人与货物完全等值的且卖方可接受的不可撤销信用证。

[2] If the buyer has any dissidence of the quality or quantity of the goods, the buyer may put forward an application, within thirty (30) days after receiving the goods, to the Commodity Inspection Bureau of China about this dissidence, and claim for compensation from the seller with the testimonial provided by the commodity inspection bureau of China.

如果买方对货物质量、数量方面有异议，买方应于收到货物之日起30日内向中国商品检验局提出申请，凭中国商品检验局出具的有效证书向卖方提出赔偿。

Review Questions

1. Do you think what questions should bethought over?

2. Please explain the meaning of the word Force Majeure.

3. What is BY T/T?

4. Should they how to be resolve if there are disputes between the parties?

5. Did you signed the agreement with other? What question should be paid attention to?

参考译文

第十五课　出口贸易合同示范文本

合同编码：＿＿＿＿＿＿　　签约日期：＿＿＿＿＿＿

签约地点：＿＿＿＿＿＿

买方：＿＿＿＿＿＿＿　　卖方：＿＿＿＿＿＿＿

地址：＿＿＿＿＿＿＿　　地址：＿＿＿＿＿＿＿

电话：＿＿＿＿＿＿＿　　电话：＿＿＿＿＿＿＿

传真：＿＿＿＿＿＿＿　　传真：＿＿＿＿＿＿＿

本合同由买卖双方缔结，有中英文两种版本，具有同等效力，卖方同意售出且买方同意购进下述条款和要求的货物。

1. 货物名称及规格(本合同所附货物技术条款是合同不可分割的一部分)

2. 生产国及制造厂商：＿＿＿＿＿＿＿＿＿＿＿＿＿＿＿＿

3. 单价(含包装费)：＿＿＿＿＿＿＿＿＿＿＿＿＿＿＿＿＿

4. 数量：_____

5. 总值：_____

6. 包装：_____

7. 发货标记（唛头）：_____

8. 发运时间

　　_____分运

　　_____转运

9. 发运港：_____

10. 目的港：_____

11. 付款条件：_____

　　卖方开户行：_____

　　卖方银行账户：_____

　　卖方公司：_____

　　卖方地址：_____

11.1 电汇，或者不可撤销、即期信用证。

买方应当在本国一流银行或国际一流银行开具以卖方为受益人与货物完全等值的且卖方可接受的不可撤销信用证。开证银行应该在见到卖方即期汇票以及运输单证后立即对100%发票进行议付。应付款项由开证银行应在卖方交单后付款。信用证必须在发货后15天内有效。

11.2 一切在中国境内的银行费用由卖方承担，一切在中国境外的银行费用由买方承担。

12. 装运条款（除非另有约定，所有条款应符合国际商会制定的《国际贸易术语解释通则2000》）：_____。

13. 价格条款（除非另有约定，所有条款应符合国际商会制定的《国际贸易术语解释通则2000》）：_____。

14. 货物检验条款。

14.1 货物质量符合本合同及制造商的技术标准。

14.2 如果买方对货物质量、数量方面有异议，买方应于收到货物之日起30日内向中国商品检验局提出申请，凭中国商品检验局出具的有效证书向卖方提出赔偿。买方对运输中货物或包装的损坏、遗失所提任何异议应由保险公司、运输机构或邮递机构负责，卖方不负任何责任。买方未在规定时间内提出异议，则视为卖方货物符合合同约定。

15. 赔偿。

15.1 因"不可抗力"而推迟或不能交货外，如果卖方所交货物不符合合同约定，卖方应负责向买方赔偿由此而引起的一切直接损失。

15.2 不可抗力。

在合同执行过程中，如果发生通常认为的"不可抗力"，则任何一方都不对合同全部或部分的不履行负责。但卖方应在事件发生后迅速通过传真或航空邮件通知对方，并在其后15天内提供证明由事故发生地的政府机关或商会出具的关于该不可抗力发生及其持续时间的足够证据。如果上述"不可抗力"持续存在60天以上，买方有权撤销合同的全部或还未履约的部分。

16. 通知。

所有通知应用英文写成并按照对方提供的联系方式送达给另一方。如果地址有变更，一方应在变更后15日内通知另一方。

17. 除非本合同另有约定,本合同的相关专业术语和条件与国际商会制定的《国际贸易术语解释通则 2000》相一致。

18. 仲裁。

双方同意对一切因执行和解释本合同条款所发生的争议,努力通过友好协商解决。在争议发生的通知之日起一个合理的时间内,最多不超过 90 天,协商不能取得对买卖双方都满意的结果时,除非双方另有协议,否则该争议应提交在中国北京的中国国际经济贸易仲裁委员会依据仲裁规则进行仲裁。仲裁用中文进行,英文作为参考。该仲裁为终局裁决,对双方均有约束力。任何一方不得寻求法庭或其他机构更改仲裁裁决。仲裁费用由败诉一方负担,另有约定除外。

19. 本合同适用中华人民共和国法律。

20. 本合同自_____之日起生效。本合同正本一式4份,合同双方各执2份。每份合同正本具有同等效力。

卖方:_____公司

代表:

买方:_____公司

代表:

Lesson 16　Notes to A Motor Vehicle Owner

The State applies a system of registration to motor vehicles. A motor vehicle is not allowed to run on road until it has been registered by the traffic administrative department of the public security organ. If an unregistered motor vehicle needs to run on road temporarily, it shall have a temporary passage certificate.

Whoever applies for the registration of a motor vehicle shall submit the following proofs and certificates:

(1)identification proof of the owner of the motor vehicle;

(2)proof on the provenance of the motor vehicle;

(3)proof on being qualified when the whole motor vehicle left factory or import documentation on the imported motor vehicle;

(4)proof on payment of vehicle purchase tax or documentation on tax-exemption;

(5)other proofs and certificates prescribed by any law or administrative regulation to be submitted for the registration of the motor vehicle.

The traffic administrative department of the public security organ shall, within 5 working days as of accepting an application, complete the registration and examination of the motor vehicle, and shall issue the motor vehicle registration certificate, the plate and the driving permit if the vehicle meets the conditions prescribed in the preceding paragraph; or shall state the reason of rejecting registration to the applicant if the vehicle fails to meet the conditions prescribed in the preceding paragraph.

A motor vehicle which is permitted to be registered shall meet the national technical standards for the safety of motor vehicles. At the time of application for the registration of a motor vehicle, the applicant shall accept the technical inspection of safety on the motor vehicle. However, if a type of new motor vehicle which is produced by an enterprise ascertained by the administrative department of the State for motor vehicle products according to the national technical standards of safety of motor vehicles is found upon inspection to have met such national technical standards when it leaves the factory and a conformity inspection certificate has been obtained, the technical inspection of safety may be exempted. [1]

Whoever drives a motor vehicle on road shall hang a motor vehicle plate, place the conformity inspection mark and the insurance sign, as well as bring with him the driving permit for the motor vehicle.

A motor vehicle plate shall be hung in accordance with the provisions and be kept clear and integral, instead of being intentionally sheltered or smeared.

No entity or individual shall confiscate or detain any motor vehicle plate.

In case any of the following circumstances occurs, the corresponding registration shall be made:

(1) the ownership of a motor vehicle is transferred;
(2) any registered content of a motor vehicle is modified;
(3) a motor vehicle is mortgaged;
(4) a motor vehicle is discarded as unserviceable.

For the motor vehicles running on road after registration, technical inspections of safety shall be carried out in accordance with the laws and administrative regulations and in light of such different particulars as the purpose of use, the number of passengers or quantity of goods carried, the service life, and etc., of the vehicles. If a driving permit or a compulsory third party liability insurance policy for a motor vehicle is provided, the institution for the technical inspection of safety of motor vehicles shall carry out the inspection, and no entity may set any other conditions. If a motor vehicle meets the national technical standards for safety, the traffic administrative department of the public security organ shall issue the conformity inspection mark.

The State applies a system of compulsory discarding unserviceable to motor vehicles, and prescribes different standards for discarding motor vehicles as unserviceable in light of their safety and technical conditions as well as their different purposes of use. [2]

For a motor vehicle which ought to be discarded as unserviceable, it must be deregistered in good time.

A motor vehicle which reaches the standards for being discarded as unserviceable shall not run on road. The large passenger vehicles, wagons and other commercial operating vehicles which have been discarded as unserviceable shall be disassembled under the supervision of the traffic administrative department of the public security organ.

Police cars, fire engines, ambulances and engineering emergency vehicles shall be painted with marked patterns and be installed with alarms and identification lamps in accordance with relevant provisions. Other motor vehicles shall not be painted or installed with or use any of the marked patterns, alarms or identification lamps specifically used by or similar to those of the aforementioned vehicles.

Police cars, fire engines, ambulances and engineering emergency vehicles shall be used strictly pursuant to the prescribed purposes and conditions.

No entity or individual may:

(1) assemble any motor vehicle or discretionarily change the registered structure, framework or features of any motor vehicle;

(2) change the motor vehicle type, engine number, chassis number or vehicle identification number;

(3) forge, alter or use forged or altered registration certificate, plate, driving permit, conformity inspection mark or insurance sign of any motor vehicle;

(4) use the registration certificate, plate, driving permit, conformity inspection mark or insurance sign of any other motor vehicle.

The State applies a compulsory third party liability insurance system to motor vehicles, and establishes social assistance funds for road traffic accidents. The specific measures shall be formulated by the State Council.

New Words

provenance ['prɔvinəns]	n. 出处,起源
exemption [ig'zempʃən]	n. 免除
administrative [əd'ministrətiv]	adj. 行政的,管理的
supervise ['sju:pəvaiz]	v. 监督,管理,指导
ascertain [æsə'tein]	v. 确定,探知,认定
conformity [kən'fɔ:miti]	n. 适合,一致,相似
integral ['intigrəl]	adj. 构成整体所必需的,完整的
	n. [数学]积分,完整,部分
intentionally [in'tenʃənli]	ad. 有意地,故意地
shelter ['ʃeltə]	n. 庇护所,避难所,庇护
	v. 庇护,保护,隐匿
smear [smiə]	v. 涂,擦上,抹擦使变模糊
	n. 油迹,污点,诋毁,诽谤
confiscate ['kɔnfiskeit]	v. 没收,充公,查抄
mortgage ['mɔ:gidʒ]	n. 抵押
	v. 抵押
formulate ['fɔ:mjuleit]	v. 用公式表示,明确的叙述
comply [kəm'plai]	v. 顺从,答应
ratify ['rætifai]	v. 批准,认可

deregister [di'redʒistə]	vt. 撤销……的登记
disassemble [,disə'sembl]	v. 解开,分解;[计算机] 反汇编
provision [prə'viʒən]	n. 规定,条款,准备,食物,供应品
aforementioned [ə'fɔː,menʃənd]	adj. 上述的,前述的
pursuant [pə'sjuːənt]	adj. = according to 按照(根据,与……致,合乎,和……一致)
discretionarily [di'skreʃənərili]	ad. 任意地,自由决定地
forge [fɔːdʒ]	n. 熔炉,铁工厂
	v. 打制,想出,伪造
lawfully ['lɔːfuli]	ad. 依法地,法定地,合法地

Phrases and Expressions

the traffic administrative department of the public security organ	公安机关交通管理部门
vehicle purchase tax	车辆购置税
as of	到……时止
driving permit	行驶证
a motor vehicle plate	车牌
in light of	考虑(从……观点,由于……结果)
engineering emergency vehicles	工程救险车
chassis number	车架号

Notes to the Text

[1] However, if a type of new motor vehicle which is produced by an enterprise ascertained by the administrative department of the State for motor vehicle products according to the national technical standards of safety of motor vehicles is found upon inspection to have met such national technical standards when it leaves the factory and a conformity inspection certificate has been obtained, the technical inspection of safety may be exempted.

但是,经国家机动车产品主管部门依据机动车国家安全技术标准认定的企业生产的机动车型,该车型的新车在出厂时经检验符合机动车国家安全技术标准,获得检验合格证的,免予安全技术检验。

[2] The State applies a system of compulsory discarding unserviceable to motor vehicles, and prescribes different standards for discarding motor vehicles as unserviceable in light of their safety and technical conditions as well as their different purposes of use.

国家实行机动车强制报废制度,根据机动车的安全技术状况和不同用途,规定不同的报废标准。

Review Questions

1. May an unregistered motor vehicle run on road ? Why ? How to drive home before

the new car was registered by the traffic administrative department of the public security organ?

2. What we should do if the ownership of a motor vehicle is transferred?

3. What should we submit when we apply for the registration of a motor vehicle?

4. Whether may my car be installed with alarms while I have pressing thing on road? Why?

5. What is the temporary passage certificate?

参考译文

第十六课　机动车所有者须知

国家对机动车实行登记制度。机动车经公安机关交通管理部门登记后,方可上道路行驶。尚未登记的机动车,需要临时上道路行驶的,应当取得临时通行牌证。

申请机动车登记,应当提交以下证明、凭证:

(1)机动车所有人的身份证明;

(2)机动车来历证明;

(3)机动车整车出厂合格证明或者进口机动车进口凭证;

(4)车辆购置税的完税证明或者免税凭证;

(5)法律、行政法规规定应当在机动车登记时提交的其他证明、凭证。

公安机关交通管理部门应当自受理申请之日起五个工作日内完成机动车登记审查工作,对符合前款规定条件的,应当发放机动车登记证书、号牌和行驶证;对不符合前款规定条件的,应当向申请人说明不予登记的理由。

准予登记的机动车应当符合机动车国家安全技术标准。申请机动车登记时,应当接受对该机动车的安全技术检验。但是,经国家机动车产品主管部门依据机动车国家安全技术标准认定的企业生产的机动车型,该车型的新车在出厂时经检验符合机动车国家安全技术标准,获得检验合格证的,免予安全技术检验。

驾驶机动车上道路行驶,应当悬挂机动车号牌,放置检验合格标志、保险标志,并随车携带机动车行驶证。

机动车号牌应当按照规定悬挂并保持清晰、完整,不得故意遮挡、污损。

任何单位和个人不得收缴、扣留机动车号牌。

有下列情形之一的,应当办理相应的登记:

(1)机动车所有权发生转移的;

(2)机动车登记内容变更的;

(3)机动车用作抵押的;

(4)机动车报废的。

对登记后上路行驶的机动车,应当依照法律、行政法规的规定,根据车辆用途、载客载货数量、使用年限等不同情况,定期进行安全技术检验。对提供机动车行驶证和机动车第三者责任强制保险单的,机动车安全技术检验机构应当予以检验,任何单位不得附加其他条件。

对符合机动车国家安全技术标准的,公安机关交通管理部门应当发予检验合格标志。

国家实行机动车强制报废制度,根据机动车的安全技术状况和不同用途,规定不同的报废标准。

应当报废的机动车必须及时办理注销登记。

达到报废标准的机动车不得上道路行驶。报废的大型客、货车及其他营运车辆应当在公安机关交通管理部门的监督下解体。

警车、消防车、救护车、工程救险车应当按照规定喷涂标志图案,安装警报器、标志灯具。其他机动车不得喷涂、安装、使用上述车辆专用的或者与其相类似的标志图案、警报器或者标志灯具。

警车、消防车、救护车、工程救险车应当严格按照规定的用途和条件使用。

任何单位或者个人不得有下列行为:

(1)拼装机动车或者擅自改变机动车已登记的结构、构造或者特征;

(2)改变机动车型号、发动机号、车架号或者车辆识别代号;

(3)伪造、变造或者使用伪造、变造的机动车登记证书、号牌、行驶证、检验合格标志、保险标志;

(4)使用其他机动车的登记证书、号牌、行驶证、检验合格标志、保险标志。

国家实行机动车第三者责任强制保险制度,设立道路交通事故社会救助基金。具体办法由国务院规定。

Lesson 17 Auto Market Assault

With today's automobiles acting as mass-produced rolling showcases of electronic technology, winning sockets in automotive electronics applications has become a major goal of just about every semiconductor company. The draw is enormous.[1] In many countries, consumers pour a huge chunk of their monthly budgets into automobiles, and the percentage of that money that flows into electronics is also rapidly increasing. We have reached a sweet spot in electronic technology capabilities where the number of new, useful features that can be added to automobiles with advanced electronics is exploding.

FPGA and programmable logic vendors are attracted to automobile applications (and automotive engineers are attracted to FPGAs) for a variety of good reasons. Programmability offers the potential for easy and inexpensive field upgrades and fixes, the ability to create multiple product variants with a single piece of hardware, and the flexibility to qualify and inventory a single piece of silicon for a large number of applications in the auto's bill of materials (BOM).

This week, Actel announced a new qualification of its ProASIC3 family for automotive applications—AEC-Q100 Grade 2 and Grade 1. Even though the automotive industry represents a potentially lucrative semiconductor market, it also has one of the most difficult and complex sets of qualification standards in the industry—rivaling and sometimes even surpassing standards for military and aerospace applications. The significance of Actel's announcement is that their ProASIC3 devices can now be used in a wide variety of automotive applications, including many "under the hood" sockets that previously were unavailable to FPGAs.

The "Grade" designations are for automotive ambient temperature ranges: Grade 0 = +150℃, Grade 1 = +125℃, Grade 2 = +105℃, Grade 3 = +85℃, and Grade 4 = +70℃. The temperature figures can be confusing because suppliers may quote (or qualify) either ambient or junction temperatures for automotive products. Generally, junction temperatures run 10℃~25℃ higher than ambient. The low power consumption (particularly the static power performance) of the Actel devices help to combat reliability problems related to high junctions temperatures which can, in the extreme case, lead to thermal runaway.

Certainly Actel's announcement does not represent the first foray of FPGAs or CPLDs into AEC-Q100 qualification. Altera, Xilinx, and Lattice Semiconductor all boast FPGA lines with AEC-Q100 qualification. Counting CPLDs, programmable logic devices have been AEC-Q100 qualified for years. Even the question of whether this is the first "Grade 1" qualification of an FPGA is little more than a semantic exercise for FPGA marketing professionals.[2] What is significant about Actel's announcement, however, is that an additional barrier to the penetration of programmable logic into our automobiles has been removed.

Actel's devices always bring a unique value proposition to the table. Because their ProASIC3 (as well as their mixed-signal Fusion) devices use flash cells to hold the configuration, they have certain advantages such as non-volatility (they are live at power-up and do not require configuration at system start time), low static power consumption, and increased immunity to transient configuration errors such as neutron-induced single-event upsets (SEUs). The tradeoff for these features is generally lower performance and density compared with SRAM-type FPGAs, and because flash technology is more difficult on the process side, they lag by a couple of process nodes behind mainstream CMOS logic.

For parts of the automotive market, however, these are attractive tradeoffs. The low cost, small footprint, low power consumption, and non-volatility make flash FPGAs a very good fit in many parts of the auto where other FPGAs might not work well. The Grade 1 qualification allows these devices into many safety-critical and "under the hood" areas in addition to FPGAs' traditional automotive strongholds such as infotainment.

In many markets, success of semiconductors depends on far more than the device alone. Supply chain considerations, qualification, and proof of prior success in an area make up a second leg of the triangle. Along with the certification, Actel announced that they have won design slots from Magna Electronics in their automotive vision systems, and that Delphi will be using the devices in engine control modules. Both of these applications take advantage of the unique properties of flash-based programmable logic.

Once these devices get a foothold under the hood, we would also expect a new crop of application-specific IP, development kits, reference designs, and prototyping boards to emerge. It is with the introduction of these remaining elements that the triangle of new market penetration will be complete, and we would expect a rapid ramp in adoption of the technology. At first, when only silicon is available, the innovators and early-adopters (and in the automotive world, these are few and far-between) kick the tires on the new technology.

The certification of ProASIC3 has us wondering if and when Actel's Fusion devices will follow the same course. Given the plethora of automotive applications that involve analog sensors and other legacy components that speak languages other than binary, Fusion would seem an ideal platform for automotive integration. We would not be too surprised to see that platform getting automotive qualified as well.

Go to any FPGA vendor's website these days and you will find a major section dedicated to automotive applications. With Actel diving under the hood, we may expect other vendors to answer with new applications of their own. The modern auto is no longer a collection of disparate electronic technologies driving in close formation. The proliferation of networked and integrated systems in cars makes an ideal target for FPGAs' flexibility in areas like networking, embedded processing, digital signal processing, and general system-level glue.

Traditionally, the automotive electronics space has been somewhat laggardly in its adoption of new technologies—the liability concerns and massive international regulation of the industry often keeping technical advances coming at a veritable snail's pace. Because of this, programmable logic is really just at the beginning of the kind of heyday in the automotive industry that it experienced in prior decades in industries such as network infrastructure. While we have marveled in the past at the number of microprocessors in a typical new automobile, we may well be making similar remarks soon about the number of FPGAs to be found there.

New Words

assault [ə'sɔːlt]	n. 攻击，突袭
	v. 袭击，突袭
socket ['sɔkit]	n. 插座，插口
semiconductor ['semikən'dʌktə]	n. 半导体
vendor ['vendɔː]	n. 小贩；卖方，卖主（亦作：vender）
programmability	n. 可编程序性
inventory ['invəntri]	n. 详细目录，存货清单
application [,æpli'keiʃən]	n. 申请，应用软件程序
lucrative ['luːkrətiv, ljuː-]	adj. 有利的，赚钱的，合算的，待遇好的，值得作为目标的
rival ['raivəl]	n. 对手，竞争者
	adj. 竞争的
	vt. 与……相匹敌，比得上
confuse [kən'fjuːz]	v. 混乱，狼狈，困惑
quote [kwəut]	n. 引用
	v. 引述，举证，报价

hood [hud]	n. 车盖、车篷;(汽车的)发动机罩;(机)罩;整流罩;(机身)成形架
ambient [ˈæmbiənt]	adj. 周围的,外界的
junction [ˈdʒʌŋkʃən]	n. 联接,会合处,交叉点
thermal [ˈθəːməl]	adj. 热的,热量的
	n. 上升的热气流
foray [ˈfɔrei]	v. 侵略,劫掠
	n. 侵掠,侵略,攻击
penetration [peniˈtreiʃən]	n. 渗透,浸透,侵入
proposition [ˌprɔpəˈziʃən]	n. 建议,命题,主张
	v. 向……提议,向……调情
semantic [siˈmæntik]	adj. 语义的,语义学的
volatility [vɔləˈtiliti]	n. 挥发性[度],轻快,快活
immunity [iˈmjuːniti]	n. 免疫,免疫性,免除
transient [ˈtrænziənt]	adj. 短促的,片刻的,一瞬间的;易逝的,虚无的;不稳定的;过渡的
tradeoff [ˈtreidˌɔːf]	n. 权衡(折中,换位,比较评定,放弃,交换)
slot [slɔt]	n. 水沟,细长的孔,狭缝,硬币投币口
	v. 组织、系统中的一个位置或空位;留细长的孔
foothold [ˈfuthəuld]	n. 立足处,据点,根据地
prototyping	n. 原型机制造,样机研究
ramp [ræmp]	n. 斜坡,坡道,诈欺
	v. 狂跳乱撞,乱冲,造倾斜路面
plethora [ˈpleθərə]	n. 过剩,过多
legacy [ˈlegəsi]	n. 祖先传下来之物,遗赠物
disparate [ˈdispərit]	adj. 不同的,全异的,乖离的
laggardly	adj. 缓慢的,落后的
	ad. 行动缓慢地
heyday [ˈheidei]	n. 全盛时期;最高潮

Phrases and Expressions

mass-produced.	大量生产的
sweet spot	有效(击球)点
CPLD=Complex Programmable Logic Device	可编程逻辑器件的两种主要类型是现场可编程门阵列(FPGA)和复杂可编程逻辑器件(CPLD)
FPGA=Field-Programmable Gate Array	现场可编程门阵列
Bill of Material	中文翻译为BOM,计算机可以识别的产品结构数据文件
infotainment=information entertainment	信息性娱乐

| far-between | 稀有的,远隔的 |

Notes to the Text

[1] With today's automobiles acting as mass-produced rolling showcases of electronic technology, winning sockets in automotive electronics applications has become a major goal of just about every semiconductor company. The draw is enormous.

随着汽车成为大批量生产的电子技术"展示柜",占领汽车电子产品市场已经成为每个半导体公司的重要目标。其前景十分广阔。

[2] Even the question of whether this is the first "Grade 1" qualification of an FPGA is little more than a semantic exercise for FPGA marketing professionals.

至于这是否是FPGA首次通过一级认证,不过是FGPA的市场营销人员的文字游戏而已。

Review Questions

1. Do you know any other information about auto technology?
2. What is the meaning of the word "infotainment"?
3. What did you think about after reading this text?
4. What is the character of ProASIC3 family?
5. Why do Actel's devices always bring a unique value proposition to the table?

参考译文

第十七课　汽车对电子市场的冲击

随着汽车成为大批量生产的电子技术"展示柜",占领汽车电子产品市场已经成为每个半导体公司的重要目标。其前景十分广阔。在许多国家,消费者每月拿出生活预算的一大部分用于汽车,其中用于汽车电子产品的比例也在迅速增长。电子技术能力已达到了非常高的水平,一大批新型实用的高级电子产品正应用到汽车上。

由于各种利好原因,FPGA和可编程逻辑销售商被吸引到汽车的应用上(同时,汽车工程师也被FPGA吸引)。可编程控制为简单便宜地现场升级改造使用同一硬件开发多种不同产品提供了能力,也为硅片在汽车BOM中的大量应用提供了可能。

本周,Actel公司宣布了该公司的ProASIC3系列产品达到了应用于汽车上的要求,通过了AEC-Q100二级和一级认证。尽管汽车产业是一个极具潜力的半导体市场,它也有一套最难和最复杂的认证标准——可以与军用和航空标准匹敌,甚至有些方面超过它们。Actel的意义在于ProASIC3系列产品现在可以广泛地在汽车上应用,包括在FPGA以前难以做到的许多发动机舱内插座上的应用。

"等级"用来指示汽车周围环境温度范围:0级＝＋150℃,1级＝＋125℃,2级＝＋105℃,3级＝＋85℃,4级＝＋70℃。直接用温度数字表示容易混淆,因为供应商提供的可能是环境温度也可能是连接点温度。一般来说,连接点温度比周围环境温度高10℃～25℃。在极端情况下,若连接点的温度过高有可能导致热失控,Actel设计在低功耗(尤其是静态功率性能)下有助于解决连接点温度高时带来的可靠性问题。

当然 Actel 的发布并不代表 FPGAs 或 CPLDs 首次通过 AEC-Q100 认证。Altera 公司、Xilinx 公司和 Lattice 半导体公司都以 FPGA 线路符合 AEC-Q100 的技术条件而自豪。CPLDs 算在内，可编程逻辑器件通过 AEC-Q100 认证多年了。至于这是否是 FPGA 首次通过一级认证，不过是 FGPA 的市场营销人员的文字游戏而已。总之，Actel 发布的意义在于可编程序逻辑控制在汽车上应用的又一个障碍被消除了。

Actel 的产品总是成为具有独特价值的议题。因为他们的 ProASIC3（及其混合信号合成）设备使用闪存单元维持配置，它们具有特定的优势，例如非挥发性（在通电时，它们是活性的，系统启动时不需要配置），较低的静态功率消耗，提高了抵抗诸如中子诱发单一事件扰乱现象（SEUS）的瞬时配置错误的能力。与 SRAM 型 FPGAs 相比，这些特征伴随着较低的性能和密度，因为闪存技术在过程控制方面更困难，他们落后于主流的 CMOS 逻辑节点。

然而，对于部分汽车市场来说，这些特征是具有吸引力的。低成本、结构紧凑、低功耗和非挥发性使闪存 FPGAs 在其他的 FPGAs 不适合的汽车配件上发挥很好的作用。一级认证使这些器件可以应用在许多要求严格安全的地方和发动机舱，以及一直应用 FPGAs 的信息娱乐系统。

在许多应用市场上，半导体的成功不仅依靠设备本身。供应链、资格认证、在某一领域成功的证据构成了另一支撑。随着通过 Grade 1 认证，Actel 公司宣布 Magna Electronics 公司已选用 Actel 的 ProASIC3 FPGA 来设计汽车视觉系统，Delphi 公司也将在发动机控制模块中运用这种设备。这两种应用都利用了基于闪存的可编程逻辑的特有性能。

一旦这些装置成功应用到发动机罩下，我们将期望一批新的应用——特定的 IP、开发工具箱、设计样本和样机的涌现。随着这些应用的实现，新市场的普及也将完成，我们预期在技术上会有一个快速的提升。首先，在只有硅可利用的时候，创新者和早期采用者（在整个汽车世界是非常少的）尝试这些新技术。

ProASIC3 的认证让我们想到 Actel 的混合信号合成装置是否、何时遵循同样的过程。由于汽车应用中模拟传感器和使用非二进制语言的其他传统组件太多，混合信号合成似乎成为汽车电器集成的理想平台。看到混合信号合成装置成为专用于汽车的平台，不必太惊讶。

现在，登录任何一个 FPGAs 的供应商网站，会看到一个重要的汽车应用区域。随着 Actel 深入到发动机罩下的应用，我们期望其他厂商把他们自己的新产品应用进来。现代汽车已不再是完全不同的电子技术的齐头并进。汽车上各种网络和集成系统的增多，为 FPGAs 在网络、嵌入式处理、数字信号处理和一般系统之间的结合等方面的灵活应用提供了用武之地。

传统上，汽车电子领域在新技术的采用总是有些滞后——责任关系和繁杂的国际惯例经常使技术进步推广缓慢。正因为如此，汽车工业中的可编程逻辑刚刚处在全盛时期的开端，就像数十年前网络基础设施在工业中经历的过程一样。过去我们惊叹大量的微处理器在新车型上的应用，也许不久我们也会为关于 FPGA 在汽车上的大量应用而惊诧。

Unit 4 Automobile Insurance

Lesson 18 Property Insurance Contract

A property insurance contract is an insurance contract with the property or related interests as the object of insurance. The property insurance contract that appears in this section is called "contract" for short, except otherwise specified.

The insurer shall be notified of the transfer of the objects of insurance and the insurance contract shall be altered with the consent of the insurer to continue to underwrite the policy. [1] But the transport insurance contracts and contracts with otherwise agreements are exceptions.

When the insured liability starts for the transport insurance contract and the voyage insurance for means of transport, the parties to the contract may not terminate the contract.

The insured shall observe the relevant regulations on fire, safety, production operations and labor protection and protect the objects insured.

According to the contract, the insurer may carry out safety checks of the objects insured and timely put forward written proposals to the insurant or the insured to eliminate unsafe factors or hidden dangers.

If the insurant or the insured has failed to perform its due obligations concerning the safety of the objects insured, the insurer has the right to demand additional insurance premiums or terminate the contract.

The insurer may, with the consent of the insured, adopt precautionary measures in order to safeguard the objects insured.

If, before the insured liability starts, the insurant demands termination of the contract, the insurant shall pay commissions to the insurer and the insurer shall return the premiums paid. If, after the insured liability starts, the insurant demands the termination of the contract, the insurer may collect the insurance premiums due for the period from the date when the insured liability starts to the date of the termination of the contract, with the remaining returned to the insurant. [2]

The insured value of the objects insured shall be agreed upon between the insurant and the insurer and specified in the contract or determined according to the actual value of the objects of insurance at the time when the insured risks occur.

The insured amount shall not exceed the insured value. If it exceeds the insured value, the part in excess shall be invalid.

If the insured amount is less than the insured value, except otherwise provided for, the insurer shall undertake to compensation according to the proportion between the insured amount and the insured value.

When an insured risk occurs, the insured shall be obliged to adopt all necessary measures to prevent or mitigate losses.

After an insured risk occurs, all the necessary and reasonable cost paid by the insured to prevent or mitigate the losses of the objects insured shall be covered by the insurer. The amount undertaken by the insurer shall be calculated separately from the compensation for the losses of the objects insured, with the maximum amount not exceeding the insured amount.

If part of the objects insured sustains losses, the insurant may terminate the contract within 30 days after the insurer pays the indemnities. Except otherwise provided for, the insurer may also terminate the contract. In the case in which the insurer terminates the contract, the insurer shall notify the insured 15 days in advance and return the premiums on the part not sustaining losses to the insured after deducting the part receivable from the date when the insured liability starts to the date when the contract is terminated.

If, after an insured risk occurs, the insurer has paid up all the insured amount and the insured amount is equal to the insured value, all the rights of the objects insured sustaining losses shall be in the possession of the insurer. If the insured amount is less than the insured value, the insurer shall retain part of the rights according to the proportion between the insured amount and the insured value.

If an insured risk occurs due to the damage of the objects insured by a third party, the insurer shall, starting from the date of paying the indemnities, subrogate the insured to exercise the right to indemnities from the liable third party.

If, after the insured risk occurs as provided for in the preceding paragraph, the insured has already obtained indemnities from the third party, the insurers may pay the indemnities in the amount after the indemnities paid by the third party to the insured are deducted.

The subrogation of the insurer to exercise the right to claim for indemnities according to the provisions of the above paragraph of this article shall not affect the right of the insured to claim for indemnity from the third party on the part not compensated for.

If, after an insured risk occurs, the insured has forfeited the right to claim for indemnities from the third party before the insurer pays the insurance money, the insurer shall not undertake to indemnities.

If, after the insurer has paid indemnities to the insured, the insured forfeits the right to indemnities from the third party, without the insurer's consent, the act is invalid.

If, due to the fault of the insured, the insurer cannot subrogate the insured to exercise the right to claim for indemnities, the insurer shall reduce the payment of insurance money correspondingly.

When the insurer exercises the right of subrogation to indemnity claims, the insured shall provide the insurer with necessary documents and the related information in its knowledge.

The necessary and reasonable expenses paid by the insurer and the insured for investigating and establishing the nature and the causes of the insured risks and the losses of the objects of insurance shall be covered by the insurer.

The insurer shall, according to the provisions of law or the agreement in the contract, directly pay insurance money to the third party if damages are caused by the insured covered by the liability insurance.

Liability insurance refers to insurance that makes the liability to indemnities of the insured to the third party as the object.

If the insured risk that has caused harm to the third party due to the insured is brought for arbitration or before the court, the necessary and reasonable expenses as arbitration fees or the litigation expenses paid by the insured shall be covered by the insurer.

New Words

consent [kən'sent]　　　　　n. 同意,许可
　　　　　　　　　　　　　v. 同意,承诺
terminate ['tə:mineit]　　　 adj. 有结尾的,有限的
　　　　　　　　　　　　　v. 结束,终止,满期
obligation [.ɔbli'geiʃən]　　 n. 义务,责任
premium ['primjəm]　　　 n. 额外费用,奖金,保险费
contingency[kən'tindʒənsi]　n. 意外,意外事故;可能,可能性;偶然,偶然性;临时费;应急费;意外费用;偶然误差,偶然错误
markedly['ma:kidli]　　　　ad. 显著地,醒目地,明显地
commission[kə'miʃən]　　 n. 委任状,任官令,佣金
　　　　　　　　　　　　　v. 委任,委托,使服役
indemnity [in'demniti]　　　n. 保证(赔偿,免罚)
deduct[di'dʌkt]　　　　　　v. 扣除
retain(=keep) [ri'tein]　　 vt. 保留[持];不忘;记住;雇用,聘请(律师等)
subrogate ['sʌbrə,geit]　　 vt. 取代,接替(别人);【律】(担保人清偿债务后)取代(债权人)
indemnity[in'demniti]　　　n. 保护[障,险];赔偿,补偿;[pl.]赔偿金;赔款;免罚,赦免;免除债务
forfeit['fɔ:fit]　　　　　　　vt. (因被罚而)丧失(所有权);(因犯罪等而)失去(职位、生命等);(因过劳等而)失掉(健康等)

deliberately [di'libərətli]　　　　　ad. 故意地
provision [prə'viʒən]　　　　　　　n. 规定,条款,准备,食物,供应品
litigation [liti'geiʃən]　　　　　　　n. 诉讼,起诉

Phrases and Expressions

property insurance contract	财产保险合同
transport insurance contract	运输保险合同
the object of insurance ＝ the objects insured	保险标的
insurance premium	保费
the insured risk	保险事故
insured amount	保险金额
insured value	保险价值
insurance money	保险金
arbitration fee	仲裁费
litigation expense ＝ litigation cost	诉讼费用
the right of subrogation to indemnity claims	代位求偿权

Notes to the Text

[1] The insurer shall be notified of the transfer of the objects of insurance and the insurance contract shall be altered with the consent of the insurer to continue to underwrite the policy.

保险标的的转让应当通知保险人,经保险人同意继续承保后,依法变更合同。

[2] If, after the insured liability starts, the insurant demands the termination of the contract, the insurer may collect the insurance premiums due for the period from the date when the insured liability starts to the date of the termination of the contract, with the remaining returned to the insurant.

保险责任开始后,投保人要求解除合同的,保险人可以收取自保险责任开始之日起至合同解除之日止期间的保险费,剩余部分退还投保人。

Review Questions

1. What is liability insurance?

2. When the insurer may subrogate the insured to exercise the right to indemnities from the third party?

3. If within the validity period of the contract, the risks of the objects of insurance have increased, but the insured did not notify the insurer in good time, may the loss not be covered by the insurer?

4. What is the right of subrogation to indemnity claims?

5. If the insured amount of double insurance exceeds the insured value, how much each insurer should undertake to compensation?

参考译文

第四单元　汽车保险

第十八课　财产保险合同

　　财产保险合同是以财产及其有关利益为保险标的的保险合同。本节中的财产保险合同,除特别指明的外,简称合同。

　　保险标的的转让应当通知保险人,经保险人同意继续承保后,依法变更合同。但是,货物运输保险合同和另有约定的合同除外。

　　货物运输保险合同和运输工具航程保险合同,保险责任开始后,合同当事人不得解除合同。

　　被保险人应当遵守国家有关消防、安全、生产操作、劳动保护等方面的规定,维护保险标的的安全。

　　根据合同的约定,保险人可以对保险标的的安全状况进行检查,及时向投保人、被保险人提出消除不安全因素和隐患的书面建议。

　　投保人、被保险人未按照约定履行其对保险标的安全应尽的责任的,保险人有权要求增加保险费或者解除合同。

　　保险人为维护保险标的的安全,经被保险人同意,可以采取安全预防措施。

　　保险责任开始前,投保人要求解除合同的,应当向保险人支付手续费,保险人应当退还保险费。保险责任开始后,投保人要求解除合同的,保险人可以收取自保险责任开始之日起至合同解除之日止期间的保险费,剩余部分退还投保人。

　　保险标的的保险价值,可以由投保人和保险人约定并在合同中载明,也可以按照保险事故发生时保险标的的实际价值确定。

　　保险金额不得超过保险价值;超过保险价值的,超过的部分无效。

　　保险金额低于保险价值的,除合同另有约定外,保险人按照保险金额与保险价值的比例承担赔偿责任。

　　保险事故发生时,被保险人有责任尽力采取必要的措施,防止或者减少损失。

　　保险事故发生后,被保险人为防止或者减少保险标的的损失所支付的必要的、合理的费用,由保险人承担。保险人所承担的数额在保险标的的损失赔偿金额以外另行计算,最高不超过保险金额的数额。

　　保险标的发生部分损失的,在保险人赔偿后 30 日内,投保人可以终止合同。除合同约定不得终止合同的以外,保险人也可以终止合同。保险人终止合同的,应当提前 15 日通知投保人,并将保险标的的未受损失部分的保险费,扣除自保险责任开始之日起至终止合同之日止期间的应收部分后,退还投保人。

　　保险事故发生后,保险人已支付了全部保险金额,并且保险金额相等于保险价值的,受损保险标的的全部权利归于保险人;保险金额低于保险价值的,保险人按照保险金额与保险价值的比例取得受损保险标的的部分权利。

　　因第三者对保险标的的损害而造成保险事故的,保险人自向被保险人赔偿保险金之日起,在赔偿金额范围内代位行使被保险人对第三者请求赔偿的权利。

前款规定的保险事故发生后,被保险人已经从第三者取得损害赔偿的,保险人赔偿保险金时,可以相应扣减被保险人从第三者已取得的赔偿金额。

　　保险人依照上述行使代位请求赔偿的权利,不影响被保险人就未取得赔偿的部分向第三者请求赔偿的权利。

　　保险事故发生后,保险人未赔偿保险金之前,被保险人放弃对第三者的请求赔偿的权利的,保险人不承担赔偿保险金的责任。

　　保险人向被保险人赔偿保险金后,被保险人未经保险人同意放弃对第三者请求赔偿的权利的,该行为无效。

　　由于被保险人的过错致使保险人不能行使代位请求赔偿的权利的,保险人可以相应扣减保险赔偿金。

　　在保险人向第三者行使代位请求赔偿权利时,被保险人应当向保险人提供必要的文件和其所知道的有关情况。

　　保险人、被保险人为查明和确定保险事故的性质、原因和保险标的的损失程度所支付的必要的、合理的费用,由保险人承担。

　　保险人对责任保险的被保险人给第三者造成的损害,可以依照法律的规定或者合同的约定,直接向该第三者赔偿保险金。

　　责任保险是指以被保险人对第三者依法应负的赔偿责任为保险标的的保险。

　　责任保险的被保险人因给第三者造成损害的保险事故而被提起仲裁或者诉讼的,除合同另有约定外,由被保险人支付的仲裁或者诉讼费用以及其他必要的、合理的费用,由保险人承担。

Lesson 19　Auto Insurance Basics

Auto insurance is a contract that protects your financial security in case of an accident. Although it is not mandated by federal law, the purchase of auto insurance is usually a requirement in most states; every state (with the exception of New Hampshire and Wisconsin) have minimum insurance laws. [1] If said owner cannot produce proof of satisfactory assets, then he must buy an auto insurance policy. [2] Regardless of the law, having good auto insurance is practical for the driver who wishes to avoid lawsuits or immense repair bills.

　　According to the Insurance Information Institute, a basic auto insurance policy is comprised of six basic types of coverage. While some of these types of coverage are required by state law, some are considered optional. These are:

　　(1) bodily injury liability;

　　(2) property damage liability;

　　(3) medical payments or Personal Injury Protection (PIP);

　　(4) collision;

　　(5) comprehensive;

　　(6) uninsured/underinsured motorists coverage.

1. Liability Insurance

Liability coverage limits (that is for the damage you do to others) are usually presented as a series of three numbers. For example, your agent might say that your policy carries liability limits of 20/40/10. That stands for $20,000 in bodily injury coverage per person, $40,000 in bodily injury coverage per accident, and $10,000 in property-damage coverage per accident.

Liability insurance (both bodily injury and property damage) is the foundation of most auto insurance policies. Every state that requires auto insurance mandates the purchase of property damage liability, and Florida is the only state that requires auto insurance but does not call for bodily injury liability. If you are at fault in an auto accident, your liability coverage will pay all the expenses, bodily injury, property damage, and any legal bills. The bodily injury coverage would pay for medical bills and lost wages; the property damage coverage would pay for any auto repairs, or replacement. Property damage liability usually repairs damage to other vehicles, but can also cover damages to things such as lamp poles, fences, buildings, or anything else that your car may have struck. The other party may also decide to sue you to collect "pain and suffering" damages.

See the minimum levels of required auto liability insurance to find out what is required where you live. Remember, if you cause a serious accident, minimum insurance may not cover you adequately. That is why it is a good idea to buy more than what your state requires. If you own a home and have nest egg and a savings account, you should consider more liability insurance.

Because, in most states, drivers are allowed to sue other drivers who injure them in car accidents. If you are sued and your liability insurance doesn't pay for all of the damages, your personal finances are on the hook, and it is likely you will become a target.

2. Collision and Comprehensive Coverages

If you cause an accident, collision coverage will pay to repair your vehicle. You usually can not collect any more than the actual cash value of your car, which is not the same as the car's replacement cost. Collision coverage is normally the most expensive component of auto insurance. By choosing a higher deductible, say $500 or $1000, you can keep your premium costs down. However, keep in mind that you must pay the amount of your deductible before the insurance company kicks in any money after an accident.

Replacement cost is the amount it would take to replace your vehicle or repair damages with materials of similar kind and quality, without deducting for depreciation. Depreciation is the decrease in vehicle value because of age or wear and tear.

Actual cash value (ACV) is the value of your property when it is damaged or destroyed. Claims adjusters usually figure ACV by taking the replacement cost and subtracting depreciation. Insurance companies often will "total" your car if the repair costs exceed a certain percentage of the car's worth. The critical damage point varies from company to company, from 55% to 90%.

Comprehensive coverage will pay for damages to your car that weren't caused by an auto accident: damages from theft, fire, vandalism, natural disasters, or hitting a deer all qualify. Comprehensive coverage also comes with a deductible and your insurer will only pay as much as the car was worth when it got wrecked.

Because insurance companies normally will not pay you more than your car's book value, it is helpful if you have a rough idea of this amount. If your car is worth less than what you are paying for the coverage, you are better off not having it.

Neither collision nor comprehension insurance is required by any of the states, but some lenders, when the owner finances the car, may require the purchase of collision and comprehensive in the loan agreement. Even when it is not required, collision and comprehensive coverage is highly recommended by the insurance industry, so that in the unforeseen event of damage or theft, the owner of the car can avoid heavy bills. Theft of cars is not as unusual as some people may think. In 2004, a car was stolen in the United States every 26 s, and a car had a 1 in 190 chance of being stolen.

3. Medical Payments, PIP, and No-fault Coverages

Medical payments (MedPay) **coverage** will pay for your and your passengers' medical expenses after an accident. These expenses can arise from accidents while you are driving your car, someone else's car (with their permission), and injuries you or your family members incur when you are pedestrians. The coverage will pay regardless of who is at fault, but if someone else is liable, your insurer may seek to recoup the expenses from him or her.

Personal Injury Protection (PIP) coverage is an extended form of MedPay. PIP may cover expenses that are related to injury, but not necessarily medical, such as lost wages, childcare and funeral costs. PIP coverage is currently required by sixteen states. If you are already insured under a good health insurance policy, then fortunately, there is no need to buy more than the minimum required amount of PIP or MedPay insurance.

4. Uninsured/Underinsured Motorists Coverages

Uninsured motorists (UM) **coverage** pays for your injuries if you are struck by a hit-and-run driver or someone who does not have auto insurance. It is required in many states.

Underinsured motorists (UIM) **coverage** will pay out if the driver who hit you causes more damage than his or her liability coverage can cover. In some states, UM or UIM coverage will also pay for property damages.

Similarly, underinsured motorists insurance will cover any damage caused when you are struck by a driver who is not insured for a sufficient amount. If you are hit, as a pedestrian, underinsured coverage will cover the expenses.

5. Add-on Features

Several supplemental auto coverages are available, either as separate premium items or included in augmented policies.

Rental reimbursement: a common add-on, covers vehicle rentals required because your car is damaged or stolen.

Coverage for towing and labor charges : in case of a road breakdown is also common.

Gap coverage: for your new car will pay the difference between the actual cash value you receive for the car and the amount left on your car loan if your vehicle is totaled in an accident.

Basic auto insurance is required by virtually every state. Proof of insurance is required at different times throughout the life of a vehicle. You may be asked for proof of insurance at any and all of these times: at vehicle registration, at the time of an accident, and any time when driving the vehicle. It is suggested that the owner of the car keeps proof of insurance in the car at all times, instead of on his or her person, so that it can be available at all times, no matter who is driving.

Any violations of state law regarding auto insurance could result in, at best, a hefty fine, and at worst, suspension of your driver's license and/or time in jail. The dire consequences of driving while uninsured are not worth the neglect of paying for insurance. The chance that an uninsured driver will avoid detection is slim; he is likely be caught and strictly punished.

New Words

satisfaction [ˌsætisˈfækʃən]	n. 满意,满足,令人满意的事物
regardless [riˈgɑːdlis]	adj. 不管,不顾,不注意
practical [ˈpræktikəl]	adj. 实际的,实践的,实用的,应用的,有实际经验的
medical [ˈmedikəl]	n. 医生,体格检查
	adj. 医学的,内科的,<古>(医)药的
payment [ˈpeimənt]	n. 付款,支付,报酬,偿还,报应,惩罚
collision [kəˈliʒən]	n. 碰撞,冲突
uninsured [ˈʌninˈʃuəd]	adj. 未保险的
motorist [ˈməutərist]	n. 乘汽车者,常坐汽车的人
liability [ˌlaiəˈbiliti]	n. 责任,义务,倾向,债务,负债,与 assets 相对
liability limit	责任限额(指保险单上规定的最高赔偿金额)
lamp [læmp]	n. 灯
	vt. 照亮
pole [pəul]	n. 棒,柱,杆,竿,极,磁极,电极
	vt. 用竿支撑,用棒推
	vi. 撑篙
depreciation [diˌpriʃiˈeiʃən]	n. 贬值,减价,跌落,折旧,轻视
lender [ˈlendə]	n. 出借人,贷方
loan [ləun]	n. (借出的)贷款,借出
	v. 借,借给
pedestrian [peˈdestriən]	n. 步行者
	adj. 徒步的,呆板的,通俗的
funeral [ˈfjuːnərəl]	n. 葬礼,出殡
rental [ˈrentl]	n. 租金额,租金收入,租赁

	adj. 租用的
breakdown ['breikdaun]	*n.* 崩溃,衰弱,细目分类

Phrases and Expressions

wear and tear	磨损,折磨
claim adjuster	理赔人
arise from	起于,由……出身
book value	净资本,资产账面价值,固定资本价值

Notes to the Text

[1] Although it is not mandated by federal law, the purchase of auto insurance is usually a requirement in most states; every state (with the exception of New Hampshire and Wisconsin) have minimum insurance laws.

尽管它没有被联邦法律所规定,但是在大多数州都要求必须购买汽车保险;各个州(新罕布什尔和威斯康星州除外)都有最低的保险要求。

[2] If said owner cannot produce proof of satisfactory assets, then he must buy an auto insurance policy.

如果没有足够证据表明车主财力满足财务责任法的要求,那么他就必须购买一份汽车保险。

Review Questions

1. Which liability insurance is required to purchase, bodily injury liability or property damage liability?

2. Why are the collision and comprehensive coverage highly recommended by the insurance industry?

3. What kind of damage will the insurer pay for if you choose the comprehensive coverage?

4. If you are not at fault in an accident, will the insurer pay for the damage on condition that you have choosen the Medpay coverage?

参考译文

第十九课 汽车保险基础

汽车保险是在事故后保证自己财产安全的合同。尽管联邦法律没有强制要求,但是在大多数州都要求必须购买汽车保险;各个州(新罕布什尔和威斯康星州除外)都有最低的保险要求。如果没有足够证据表明车主财力满足财务责任法的要求,那么他就必须购买一份汽车保险。就算没有法律规定,购买一份合适的汽车保险对驾驶员避免惹上官司和承担过多维修费来说都是非常实用的。

依据美国保险资讯中心的资料显示,一份基本的保险单应由6个险种组成。这其中有些是由州法律规定,有些是可以选择的。具体如下:

(1) 身体伤害责任险；
(2) 财产损失责任险；
(3) 医疗险或个人伤害保护险；
(4) 车辆碰撞险；
(5) 综合损失险；
(6) 无保险驾驶人或保额不足驾驶人险。

1. 责任保险

责任险的投保限额（针对投保人对他人造成的损害）一般用三个数字表示。比如，你的保险经纪人说你的保险单责任限额是 20/40/10。这就代表每个人的人身伤害责任险赔偿限额是 2 万美元，每起事故的人身伤害责任险赔偿限额是 4 万美元，每起事故的财产损失责任险的赔偿限额是 1 万美元。

责任险（人身伤害和财产损失）是大多数汽车保险单的基础。要求购买汽车保险的每个州都强令必须投保财产损失责任险，佛罗里达是唯一要求汽车保险但不要求投保人人身伤害责任险的州。如果由于你的过错造成了事故，你的责任险会承担人身伤害、财产损失和法律规定的其他费用。人身伤害责任险将赔偿医疗费和误工工资；财产损失责任险将支付车辆的修理及零件更换费用。财产损失责任险通常承担对其他车辆的维修费用，但是也可以对车辆撞坏的灯杆、护栏、建筑物等其他物品的损坏进行赔偿（不包括车辆自身）。另一方当事人也可以决定起诉你赔偿精神损失。

看看汽车责任险的最低投保要求，你就会发现在你居住的地方哪些保险是必需的。记住，如果你引起了一起严重的交通事故，最低限度的保险可能不足以支付你造成的损失。因此最好在州要求的最低限度外再买一些保险。如果你已经拥有了家庭、养老金和储蓄账户，你应该更多地考虑责任险。因为在大多数州，驾驶员们都有权利去起诉肇事驾驶员。如果你被起诉了并且你投保的保额不足以弥补各类损失，那么你有可能会成为众矢之的，个人财政将陷入麻烦。

2. 车辆碰撞险和综合损失险

如果投保人肇事，车辆碰撞险将支付你的车辆维修费。通常投保人得到的赔付不能超过车辆实际价值，这和车辆的更换费用不同。车辆碰撞险通常来说是汽车保险中最贵的险种。选择一个较高的免赔额，比如 500 美元或 1000 美元，就会使你的保费下降。不过要记住，你必须承担免赔额以内的部分，保险公司只承担超出免赔额的部分。

更换费用是重置车辆或用相同种类和质量的材料对汽车进行维修，且没有折旧扣除的总额。折旧是因使用年限或磨损等原因使汽车价值的减少。

实际价值是财产被损坏或毁坏时的实际价值。理赔人员通常会用重置成本减去折旧来确定车辆实际价值。保险公司通常在修理费用超过汽车价值一定比例的时候将车视作"车辆全损"。这个比例高低因公司不同而异，从 55%～90% 不等。

综合损失险对非交通事故原因造成投保人车辆的损失进行赔付：如偷盗、火灾、被故意破坏、自然灾害或各种意外等。综合损失险同样可以有免赔额，并在车辆毁损时保险公司仅按车辆价值赔付。

正常情况下，因为保险公司的赔偿额度不会超过汽车的账面价值，投保人最好对这个金额有个大致的了解。如果车辆的价值还不如保费高，还是不要投保的好。

任何州都不会强制投保人购买碰撞险及综合损失险，不过当车主能够负担汽车费用时，贷方可能会在贷款协议中要求车主购买碰撞及综合损失险。即使没有要求，碰撞及综合损失险也是保险业大力推荐的险种，以便在不可预知的毁损或偷盗情况下，车主可以避免重大损失。车辆偷盗现象很常见。2004年，在美国每26s中就有一辆车被盗，每辆车都有1/190的被盗概率。

3. 医疗险、个人伤害保护险和无过错险

医疗险将对被保险人及车上人员在事故后的医疗费用进行赔付。这些费用可能由于投保人驾驶自己的车或别人的车时（经他们的同意）发生事故，或者被保险人及其家庭成员在步行时受伤产生。无论过错在哪一方，保险公司都会进行赔付，但若责任由第三方造成，保险公司可以对其进行追偿。

个人伤害保护险是医疗险的一种延伸形式。它用来支付与伤害有关的费用，但并非必须是医疗的，如丧失的工资收入和幼托、丧葬支出等。目前有16个州要求购买个人伤害保护险。如果你已经投保了一份不错的身体健康保险的话，幸运的是你只需要买最低额度的医疗险或个人伤害保护险即可。

4. 无保险驾驶人险或保额不足驾驶人险

无保险驾驶人险在你被撞伤而肇事驾驶员逃逸或被没有投保汽车保险的驾驶员撞伤时进行赔付。该险种在许多州都要求购买。

保额不足驾驶人险 在肇事驾驶员所投的责任保险额不足以弥补造成的损失时，由保险公司进行赔付。在有些州，这两种险也对财产损失进行赔付。

类似的，保额不足驾驶人险也会在你遭受到一个保额不足的驾驶员撞击时给予赔付。如果你是行人遭到撞击，保额不足时驾驶人险会支付这些费用。

5. 附加条款

汽车保险有很多补充，既可作为单独险种，也可作为附加条款。

租车补偿条款：常见的附加条款，当你的车损坏或丢失而不能使用时的租车费用。

拖车和人工费条款：以防车辆途中抛锚，也很常用。

差价补偿条款：若你的新车全损，用来支付实际价值和汽车贷款余额之间的差额。

每个州都要求车主购买基本的汽车保险。在汽车的使用过程中，要求随车携带保险证明。在以下这些时候你可能要出示保险证明：汽车登记时、发生事故时、驾驶过程中。建议车主将保险证明放到车上，而不是带在身上，这样不管谁驾驶，都可以随时出示保险证明。

任何违反州法律中关于汽车保险内容的行为都会带来一些后果，轻则高额罚款，重则吊销驾照甚至入狱。这些可怕的后果说明购买汽车保险非常值得。不投保而又不被惩罚的可能性是很小的，一旦被发现将重罚。

Lesson 20　The Benefits with An Auto Insurance Contract

1. Standard Benefits

Standard benefits count in lifetime guarantee on all paint and bodywork repairs, courtesy car, 24-hour claims helpline, immediate authorization of repairs, emergency overnight accommodation, cover for personal effects, cover for medical expenses, cover for in-car audio/visual equipment, 24-hour windscreen replacement and repair helplines for legal advice, medical advice and post-accident counseling.

2. Available as Optional Extras

Available as optional extras count in Maximum No Claim Bonus for Life, Legal Assistance, Travel Accident Plan and Breakdown Cover (such as roadside, recovery and homecall).

The benefits are different with the level of coverage you (meaning the policyholder named in the schedule in this lesson) choose.

You can select the cover that suits your needs, from:

Third Party only—third party liability protection for injury or damage insured drivers may cause to others or their property.

Third Party Fire and Theft—fire and theft cover for your car and third party liability protection for injury or damage insured drivers may cause to others or their property.

Comprehensive—loss or damage cover for your car and third party liability protection for injury or damage insured drivers may cause to others or their property.

You may add the following optional extras to any of the above covers:

(1) Maximum No Claim Bonus for Life;

(2) Legal Assistance Plan;

(3) Breakdown Cover;

(4) Travel Accident Plan.

3. Some Key Benefits in a Little More Detail

We have outlined the range of benefits you can earn above. Now let us explain in a little more detail just what some of those benefits mean to you:

1) 24 Hour Claims Helpline

When you have had an accident or loss call our Claims Helpline. Speak to friendly and efficient experts 24 hours a day on helpline.

2) For Immediate Authorisation of Repairs (Comprehensive Only)

With of the insurance company an accident covered by your policy indicated in your insurance contract, if you choose to have the repairs carried out by one of recommended repairers, we (meaning the insurance company) can arrange for them to be authorised straight away. [1] The repairers are all thoroughly checked to make sure that their work is of a consistently high standard. As proof, all paint and bodywork repairs carried out by the repairers are guaranteed for the lifetime of the car. [2]

3) Courtesy Car (Comprehensive Only)

If your car is being repaired by one of the recommended repairers following an incident covered by your policy and you have an Comprehensive Cover, we will provide a small loan car whilst your own car is off the road. However, we will not provide a loan car if your own car is stolen or damaged beyond economical repair. [3]

4) Special Discount Through The Glass Helpline and 24-Hour Glass Replacement

If the windscreen, windows or glass sunroof of your car becomes cracked or broken, call the Glass Helpline available 24 hours a day. If you have our Comprehensive Cover, any repairs will be free of charge. If repairs are not possible then you will get a replacement but will have to pay the windscreen excess which is shown under "Own Damage Excess" in your schedule. If you decide not to claim, or have another type of cover, you will receive a special discount from our suppliers.

5) Vehicle Repairs

Where your policy provides cover for damage to your vehicle, the insurance company have a network of recommended repairers who will collect and redeliver your vehicle. Where provided for under your policy, they will also provide a courtesy car to keep you mobile. The repair process will commence immediately the vehicle arrives on their premises. To ensure there is no effect on any existing warranty you may have, they provide a lifetime guarantee on all paint and bodywork repairs.

Where you choose not to use one of our recommended repairers, we will arrange for the damaged vehicle to be examined by one of our motor engineers to agree the repairer cost with your nominated repairer. The inspection should happen within 2 working days of you providing repair details to us.

4. Definition of Words

"We" or "us" means the insurance company.

"You" means the policyholder named in the schedule.

"Your partner" means the partner, or husband or wife of the policyholder living at the same address as the policyholder and sharing financial responsibility. This does not include business partners or associates.

"Your car" means the car in the schedule or any courtesy car we arrange for you while your car is being repaired after you have claimed under this policy.

"Visual navigation equipment" means electronic equipment which can only be used primarily in your car for planning your routes.

"Key" means any device used for starting the car or using its locks.

"Terrorism" means using or threatening violence or action against people, property, business or everyday life for political, religious or ideological reasons.

New Words

lifetime['laiftaim]	n. 一生,终生,寿命
paint[peint]	n. 油漆,颜料,涂料
	v. 油漆,(用颜料等)画,绘,描绘,逼真地描述
courtesy ['kə:tisi]	n. 谦恭,允许,礼貌
immediate[i'mi:djət]	adj. 直接的,紧接的,紧靠的,立即的,知觉的
overnight ['əuvə'nait]	n. 头天晚上
	adj. 通宵的,晚上的,前夜的
	ad. 在前一夜,整夜,昨晚一晚上
accommodation [əkɔmə'deiʃən]	n. 住处,膳宿,(车、船、飞机等的)预定铺位,(眼睛等的)适应性调节,(社会集团间的)迁就融合
emergency [i'mə:dʒnsi]	n. 紧急情况,突然事件,非常时刻,紧急事件

optional [ˈɔpʃənəl]		adj. 选择的,随意的
extra [ˈekstrə]		adj. 额外的,不包括在价目内的,特大的,特佳的
		ad. 特别地,非常,另外
		n. 额外的人(或物),(报纸)号外,上等产品,(电影)临时演员
available [əˈveiləbəl]		adj. 可用到的,可利用的,有用的,有空的,接受探访的
insurer [inˈʃuərə]		n. 保险业者,保险公司
insured [inˈʃuəd]		n. 被保险者,保户
		adj. 加入保险的
insurance [inˈʃuərəns]		n. 保险,保险单,保险业,保险费
comprehensive [ˌkɔmpriˈhensiv]		adj. 全面的,广泛的,能充分理解的,包容的
whilst [wailst]		conj. 时时,同时
discount [ˈdiskaunt]		n. 折扣

Phrases and Expressions

count in	把……计算在内
personal effects	(衣物、化妆品等)随身物品,私人物品
no claim bonus	(因前一年未发生索赔而享受的)保险金优惠
straight away	马上

Notes to the Text

[1] With an accident covered by your policy indicated in your insurance contract, if you choose to have the repairs carried out by one of recommended repairers, we (meaning the insurance company) can arrange for them to be authorised straight away.

发生了保险单中载明的事故之后,投保人如果选择保险公司推荐的修理厂进行维修的话,保险公司将会立刻通知该修理厂提供维修服务。

[2] The repairers are all thoroughly checked to make sure that their work is of a consistently high standard. As proof, all paint and bodywork repairs carried out by our repairers are guaranteed for the lifetime of the car.

这些修理厂全部经保险公司严格检查,始终保持较高工作质量。作为证明经他们维修过的车漆或车身可以终生保修。

[3] However, we will not provide a loan car if your own car is stolen or damaged beyond economical repair.

但是,如果投保人的车由于被盗或损坏而不值得修理,保险公司将不提供代步车。

Review Questions

1. What do the standard benefits refer to with an auto insurance contract?
2. According to different level the policyholders choose, what are the difference of

coverage benefit?

3. What optional extras can the policyholders add to their covers?

4. On what conditions will the insurer not provide a loan car?

5. What insurance should be choose if the policyholder want to receive the service of a courtesy car?

参考译文

第二十课 汽车保险的益处

1. 基本保障

基本保障包括车漆及车体的终身维修、维修期间提供代步车、24小时热线服务电话、即时安排维修、晚间紧急情况下的住宿、私人随身物品的损失赔偿、医疗费用赔偿、车内音频视频设备的损失赔偿、24小时风窗玻璃的更换和提供法律和医疗方面的建议及事故后咨询的维修热线。

2. 附加保障

附加保障包括：最大限度的无赔款优待、法律帮助、旅行意外险及抛锚险（如在路边，修车时或在家抛锚的情况下提供帮助）。

投保人选择的险种不同，保障就有所不同。

投保人可以按需要从下列险种中选择：

第三者责任险——保险公司对因被保险人驾驶时的责任引起的第三方人身伤害或财产损失负赔偿责任。

第三者火灾及盗抢险——保险公司对投保人车辆在事故中遭受的火灾及盗抢负赔偿责任，以及对被保险人驾驶时引起的第三方人身伤害或财产损失负赔偿责任。

综合损失险——对被保险人的车辆损失以及被保险人驾驶时引起的他人的人身损害和财产损失提供保障。

投保人可以将下列内容补充到以上险种中：

(1)前一年度没有索赔，保险公司给予的最大限度的无赔款优待；

(2)法律帮助计划；

(3)抛锚险；

(4)旅行意外险。

3. 部分主要益处解析

上面简要介绍了保险所提供的保障。下面分别详细说明。

1) 24小时服务热线

当投保人发生了事故或遭受了损失，可以随时拨打保险公司服务热线。可以通过热线24小时向态度友好、处理高效的专家说明情况。

2) 即时安排维修（只有投保综合损失险才有此权益）

发生了保险单中载明的事故之后，投保人如果选择保险公司推荐的修理厂进行维修的话，保险公司将会立刻通知该修理厂提供维修服务。这些修理厂全部经保险公司严格检查，始终保持较高工作质量。作为证明，经他们维修过的车漆或车身可以终身保修。

3)代步车（只有投保综合损失险才有此权益）

如果投保人投保的是综合损失险，在遭受了保险责任之内的事故后，在将车交由保险公司推荐的修理厂维修的过程中，那么保险公司在车辆修好之前会提供一辆小型代步车给投保人使用。但是，如果投保人的车由于被盗或损坏而不值得修理，保险公司将不提供代步车。

4)关于热线电话给予的特别折扣及24小时更换玻璃服务

如果投保车辆的风窗玻璃，车窗及天窗玻璃损坏，被保险人可以拨打24小时玻璃热线维修。如果投的是综合损失险，所有维修都将免费。如果已经无法维修的就只能更换，超出部分的费用由投保人自己承担，超出的费用已在投保人的投保单中注明。如果投保人决定不进行索赔或通过其他险种索赔，将会得到来自供应商的额外折扣。

5)车辆维修

只要是在保险责任内车辆发生损坏事故，保险公司专门推荐的一些修理厂会集中并运送投保人的车辆。如果保单有相应记载，他们还将提供代步车给投保人使用。车辆一到修理厂马上开始维修。为了保证不影响被保险人保单的效力，修理厂将会对车漆和车身进行终生保修。

如果投保人没有选择保险公司推荐的修理厂，那么保险公司会安排一位汽车工程师对车辆进行检测，然后与投保人指定的修理厂共同定损。将在提供定损维修单后两个工作日内完成相应的检测。

4. 术语注释

"我们"指保险公司。

"你们"指被保险人。

"你的伴侣"指与投保人共同居住的并共同承担财产责任的被保险人的丈夫或妻子。这里的伴侣并不指生意上的合作伙伴。

"你的车辆"指保险标的车辆，或者在被保险人依照保险合同进行索赔后车辆在进行维修的过程中保险公司提供的代步车。

"视频导航设备"指在车辆上主要用来引领行驶路线的电子设备。

"钥匙"指任何可以启动与关闭车辆的设备。

"恐怖行动"指基于政治、宗教信仰或意识形态的原因对人们的财产及日常生活采取的暴力行为或以暴力威胁。

Lesson 21　The Cover for Your Car

The cover an insurance company provides will apply as follows depending on the level of cover shown in the schedule.

(1)**Comprehensive Policy.** If the level of cover shown in the schedule is comprehensive, section as follows applies.

(2)**Accidental Damage Fire and Theft Policy.** If the level of cover shown in the schedule is accidental damage fire and theft, section as follows applies.

(3)**Third Party Fire and Theft Policy.** If the level of cover shown in the schedule is third party fire and theft, section as follows will apply only if your car is damaged or lost by fire, lightning, explosion, theft or attempted theft.

(4)**Third Party Only Policy.** If the level of cover shown in the schedule is third party only, an insurance company will not pay for any loss or damage to your car.

1. What is Covered

1)Damage To Your Car

If your car is accidentally damaged we may choose to repair the damage or pay the amount of the loss or damage. We will repair the damage to your car unless the repair cost is more than the market value of your car less its value after the accident. [1] We may decide to use suitable parts or accessories not supplied by the original manufacturer.

If this happens or your car is stolen and not recovered we will pay the cost of replacing it with a similar one of the same quality and market value at the time of the accident or theft. [2] If you buy your car new and within 12 months it is: stolen and not recovered; or damaged and the repair cost is more than 60% of its current new list price including VAT (where appropriate); we may replace it with a new car of the same specification.

If this is not acceptable to you, we will pay the market value of your car. If we replace your car this will be instead of any payment and we must have the owner's permission if it belongs to someone else.

If we cannot replace your car with one of the same specification, we will pay the most recent new list price, including VAT (where appropriate), for that specification of car.

If your car's accessories or spare parts (including audio, telephone, visual navigation equipment, or visual-entertainment equipment, including televisions, video cassette recorders or players, DVD players and games consoles, which are permanently fitted or can only be used in your car) are accidentally damaged while they are: in or on your car; or in your garage when it is locked; we will repair the damage unless the repair cost is more than the market value of the damaged equipment.

If they are stolen in these circumstances and not recovered, we will replace them with similar equipment of the same quality and market value.

The cover provided for audio, telephone or visual-entertainment equipment (including televisions, video cassette recorders or players, DVD players and games consoles), which are permanently fitted or can only be used in your car, and visual navigation equipment, is limited to the amount shown in the schedule under Audio/Visual Cover. We will not pay more than the market value of your car (including accessories and spare parts) if it is damaged or stolen and not recovered. If the keys for your car are stolen and not recovered we will pay the cost of replacing the locks and keys.

2)Recovery And Re-delivery

As well as paying for loss or damage to your car, we will also pay reasonable costs for the following.

(1)If your car cannot be driven due to the loss or damage, removing it and taking it to one of our recommended repairers or the nearest suitable repairer. We may take your car to a safe place of storage while awaiting repair or disposal.

(2)After your car is repaired we will deliver it to you at your address.

2. What is not Covered

This policy does not provide cover for the following.

(1) The amount you have to pay, which is the first amount of any claim, shown in the schedule under own damage excess.

(2) Losing or spending money because you cannot use your car when it is damaged or stolen.

(3) Losing money because you are deceived, or do not receive all the money you agree when you sell the car.

(4) Loss or damage caused by pressure waves from aircraft and other objects in the sky travelling at sonic or supersonic speed.

(5) Loss or damage to any part caused by that part breaking down or failing.

(6) Wear and tear, or your car losing value, including any loss of value after the car has been repaired following an accident.

(7) Loss or damage while your car is being driven by or is in the charge of any person, for the purposes of being driven, who is not covered to drive according to the schedule. An example of this is a person who is insured to drive your car under an extension of his own motor insurance policy.

Exception 7 shown above does not apply if your car is: stolen or taken away without your permission provided that, if this is done by a member of your family or a person who normally lives with you, such person has been reported to the police for the purpose of a criminal prosecution and no subsequent statement is made indicating that such a person did in fact have your permission; being parked by an employee of a hotel or restaurant or car parking service; or being serviced or repaired by the motor trade.

(8) Loss or damage to visual navigation equipment that is not permanently fitted to the car and has not been stored in a locked boot or glove compartment when the car is left unattended.

3. Hire Purchase

If we know you are paying for your car by hire purchase or under a leasing agreement then we will do either of the following.

(1) If we are paying the cost of replacing the car, we will pay the proceeds of the claim to the company which you are buying or leasing your car from. If you owe less than the proceeds of your claim, we will pay you the difference.

(2) If we replace the car, we must have the permission of the company you are buying or leasing your car from.

New words

accessory [ækˈsesəri]   adj. 附属的(副的,辅助的)
                         n. 附件
vat [væt]   n. (=value added tax)增值税,大桶
owner [ˈəunə]   n. 所有人,物主
permission [pəˈmiʃən]   n. 同意,许可,允许
spare [spεə]   n. 剩余,备用零件,备用轮胎

	adj. 多余的,备用的,简陋的
	v. 节约
audio [ˈɔːdiəu]	*adj.* 成音频率的,声音的
permanently [ˈpɜːməntli]	*ad.* 永久地
fit [fit]	*adj.* 适宜的,对的,准备好的
	v. 适合,安装
	n. 适宜,发作,一阵
recovery [riˈkʌvəri]	*n.* 恢复,复原,痊愈
delivery [diˈlivəri]	*n.* 递送,交付,分娩
garage [ˈgærɑː(d)ʒ]	*n.* 车库,汽车修理厂
	vt. 把……放入车库
storage [ˈstɔridʒ]	*n.* 储存体,储藏,仓库
disposal [disˈpəuzəl]	*n.* 处理,消除,销毁,处置,弃菜碾碎器
amount [əˈmaunt]	*n.* 数量,总额
	v. 总计,等于
claim [kleim]	*n.* 要求,要求权
	v. 要求,请求,主张,声称,说明,断言
deceive [diˈsiːv]	*v.* 欺骗,行骗
pressure [ˈpreʃə(r)]	*n.* 压力,压强,压迫
wave [weiv]	*n.* 波,波浪,波动
	v. 波动,挥动,起伏
aircraft [ˈeəkrɑːft]	*n.* 飞机
object [ˈɔbdʒikt]	*n.* 物,物体,目标,宾语
	v. 反对
sonic [ˈsɔnik]	*adj.* 音波的,音速的
supersonic [ˈsjuːpəˈsɔnik]	*adj.* 超音波的
failing [ˈfeiliŋ]	*n.* 失败,缺点,过失
charge [tʃɑːdʒ]	*n.* 电荷,指控,费用
	v. 控诉,加罪于,要价,赊账,充电,管理
purpose [ˈpɜːpəs]	*n.* 目的,意图
extension [iksˈtenʃən]	*n.* 延长,扩充,范围
steal [stiːl]	*v.* 偷
provide [prəˈvaid]	*vi.* 供给,提供
	vt. 提供
normally [ˈnɔːməli]	*ad.* 正常地
criminal [ˈkriminl]	*adj.* 犯罪的,刑事的
	n. 罪犯
prosecution [prɔsiˈkjuːʃn]	*n.* 实行,经营,起诉
subsequent [ˈsʌbsikwənt]	*adj.* 随后的,后来的
statement [ˈsteitmənt]	*n.* 声明,陈述

indicate [ˈindikeit]	v. 显示,象征,指示,指明,表明
report [riˈpɔːt]	n. 报告,报道,成绩单
	v. 报告,报道,记录
trade [treid]	n. 贸易,商业,交易
	v. 贸易,交易,交换
boot [buːt]	n. 靴子,[英]汽车行李舱
	vt. 踢
glove [glʌv]	n. 手套
compartment [kəmˈpɑːtmənt]	n. 间隔,个别室,小事
unattended [ˈʌnəˈtendid]	adj. 无随员的,无侍从的,无伴的
proceed [prəˈsiːd]	v. 着手进行,继续进行

Phrases and Expressions

break down	打破(减轻,坍塌,彻底失败,精神不支,中止,把分解)
glove compartment	汽车仪表板上的小柜
take away	拿走(减去,解除)
wear and tear	磨损(折磨)

Notes to the Text

[1] We will repair the damage to your car unless the repair cost is more than the market value of your car less its value after the accident.

保险公司一般会选择修理车辆,除非修理费用超过了标的车辆市场价值与受损后车辆价值的差额。

[2] If this happens or your car is stolen and not recovered we will pay the cost of replacing it with a similar one of the same quality and market value at the time of the accident or theft.

如果发生这种情况,或者投保人的车辆被偷且没有追回来,保险公司将赔付一笔费用,额度相当于更换一辆与发生事故或被偷时市场价值相当、具有相似或同等质量的车辆的费用。

Review Questions

1. Which coverage policy do you choose that the insurance company will not pay for any loss or damage to your car?

2. On what conditions the insurer will replace your car with a new one of the same specification?

3. If your car cannot be driven due to the loss or damage, what will the insurer do?

4. Will the insurer pay for the policy holder if he spends money because he cannot use his car when it is damaged?

5. What will the insurer do if they know that the policy holder pay for the car by hire purchase or under a leasing agreement?

参考译文

第二十一课 机动车保险

保险公司的承保范围与投保单中选择的险种相对应。

(1)综合损失险。如果选择了综合损失险,那么下列情况都适用。

(2)意外损失火灾及偷盗险。如果投保了意外损失火灾及偷盗险,那么下列情况也都适用。

(3)第三者火灾及偷盗险保单。如果投保的是第三者火灾及偷盗险,那么只有在你的车辆由于火灾、雷电、爆炸、偷盗或企图偷窃而导致车辆受损或丢失时适用。

(4)第三者责任险。如果只投保了第三者责任险,保险公司不会对投保人的车辆损失负赔偿责任。

1. 保险责任

1)车辆的损坏

如果投保人的车辆被意外损坏,保险公司可以选择修理车辆或赔付损失金额。保险公司一般会选择修理车辆,除非修理费用超过了标的车辆市场价值与受损后车辆价值的差额。保险公司可能用非原零件生产商生产的零部件。

如果发生这种情况,或者投保人的车辆被偷且没有追回来,保险公司将赔付一笔费用,额度相当于更换一辆与发生事故或被偷时市场价值相当、具有相似或同等质量的车辆的费用。如果标的车是新车并且使用不超过12个月;被偷且没有追回;或损坏且修理费用比它当前价格(含增值税)的60%还高的话,保险公司会赔付一辆同等规格的新车。

如果投保人不接受这种建议,保险公司将按市场价值赔付相应金额。如果保险公司为投保人更换新车,就不会再赔偿任何费用,如果它属于别人的话,保险公司必须得到车主的允许。

如果保险公司不能赔付一辆相同规格的汽车,那么他们将按照这种规格汽车的现价(含增值税)进行赔付。

如果投保人车辆的附件或零件(包括车辆原装的或只能用于投保车辆的音频设备、车载电话、视频导向设备或视频娱乐设备,如电视机、录像机、DVD播放器、游戏控制台等)是在如下情况下被意外损毁:在投保人的车里或车上或车锁着停在车库里,保险公司将在修理费用不高于毁损设备现值的情况下进行修理。

如果这些零部件在上述情况下被偷且未被找回,那么保险公司将用相同质量和市值的类似设备更换。

为投保人车辆的音响、电话和视频设备(包括车辆原装的或只能在投保车辆上使用的电视机、录像机、DVD播放器、游戏控制台等)和可视导航设备提供的保险,应在保险合同规定的音频、视频设备保额范围内。车辆(包括配件)损毁或被偷未找回时,保险公司不会提供超过车辆市值的赔偿。如果标的车辆的钥匙被盗且未找回,保险公司将赔付更换锁和钥匙的费用。

2)车辆的恢复与转移

如同保险公司会赔付车辆的损毁一样,保险公司还会为下列事项提供合理赔付。

(1)如果投保人的车辆因丢失或损毁不能被驾驶,保险公司既可以将其送到保险公司指定的修理厂或最近的适合的修理厂,也可将标的车辆转移到安全的地方等候修理或处理。

(2)车辆修理好后,保险公司会将其送还被保险人。

2. 责任免除

发生下列情况,保险公司不负责赔偿。

(1)被保险人必须承担的免赔额以内的费用。

(2)因车辆损毁或丢失投保人无法使用车辆而导致的额外费用。

(3)投保人受骗或在卖车时没有收回谈妥的全部车款而导致的损失。

(4)投保人车辆由于飞机或其他以音速或超音速飞行物的声波而造成的损坏。

(5)由于某个零部件损坏或失效而造成的其他零部件的损毁。

(6)车辆磨损或事故后修理造成的贬值。

(7)车辆由不属于保单规定的其他人驾驶造成的损坏或丢失,不予赔偿。例如,在自己的车辆保单之外附加保险驾驶他人车辆的人。

除了以上 7 种情况外,发生下面各种情况,保险公司也不予赔偿:没有被保险人的许可被盗走或开走,有证据证明是由投保人的家庭成员或日常共同居住的人所为,此人被刑事起诉过并且也无法证明其行为得到了被保险人的许可;由旅馆或饭店的雇员代为停车或其提供的泊车服务;或正在由汽车销售商进行修理。

(8)非永久固定的视频导航设备在车内没人时,没有将其锁在汽车行李舱或杂物箱中而造成的损失或毁坏。

3. 分期付款

如果保险公司得知投保人通过分期付款买车或基于租赁协议租车,保险公司根据以下情况处理。

(1)如果保险公司要赔付换车费用,保险公司将把款项付给卖车或出租的公司。如果保险赔付额超过投保人所欠债务,保险公司将差额付给投保人。

(2)保险公司欲更换标的车辆,必须征得卖车或租车的公司许可。

Lesson 22　The Legal Responsibilities to Third Parties

The cover as follows is only provided if the level of cover shown in the schedule is Comprehensive, Third Party Fire and Theft or Third Party Only.

1. What is Coverd

1)Your Cover While Driving or Using Your Car

This policy covers you for the cost of any claims if you are legally responsible for: causing injury to or the death of anyone; or the damage you cause to another person's property, including damage caused by a trailer attached to your car.

2)Your Cover While Driving Any Other Car

This policy covers you for the cost of any claims if you are legally responsible for: causing injury to or the death of anyone; or the damage you cause to another person's property. You are covered while driving any other car only if all the following apply:

(1) you are 25 years of age or older;

(2)you are driving with the owner's permission;

(3)you are not entitled to make a claim for the damage under any other policy of insurance;

　　(4)the car is not owned by (or hired under a hire purchase agreement by or leased to) you or your partner.

3)Cover for Other People

This policy also covers the following people while using your car against their legal responsibility to pay for injury or causing the death of anyone or damaging another person's property:

　　(1)any person driving your car with your permission, who is insured by this policy;

　　(2)any passenger travelling in, or getting into or out of your car.

4)Legal Costs

If any person has an accident that is covered we may arrange for legal services to be provided to: represent that person at any coroner's inquiry or fatal accident inquiry; or defend that person against a driving charge arising from the incident, if we decide there is a reasonable chance of success.

　　We will not pay any legal costs or provide legal services if that person decides to plead guilty but they want a solicitor to speak to the court on their behalf. We will not pay any legal costs or provide legal services for charges to do with speeding, driving under the influence of drink or drugs, or for parking offences.

2. What is Not Covered

This policy does not provide cover for the following:

　　(1)any person other than you, who is covered under another insurance policy;

　　(2)death of or injury to any person if the death or injury arises out of and during the course of his or her employment either with or for the driver of your car (however, this event will be covered if we must provide cover under the Road Traffic Law);

　　(3)any accident, death, injury, loss or damage caused when your car is in any area to which aircraft normally have access;

　　(4)loss or damage to your car, or any other motor car driven or towed by you;

　　(5)damage to any property which the person covered owns or is responsible for;

　　(6)we will not be liable for any consequence of terrorism unless we have to meet the requirements of any road traffic legislation.

　　Right of recovery: if, under the law of any country, we must make a payment which we would not otherwise have to make under this policy, you must repay the amount of that payment.

3. Extra Benefits

Cover only provided by Comprehensive, Third Party Fire and Theft and Third Party Only policies.

1)Emergency Treatment Fees

We will pay the cost of any emergency medical treatment required under road traffic laws. If we pay emergency treatment fees, this will not affect your No Claims Bonus.

Cover only provided by Comprehensive policies.

2) Emergency Overnight Accommodation

We will pay up to the amount shown as "Overnight accommodation" in your schedule for necessary expenses for emergency accommodation [1] if you or any other driver cannot use your car during a journey as a result of loss or damage which we cover; and cannot reach your destination.

3) Medical Expenses

We will pay benefit up to the amount shown as "Medical expenses" in your schedule for the cost of medical treatment for anyone injured in an accident in your car.

4) Personal Effects

If personal belongings or clothing are lost or damaged by fire, theft, attempted theft or accident when they are in your car, we will pay you or the owner of the property up to the amount shown in the schedule for each incident.

5) Notice

This policy does not provide cover for the following.

(1) Loss or damage to money, stamps, tickets, documents or securities;

(2) Any property stolen from an open top or convertible car unless the property was in a locked boot or glove compartment. [2]

4. No Claim Bonus

1) No Claim Bonus

If you have made no claims in this period of insurance, your No Claim Bonus will be increased at renewal up to a maximum discount of 65%. If you have made any claims, your No Claim Bonus may be reduced at your next renewal.

Claims for the following will not affect your No Claim Bonus:

(1) damage to windscreens or glass, if this is the only damage;

(2) fees for emergency treatment;

(3) a claim under the Travel Accident Plan section;

(4) a claim under the Legal Assistance Plan section.

2) Maximum No Claim Bonus Protection

If you have maximum No Claim Bonus Protection, the following will apply:

(1) we will not reduce your No Claim Bonus if a claim or claims are made under the policy;

(2) we will not increase your premium as a result of a claim or claims under the policy;

(3) we will not cancel your policy as a result of the number of claims made under the policy.

The following also apply:

(1) your maximum No Claim Bonus Protection may end if we are told of a change in your circumstances that makes you ineligible or if the policy runs out or is cancelled under the terms;

(2) your premium may change if we are told about a change in your circumstances or

when you renew the policy because we have increased premiums generally.

New Words

legal ['li:gəl]	*adj.* 法律的,合法的,法定的
responsibility [ris,pɔnsə'biliti]	*n.* 责任
trailer ['treilə]	*n.* 追踪者,拖车,电影预告片
hire ['haiə]	*n.* 租金,租用,雇用
	v. 雇请,出租
represent [ripri'zent]	*vt.* 表现,表示,描绘,代表
	vi. 提出异议
coroner ['kɔrənə]	*n.* 验尸官
inquiry [in'kwaiəri]	*n.* 打听,询问,调查,查问
defend [di'fend]	*v.* 防护,辩护,防卫
plead [pli:d]	*v.* 辩护,恳求,托称
guilty ['gilti]	*adj.* 有罪的,内疚的
solicitor [sə'lisitə]	*n.* 律师
influence ['influəns]	*v.* 影响,感化
	n. 影响力,感化力,势力,权势
offence [ə'fens]	*n.* 过错(攻击,令人讨厌的事物)
park [pɑ:k]	*n.* 公园,停车处
	v. 停车,置于,停车
employment [im'plɔimənt]	*n.* 工作,职业,雇用,使用
access ['ækses]	*n.* 通路,进入,使用之权
	v. 存取
tow [təu]	*n.* 拖,拖曳所用之绳,麻的粗纤维
	v. 拖,曳
terrorism ['terəriz(ə)m]	*n.* 恐怖统治,恐怖行动
otherwise ['ʌðəwaiz]	*ad.* 否则,要不然,不同地,别的方式
extra ['ekstrə]	*adj* 额外的
	ad. 特别地
	n. 额外的事物
benefit ['benifit]	*n.* 利益
	v. 获益
emergency [i'mə:dʒnsi]	*adj.* 紧急的
	n. 紧急情况,突发事件
treatment ['tri:tmənt]	*n.* 治疗
overnight ['əuvə'nait]	*n.* 前晚
	adj. 通宵的,晚上的,前夜的
	ad. 在前一夜,整夜,昨晚一晚上
journey ['dʒə:ni]	*n.* 旅程,旅行,行程

	v. 旅行
personal [ˈpəsənl]	*adj.* 私人的,个人的
	n. 私人信息启示
ticket [ˈtikit]	*n.* 票,券
security [siˈkjuəriti]	*n.* 安全,保证金,抵押品,债券,证券
top [tɔp]	*n.* 顶端,极点,最高地位;陀螺
	adj. 最高的,顶上的
	v. 高耸,加以顶端,超越
convertible [kənˈvətəbl]	*adj.* 可改变的,可交换的,同意义的
	n. 有活动摺篷的汽车
renewal [riˈnjuːəl]	*n.* 更新,革新,复兴
maximum [ˈmæksiməm]	*n.* 极点,最大量,极大
	adj. 最高的,最大极限的
documentation [ˌdɔkjumenˈteiʃən]	*n.* 文件
additional [əˈdiʃənl]	*adj.* 附加的,另外的
introductory [ˌintrəˈdʌktəri]	*adj.* 介绍的,引导的,开端的
ineligible [inˈelidʒəbl]	*adj.* 无被选任资格的,不适任的,不适当的
	n. 无被选任资格的人,不合录用资格的人
boot [buːt]	*n.* 靴子,[英]汽车行李箱

Phrases and Expressions

legal cost	诉讼费
no claim bonus	(因前一年未发生索赔而享受的)保险金优惠
open top	敞口式的
convertible car	活顶汽车,两用车,折合式敞篷汽车,敞篷小汽车
emergency treatment	急救措施,急症治疗,抢救
run out	伸出(消退,偏转,振摆,滑动,空刀);用尽,耗尽
glove compartment	汽车仪表盘上的小柜

Notes to the Text

[1] We will pay up to the amount shown as "Overnight accommodation" in your schedule for necessary expenses for emergency accommodation...

……shown as……引导状语成分修饰前面的主句 We will pay up to the amount,意思是"如同……所显示的……"

[2] Any property stolen from an open top or convertible car unless the property was in a locked boot or glove compartment.

由于该句属于上句列举的内容,不具有独立的句子结构,中心词是 any property,stolen from an open top or convertible car 作后置定语修饰中心词,指任何财产的范围是从开着车门的车或敞篷车中偷盗的。unless the property was in a locked boot or glove compartment 是状语修饰整个前半句话,任何从开着车门的车或敞篷车中偷盗的财产,条件是这些没有被锁在汽车行李舱和仪表盘的小柜中。

Review Questions

1. Will the insurer pay for the damage caused by a trailer attached to your car if you choose the third party only?

2. Will the insurer pay for the damage caused by a driver who is not the policy holder and without the owner's permission?

3. On what conditions will the insurer not pay for the legal cost?

4. If you purchase the third party only, will you receive the service of emergency overnight accommodation?

5. What is the meaning of No Claim Bonus?

参考译文

第二十二课 投保人对第三者的法律责任

以下保险内容只有投保综合损失险、第三者火灾及偷盗险和第三者责任险才适用。

1. 保险责任

1)投保人驾驶或使用自有车辆

保险公司可为投保人在承担如下法律责任时进行赔偿:造成他人的伤害或死亡;造成他人财产的损失,包括由标的车拖曳物造成的他人财产的损失。

2)被保险人驾驶他人车辆

只有被保险人驾驶车辆造成他人伤害或死亡、造成他人财产损失,并符合下列条件,保险公司为投保人在承担如下法律责任时进行赔偿:

(1)已满25周岁;

(2)经车主允许驾驶其车辆;

(3)没有以其他保单提起索赔;

(4)驾驶的车辆不是由被保险人或其搭档拥有(或由租赁协议租赁)。

3)对其他人的保险责任

保险公司同样为使用被保险人车辆造成他人人身伤亡或财产损失的下列人员进行赔付:

(1)任何经被保险人允许驾驶其车辆的人;

(2)所有标的车上的旅客及上下车的乘客。

4)诉讼费

如果被保险人发生了所列明的事故,在以下情况保险公司会为其提供诉讼服务:被保险人因死亡事故或重大事故受到质问时;或由驾驶产生的事故诉讼需辩护且保险公司认为足够有胜诉可能时。

若被保险人决定服罪只是需要一个律师为其辩护,保险公司不会提供诉讼费或法律服务。如果被保险人因超速驾驶、酒后及用药后驾驶或违章停车被起诉,保险公司不会提供诉讼费用或法律服务。

2. 责任免除

以下情况保险公司不负责赔偿：

(1) 由其他险种承保的被保险人以外的人；

(2) 由于职务原因驾驶标的车辆并在工作过程造成的伤亡事故（道路交通法律规定保险公司必须赔偿的除外）；

(3) 车辆在飞机正常进入的地区停放时发生的意外事故、死亡、伤害、损失或毁损；

(4) 被保险人驾车牵引或拖拽作业造成标的或其他车辆的损失；

(5) 被保险人驾驶他人车辆造成的财产损失；

(6) 保险公司不会承担恐怖事件造成的损失，除非道路交通法律另有规定。

追偿的权利：基于任何国家的法律，保险公司必须支付，但依保单不需支付的，投保人必须返还。

3. 额外利益

以下内容只有投保综合损失险、第三者火灾及偷盗险和第三者责任险才可享有。

1) 抢救费用

保险公司将会提供道路交通法要求支付的紧急抢救费用。如果保险公司支付了这笔费用，并不影响投保人的无赔款优待。

只有投保综合损失险才可享受该利益。

2) 紧急情况下的住宿费

由于标的车辆损坏导致被保险人或其他驾驶者不能继续开车前行，无法到达目的，保险公司将按合同中规定的数额赔付在紧急情况下的住宿费用。

3) 医疗费用

保险公司将按合同中的规定支付在事故中受伤的标的车辆乘员的医疗费用。

4) 个人财物

如果车上人员放在车内的私人物品或衣服等遭火灾、偷盗等意外损坏或丢失，保险公司将依合同规定的每起事故赔偿的金额进行赔偿。

5) 注意

这份保单对以下内容不予承保：

(1) 金钱、邮票、票据、文件或有价证券的毁损与灭失；

(2) 在敞篷车中丢失的财物，除非它被锁在行李舱或仪表盘的小柜中。

4. 无赔款优待

1) 无赔款优待

如果投保人在这个保险期间内没有提起索赔，则保费优惠幅度最大可达到65％。如果投保人提出了索赔，那么该优惠幅度会在下一年度有所降低。

以下情况不会影响无赔款优待：

(1) 只是风窗玻璃或玻璃损坏；

(2) 紧急救护的费用；

(3) 旅行意外伤害险的索赔；

(4) 法律援助中的索赔。

2) 无赔款优待最大程度的保护

如果被保险人享有最大程度的保险金优惠保护，那么以下款项适用：

(1)依上述情况提出的索赔要求,保险公司不会降低优惠;

(2)以上述情况提出的索赔要求,保险公司不会提高保费;

(3)以上述情况提出的索赔要求,保险公司不会取消保险合同。

以下款项同样适用:

(1)若保险公司被告知被保险人的情况有变已经不符合条件或者保险合同已经到期或被取消,被保险人的最大程度保费优惠保护就会终结;

(2)如果保险公司获知被保险人的情况有变化,或因公司普遍提高了保费使被保险人更改了投保内容,投保人的最大程度保费优惠保护也会终结。

Unit 5 Assessment of Automobile

Lesson23 New Car Assessment Program

NCAP stands for New Car Assessment Program. If you have heard of "government 5-star ratings", you should know NCAP. NCAP is organized by the National Highway Traffic Safety Administration, which belongs to the U. S. Department of Transportation.

NCAP has actually been around for a while. NCAP was initiated in 1978 with the primary purpose of providing consumers with a measure of the relative safety potential of vehicles in frontal crashes. Side crash rating results were added to the program beginning with model year 1997 vehicles and rollover ratings were added beginning with model year 2001 vehicles.

The ultimate goal of NCAP is to improve occupant safety by providing market incentives for vehicle manufacturers to voluntarily design their vehicles to better protect occupants in a crash and be less susceptible to rollover, rather than by regulatory directives. [1]

NCAP provides consumers with vehicle safety information, primarily front and side crash rating results, and more recently rollover ratings, to aid consumers in their vehicle purchase decisions. The rating results are relayed to consumers via an easily recognizable star rating system from 1 to 5 stars, with 5 being the highest. [2]

For frontal crash ratings, crash-rating dummies representing an average-sized adult are placed in driver and front passenger seats and secured with the vehicle's seat belts. Vehicles are crashed into a fixed barrier at 35 miles per hour (mph), which is equivalent to a head-on collision between two similar vehicles each moving at 35 mph. Since the rating reflects a crash between two similar vehicles, make sure you compare vehicles from the same weight class, plus or minus 250 lbs., when looking at frontal crash star ratings.

Instruments measure the force of impact to each dummy's head, neck, chest, pelvis, legs and feet. Frontal star ratings indicate the chance of a serious head and chest injury to the driver and right front seat passenger. A serious injury is one requiring immediate hospitalization and may be life threatening.

　　　　★★★★★　　　10% or less chance of serious injury
　　　　★★★★　　　　11% to 20% chance of serious injury

★★★	21% to 35% chance of serious injury
★★	36% to 45% chance of serious injury
★	46% or greater chance of serious injury

For side crash ratings, crash-rating dummies representing an average-sized adult are placed in the driver and rear passenger seats (driver's side) and secured with the vehicle's seat belts. The side crash rating represents an intersection-type collision with a 3 015 pound barrier moving at 38.5 mph into a standing vehicle. Since all rated vehicles are impacted by the same size barrier, it is possible to compare all vehicles with each other when looking at side crash protection ratings.

Instruments measure the force of impact to each dummy's head, neck, chest, and pelvis. Side-collision star ratings indicate the chance of a serious chest injury for the driver, front seat passenger, and the rear seat passenger (first and second row occupants). Head injury, although measured, is not currently included in the star rating. An excessive head injury score (HIS greater than 1 000) is reported separately as a safety concern. As with the frontal crash ratings, a serious injury is one requiring immediate hospitalization and may be life threatening.

★★★★★	5% or less chance of serious injury
★★★★	6% to 10% chance of serious injury
★★★	11% to 20% chance of serious injury
★★	21% to 25% chance of serious injury
★	26% or greater chance of serious injury

NHTSA's New Car Assessment Program has a limited budget and must concentrate its ratings on front and side-impact crashes which every year are responsible for the highest percentage of deaths and serious injuries. [3]

NCAP was initiated in America in 1978, and established in Europe and Japan after 1990th, which named NHTSA—NCAP, Euro—NCAP and J—NCAP.

Euro—NCAP: it includes front collision tests(at a speed of 64 km/h) and side collision tests(at a speed of 50 km/h). Measuring the injury with 5 stars being the highest and 1 star being the lowest.

J—NCAP: it includes front collision tests(at a speed of 55 km/h), offset frontal collision test(at a speed of 64 km/h), side collision tests(at a speed of 55 km/h) and braking performance tests(at a speed of 100km/h). Measuring the injury with 6 stars being the highest and 1 star being the lowest.

New Words

initiate [ɪˈnɪʃieɪt]	vt. 开始,发起
primary [ˈpraɪməri]	adj. 第一位的,主要的,初步的,初级的,原来的,根源的
rollover [ˈrəulˌəuvə]	n. 翻滚
ultimate [ˈʌltimit]	adj. 最后的,最终的,根本的

	n. 最终
incentives [insentiv]	*n.* 动机
	adj. 激励的
susceptible [səseptəbl]	*adj.* 易受影响的,容许……的
	n. (因缺乏免疫力而)易得病的人
purchase [pəːtʃəs]	*vt.* 买,购买
	n. 买,购买
via [vaiə, viːə]	*prep.* 经,通过,经由
dummy [dʌmi]	*n.* 哑巴,傀儡,假人,假货
	adj. 虚拟的,假的,虚构的
equivalent [ikwivələnt]	*adj.* 相等的,相当的,同意义的
	n. 等价物,相等物
impact [impækt]	*n.* 碰撞,冲击,冲突,影响,效果
	vt. 挤入,撞击,压紧,对……发生影响
chest [tʃest]	*n.* 胸腔,胸膛,箱,柜
pelvis [pelvis]	*n.* [解]骨盆
hospitalization [ˌhɒspɪtəlaɪˈzeɪʃ(ə)n]	*n.* 医院收容,住院治疗

Phrases and Expressions

New Car Assessment Program	新车评估体系
National Highway Traffic Safety Administration	美国高速公路安全协会
the U.S. Department of Transportation	美国交通运输部
frontal crashes	正面碰撞
side crash	侧面碰撞
occupant safety	乘员安全性
seat belt	安全带

Notes to the Text

[1] The ultimate goal of NCAP is to improve occupant safety by providing market incentives for vehicle manufacturers to voluntarily design their vehicles to better protect occupants in a crash and be less susceptible to rollover, rather than by regulatory directives.

NCAP 最终的目的是,通过刺激市场使制造商自发地改善汽车的设计,以便在碰撞中更好地保护乘员,减少车辆翻滚的灵敏性,改善乘员安全性,而不是通过法律强制要求。

[2] NCAP provides consumers with vehicle safety information, primarily front and side crash rating results, and more recently rollover ratings, to aid consumers in their vehicle purchase decisions. The rating results are relayed to consumers via an easily recognizable star rating system from 1 to 5 stars, with 5 being the highest.

NCAP 为用户提供车辆的安全性信息,主要包括正面碰撞、侧面碰撞安全性等级评定结果,以及翻滚测试的等级评定,为用户选购汽车提供参考。评定等级通过容易辨认的星级反馈给用户,从1星到5星,其中5星级表示性能最好。

[3] NHTSA's New Car Assessment Program has a limited budget and must concentrate its ratings on front and side-impact crashes which every year are responsible for the highest percentage of deaths and serious injuries.

美国高速公路安全协会的新车评估体系预算费用有限,必须集中精力到每年死亡率和严重伤害最高的正面和侧面碰撞。

Review Questions

1. What is the NCAP?
2. How long has NCAP been around and what is the program's goal?
3. How does NHTSA perform the frontal crash rating and how are vehicles rated?
4. How does NHTSA perform the side crash rating and how are vehicles rated?
5. Why does not NHTSA do rear impact crash ratings?

参考译文

第五单元 汽车评估

第二十三课 新车评估体系

NCAP 是指新车评估体系。如果你听说过"政府五星等级",就会知道 NCAP。NCAP 是由所属美国交通运输部的美国高速公路安全协会组织实施的。

NCAP 实际上已经存在一段时间了。NCAP 始于 1978 年,主要的目的是为用户提供车辆在正面碰撞时的安全潜能性测评。侧面碰撞在 1997 车型年被引入到该体系中,翻滚测试的等级评定在 2001 车型年被引入到该体系中。等级评定加入到评估体系中。

NCAP 最终的目的是,通过刺激市场使制造商自发地改善汽车的设计,以便在碰撞中更好地保护乘员,减少车辆翻滚的灵敏性,改善乘员安全性,而不是通过法律强制要求。

NCAP 为用户提供车辆的安全性信息,主要包括正面碰撞和侧面碰撞的安全性等级评定结果,以及翻滚测试的等级评定,为用户选购汽车提供参考。评定等级通过容易辨认的星级反馈给用户,从1星到5星,其中5星级表示性能最好。

正面碰撞测试时,碰撞人体模型中规定坐在驾驶员和副驾驶位置的是已系好安全带的普通身材的成年人。车辆以 35 mph(56.3km/h)的速度碰向固定的障碍物,这相当于两辆车辆同时以 35 mph(56.3km/h)正面碰撞。由于碰撞程度反映了两辆相似的车的碰撞情况,当查看碰撞等级的时候务必比较车辆的载重等级,误差不超过 250 磅(113.4kg)。

通过工具测量碰撞力对人体模型的头部、颈部、胸部、骨盆、腿部和脚部的冲击。正面的碰撞星级表明了驾驶员和前排乘员头部、胸部受到严重伤害的概率。严重伤害是指需要马上送入医院治疗,并且可能会危及生命的伤害。

★★★★★ 表示乘员受严重伤害的概率小于或等于 10%
★★★★ 表示乘员受严重伤害的概率为 11%~20%
★★★ 表示乘员受严重伤害的概率为 21%~35%
★★ 表示乘员受严重伤害的概率为 36%~45%

| ★ | 表示乘员受严重伤害的概率等于或大于46% |

侧面碰撞测试时,碰撞人体模型中规定坐在驾驶员位置和后排乘客(驾驶员这一边)的是系有安全带的普通身材成年人。侧面碰撞测试规定3015磅(1367.6kg)重的障碍物以38.5 mph(61.9km/h)的速度交叉碰向静止的车辆。由于所有类型的车辆被同一类型的障碍物碰撞,在查看侧面碰撞保护等级时可以对这些车辆进行相互比较分析。

通过工具测量碰撞力对人体模型的头部、颈部、胸部、骨盆的冲击。侧面碰撞的星级表明了驾驶员、前排乘员和后排乘员胸部受严重伤害的概率(第一排和第二排乘客)。然而,头部的伤害虽然也检测,但目前通常不包括在受伤等级程度中。头部伤害分过高(HIS超过1000)就要作为一项安全性因素单独记录在报告中。如同正面碰撞等级,严重伤害是指需要马上送入医院治疗,并且可能会危及生命的伤害。

★★★★★	表示乘员受严重伤害的概率小于或等于5%
★★★★	表示乘员受严重伤害的概率为6%~10%
★★★	表示乘员受严重伤害的概率为11%~20%
★★	表示乘员受严重伤害的概率为21%~25%
★	表示乘员受严重伤害的概率等于或大于26%

美国高速公路安全协会的新车评估体系预算费用有限,必须集中精力到每年死亡率和严重伤害最高的正面和侧面碰撞。

NCAP最早于1978年出现在美国,进入20世纪90年代后,欧洲、日本也相继建立了自己的NCAP体系,其分别被称为NHTSA—NCAP、Euro—NCAP和J—NCAP。

Euro—NCAP:包括正面碰撞测试(以64km/h的速度)和侧面碰撞(以50km/h的速度)。伤害程度评定,最高5星,最低1星。

J—NCAP:包括正面碰撞(以55km/h的速度)、偏置碰撞(以64km/h的速度)、侧面碰撞(以55km/h的速度)和制动性能(以100km/h的速度)。伤害程度评定,最高6星,最低1星。

Lesson 24   Estimating for Automobile Repair

1. Estimating Guides

Collision estimating guides (also called collision manuals or crash guides) are the single most important tools used by damage report writers and appraisers. The Mitchell Collision Estimating Guide, published by Mitchell International Inc., and the Motor Crash Estimating Guide published by the Hearst Corporation are the two most popular estimating guides in use today. They contain vital crash and repair information on both domestic and import passenger cars, vans, and light trucks.

Publishers constantly update and reissue their guides to keep abreast of changing prices, revised Labor hours, and new and discontinued components. With up to 16 updates per year for current models, it is important for all involved in the industry to use the most up-to-date manuals when compiling and comparing estimates.[1] The guides list the OEM parts prices and information for the past seven or eight model years. Early model guides are also available for vehicles up to 14 years old.

As mentioned earlier, publishers strive to organize their manuals in a logical, easy-to-use manner. Although slight differences exist between manuals, information is generally first divided by vehicle year and vehicle model. Within each of these divisions, information is then categorized under major assemblies (such as the bumper or hood) or major systems (such as the air conditioner, heater, or exhaust). An exploded-view illustration of the assembly or system shows the relative position of the parts and gives their industry-accepted names and manufacturer's reference numbers. The parts in the exploded views are keyed to the pricing and flat rate labor allowances that accompany each illustration.

It is important to remember that the flat rate Labor hours provided by the manuals give times for the removal and replacement of new and undamaged parts on undamaged vehicles are vital. But actual Labor hours needed to remove heavily damaged parts or parts frozen by rust or corrosion may vary. [2]

It is impossible to establish accurate Labor hours for all operations. Jobs such as transferring brackets, braces, reinforcements, or ornaments from old to new parts vary in difficulty depending on the particular job. Removing undercoating, restoring corrosion protection, and filling or plugging unneeded holes on new parts are other examples of labor allowances not included in the published Labor hours.

A full listing of times not included in published Labor hours is given in the collision estimating guide. Guides also do not list any Labor hours for the straightening or repair of frame, sheet metal components, or plastics. Labor allowances for these repairs are referred to as judgement Labor hour. Allowances for judgement Labor hour and other nonincluded operations are determined through experience and careful calculation of all factors involved. Reaching an agreement concerning nonincluded labor allowances is often the most difficult part of shop/adjuster negotiations. [3]

Part prices listed in the manuals are for new OEM parts. Glass listings give both the manufacturer's and National Auto Glass Specifications (NAGS) part numbers and prices.

Individual crash guides also include most, if not all, of the following:

(1) detailed step-by-step instructions on how to use the guide effectively;

(2) definition of the terms used in the guide;

(3) guidelines for computing Labor hours for overlapping operations;

(4) abbreviation explanations;

(5) guidelines for vehicle identification, including how to interpret vehicle identification numbers (VINs);

(6) cooling capacity information;

(7) air conditioner refrigerant capacity listings;

(8) underhood diagrams;

(9) conversion tables for quickly determining labor prices;

(10) sectioning information (when available from OEM);

(11) listings of part numbers that can be interchanged between related models.

It is easy to see why damage report writers and appraisers must be totally familiar with the information in the most up-do-date guides. It is provided to make your job easier. Unfortunately, one of the most common complaints about incompetent adjusters and facility personnel is the inability to use the collision estimating guides.

The information in the guides also serves as the data base for most computerized estimating programs. Computerized estimating vastly reduces the time needed to prepare a damage report, and also lowers the likelihood of math errors, omitted operations and inaccurate overlap computation.

Warning: verbal, nonwritten estimates should never be made. They often lead to misunderstandings that generate customer disloyalty and possible legal action.

2. The Estimator's Tools

The estimator needs several tools when making an analysis of damage. Here is a list of the basic equipment required to complete a thorough damage analysis.

(1) The estimator will need several methods of recording information. Depending on the extent of damage, the estimator can simply use a note pad and pencil; or the damage can be verbally recorded on a tape recorder and transcribed later. Those with access to a computerized estimating program can use computer-generated exploded parts illustrations and estimating worksheets or even enter parts codes into a hand-held computer.

(2) The estimator needs manufacturer's parts lists and specification sheets to assist in the identification of parts and in the measuring of critical dimensions.

(3) Measuring tools are essential to accurately analyzing damage. A tram gauge and a twelve-foot steel tape with both metric and fractional-inch (SAE) dimensions are necessary. Most manufacturer's specifications are given in the metric system.

(4) The estimator must have at his or her disposal a lift (or jack) and support stands to raise the vehicle. In all but the very light collision damage, it is necessary to perform underbody visual inspections and measurements.

(5) The estimator should have at hand common mechanics hand tools, such as wrenches (both metric and SAE), screwdrivers, and pliers. These are sometimes necessary for disassembly and removal of parts on a vehicle that might be obstructing visual ormeasurement checks. Stools, creepers, trouble lights, and extension cords should also be accessible in the estimating area.

New Words

appraiser [əˈpreɪzə(r)]	n. 评估鉴定员
vital [vaitl]	adj. 致命的,极其重要的
domestic [dəˈmestɪk]	adj. 国产的,国内的,家庭的
van [væn]	n. 运货车;前卫,先头部队,先锋
	vt. 用车搬运
constantly [ˈkɒnstəntli]	ad. 坚定地,坚决地;始终如一地;忠诚地;不断地
reissue [riːˈɪʃuː]	vt. 再发出;重新发行
	vi. 重新发行

	n. 新发行本
abreast [əˈbrest]	ad. &adj. 朝同方向并列(的),并肩(的)
revised [riˈvaizd]	adj. 修订过的,改订的
discontinued [diskənˈtinju:d]	adj. 不连续的
compiling [kəmˈpailiŋ]	n. 编纂
strive [straiv]	vi. 努力,奋斗,力求;斗争,反抗
illustration [iləsˈtreiʃən]	n. 说明,图解,例证,实例,插图
frozen [ˈfrəuzən]	adj. 结冰的;冻死的,冻伤的;严寒的;冷藏的;不能动用的;冷淡的
rust [rʌst]	n. 铁锈;铁锈色
	vi. 生锈;(脑子等)发锈,衰退
	vt. 使生锈
corrosion [kəˈrəuʒən]	n. 腐蚀,侵蚀;(渐渐的)损坏,消损;铁锈
brackets [ˈbrækit]	n. 托架;括号;(收入额等)等级,档次
	vi. 给……装托架;把……括在括号内;把……相提并论;把……围住;把……放在考虑之外;对……作界定
brace [breis]	n. 支柱,支架;摇钻,大括号
	vt. 拉紧,支住,激励,加强,使经受锻炼;打起精神
	vi. 做好准备
	adj. 曲柄的
reinforcement [ri:inˈfɔ:s]	vt. 增援,支援;增强,增加
	vi. 求援,得到加强
	n. 加固物
ornament [ˈɔ:nəmənt]	n. 装饰品,点缀品
	vt. 装饰,美化;为……增光
undercoating [ˈʌndəkəutiŋ]	n. (涂在车辆底部、通常以柏油打底的)防水底涂层
abbreviation [əˌbri:viˈeiʃn]	n. 缩写,缩短;缩写式

Phrases and Expressions

collision estimating guides	碰撞评估指南
Mitchell Collision Estimating Guide	米切尔碰撞评估指南
Motor Crash Estimating Guide	发动机碰撞修理评估指南
up-to-date	最时新的
National Auto Glass Specifications	国家汽车玻璃技术规范

Notes to the Text

[1] With up to 16 updates per year for current models, it is important for all involved in the industry to use the most up-to-date manuals when compiling and comparing estimates.

现在的评估指南平均每年更新多达16次,业内人士在制作和比较评估报表时选用最新评估指南至关重要。

[2] It is important to remember that the flat rate Labor hours provided by the manuals give times for the removal and replacement of new and undamaged parts on undamaged vehicles are vital. But actual Labor hours needed to remove heavily damaged parts or parts frozen by rust or corrosion may vary.

记住评估指南中列出的在一辆完好无损的汽车上拆卸并更换上合格新配件所花费的时间非常重要。而实际上拆卸一个受损严重或锈死的零件所需要的时间可能有所不同。

[3] Reaching an agreement concerning nonincluded labor allowances is often the most difficult part of shop/adjuster negotiations.

对这部分劳动的报酬问题达成一致往往是修理企业和理赔员谈判过程中最棘手的问题。

Review Questions

1. List the tools needed to platform a complete damage inspection.
2. Explain the important role estimating guides play in the collision repair industry.
3. What is the flat rate Labor hours?
4. Can you recognize certain ethical dilemmas that can occur in the present system of automobile repair?

参考译文

第二十四课　汽车修理评估

1. 评估指南

碰撞评估指南(也称为碰撞手册或碰撞指南)是车损报告员或鉴定员最重要的工具,由米切尔国际联合公司出版的米切尔碰撞评估指南和由赫斯特公司出版的发动机碰撞修理评估指南是现在使用最广泛的两种评估指南。它们都包含了国产和进口乘用车、货车和轻型卡车的一些严重碰撞情形和修理信息。

出版商不断更新和修订他们的评估指南,以适应不断变化的价格和修正工时定额,删除已经停产的配件并填补新型配件。现在的评估指南平均每年更新多达16次,业内人士在制作和比较评估报表时选用最新评估指南至关重要。评估指南列举了各原厂配件的价格和近七八年内车型变化的信息。早期的评估指南可提供近14年内的相关信息。

如前所述,各出版商总是力求自己的评估指南条理清晰,易于查阅。尽管各评估指南之间存在一些细微差别,但他们编排内容时大多都是首先按照车辆出产年份和车辆模型进行分类的。在每一个分类中,再将信息按照主要总成(如减振器或发动机罩)或主要系统(如空调、加热器或排气系统)分门别类。一个总成或系统的分解图展示了各零件的位置,并注明了其专业名称,标注了生产编号。这些分解图中的零件与价格及正常工时费率相对应。

记住评估指南中列出的在一辆完好无损的汽车上拆卸并更换上合格新配件所花费的时间非常重要。而实际上拆卸一个受损严重或锈死的零件所需要的时间可能有所不同。

估量出每一道工序所需要的准确时间是不可能的。例如更换托架、拉杆、加强件或更新各种饰件等作业所需时间长短视操作难易程度而定。拆卸车身底层、修理防腐层、填堵新配件上多余的小洞等所花费时间不计入手册中所述的工时。

碰撞评估指南中列出了完整的时间明细表,其并不包含工时手册中所列的工时定额。评估指南也无没有列出加固或者修理车架、钣金构件或塑料零件所需的工时。这些修理工作的劳动报酬应根据工时而定。根据工时和其他一些未考虑在内的工作支付的报酬,应根据经验和仔细计算各相关因素合计得出。对这部分劳动的报酬问题达成一致往往是修理企业和理赔员谈判过程中最棘手的问题。

评估指南中所罗列的部分零件价格指的是原厂新配件的价格。车用玻璃列表中既有制造商提供的价格,又包括国家汽车玻璃技术规范中的产品批号和价格。

个人碰撞评估指南中几乎涵盖了所有下面所列的内容:
(1)评估指南使用步骤详解;
(2)手册中所使用的各专有名词的定义;
(3)计算交叉作业所用工时;
(4)对所使用的缩略语的注释;
(5)车辆识别方法,包括如何解释车辆识别号码(VINS);
(6)制冷能力信息;
(7)空调制冷剂容量清单;
(8)发动机罩内结构图解;
(9)便于快速查对的劳动价格换算表;
(10)切割信息(当可以获取原厂配件的此类信息时);
(11)相关型号间可以互相替换的零件代码清单。

显而易见,为什么车损报告编制员和鉴定员必须精通最新的评估指南中的信息。它能使其工作变得更加轻松自如。遗憾的是,客户常常抱怨一些不称职的理赔员和修理企业员工不会使用碰撞评估指南。

评估指南中的信息也作为大多数电脑评估系统的数据源。电脑评估系统大大缩短了车损报告的编制时间,同时也减少了计算失误、遗漏工序、重复作业和计算不准确的可能性。

注意:千万不要只作一些口头上的、非书面上的评估。这样常常产生误解,容易使客户见利忘义,并引起法律纠纷。

2. 评估工具

评估员进行损坏分析时,需要一些工具。这里列出的是完成损坏分析必需的一系列基本仪器。

(1)评估员记录数据的一些方法。依据损坏的程度,评估员可简单地使用笔记本和铅笔对损坏情况进行记录;损坏情况也可以用口述的方式录制到带式录音机上,然后抄写下来。损坏评估可借助计算机辅助评估程序,用计算机生成零件构造图和评估工作表,甚至只需在手提电脑上输入零件代码。

(2)评估员需要制造商的产品零件目录和技术规格表来帮助辨别零件和对关键尺寸进行测量。

(3)测量工具是正确地分析损坏所必需的。一个滑规式标尺和一个两面分别为公制和SAE两种单位的12英尺钢卷尺必不可少。大多数制造厂商的技术规格采用公制。

(4)评估员必须配置可自行支配的举升器(或千斤顶),便于举升车辆。除了轻微碰撞之外,几乎所有的损坏都需要对车身底部进行检查和测量。

(5)评估员应该备有常用工具,例如扳手(公制和 SAE 标准)、旋具和手钳。有时需要对妨碍检视和测量的某些汽车零件进行解体或拆卸。垫板、躺板、故障检视灯以及延长电线也应放在评估区内。

Lesson 25   Assessment of Labor Hour Cost

1. Labor Hours

When the decision has been made to replace a damaged panel, the estimator will find labor allowance times listed in the crash guides. The operation times are listed in hours and tenths of an hour. For example, the Labor hour allotted for removing and replacing a headlight assembly might be 0.4 hours, which is equivalent to 24 minutes. A Labor hour of 3.5 hours is equal to 3 hours and 30 minutes.

Labor hours are based on information supplied by vehicle manufacturers and time studies. The manufacturers arrive at the times by performing each operation under normal shop conditions. The average mechanic, working under average conditions and following procedures outlined in the manufacturer's service manuals, should be able to complete the operation within the time allotted. The Labor hour studies include time for gathering tools and materials in preparation for the operation.

The Labor hours suggested by the vehicle manufacturer are for the removal and replacement of new, undamaged OEM parts from new, undamaged vehicles. Sometimes the manufacturers' operation times are proven by field experience to be unrealistic when performed on damaged vehicles. Therefore, the publishers of the collision estimating guides are constantly collecting data from the collision repair industry, comparing the quoted times with actual performance in the field. Time studies are performed in an actual body shop environment to validate the operation times listed in the collision estimating guides. These time studies centers are performed throughout the country and cover a multiplicity of operations in a variety of environments. These "hands-on" experiences, in addition to industry surveys and technical input from collision repair facilities, are used to develop the labor allowance illustrated in the collision estimating guides.

2. Additional Time Allowances

Operation times are based on new, undamaged parts installed as an individual operation. These times apply only to standard OEM stock items. The times do not apply to vehicles with equipment other than that supplied by the manufacturer as standard or regular production options. If other parts or equipments must be replaced, the operation times should be adjusted to compensate for the increased labor. For example, if the decision is made to replace a damaged part with an aftermarket or salvage part, additional time might be justified for adjusting and aligning the part to the car.

Additional time may also be required for operations not included in the quoted times. There are a variety of vehicle conditions and a wide range of collision damages that simply cannot be anticipated by the publishers of the collision estimating guides. [1] Therefore, the following items are not taken into consideration when formulating the operation times.

(1) Access Time. Remove extensively damaged parts by cutting, pushing, pulling, and etc.

(2) Anticorrosion Rust-Resistant Material. Remove or apply weldable zinc primers, wax, petroleum based coating, undercoating or any type of added conditioning.

(3) Broken Glass Cleanup.

(4) Detail. Clean vehicle to preaccident condition.

(5) Electronic Components.

(6) Time to remove and install as necessary, includeing wiring and/or wiring harness and computer module.

(7) Time to reset memory code function when battery has been disconnected to perform repairs.

(8) Frame Setup.

(9) Free Up Parts. Time necessary to free up parts frozen by rust or corrosion.

(10) Measure and Identify. Structural damage to unibody vehicles.

(11) Plug and Finish Holes. Time to plug and finish unneeded holes on parts being installed.

(12) Repair or Align. Parts adjacent to parts being replaced.

(13) Rework Parts. To fit a particular year or model (e. g. , cutting holes for lamps, modifying a radiator support).

(14) Tar and Grease. Removal of these or any other materials that would interfere with operation.

(15) Transfer Time. For welded or riveted brackets, braces or reinforcements from old part to new part.

It is important to refer to all pages when writing an estimate. These pages explain which operations are included or not included in an operation time. They might also specify adjustments to the operation times based on the vehicle's accessories and trim packages. Other notes give information on sectioning, pricing, ordering parts, and refinishing.

New Words

allot [ə'lɒt]	vt. (按份额)分配,分派
unrealistic ['ʌnriə'lɪstɪk]	adj. 不切实际的,不实在的
multiplicity [ˌmʌltə'plɪsɪti]	n. 多样性
anticipate [æn'tɪsɪpeɪt]	vt. 预期,期望,过早使用,占先
	v. 预订,预见,可以预料
weldable ['weldəbl]	adj. 可焊的
battery ['bætəri]	n. 电池,殴打
rivet ['rɪvɪt]	n. 铆钉
	v. 固定

brace [breis]	n. 支柱,带子,振作精神
	vt 支持,支住,撑牢,振作起来,奋起
	adj. 曲柄的
reinforcement [ˌriːinˈfɔːsmənt]	n. 增援,加强,加固,援军

Phrases and Expressions

Labor hour	作业工时
additional time allowances	附加工时定额

Notes to the Text

[1] There are a variety of vehicle conditions and a wide range of collision damages that simply cannot be anticipated by the publishers of the collision estimating guides.

各种复杂的汽车状况和相差巨大的碰撞损失,是碰撞评估指南出版商所无法简单预见的。

Review Questions

1. How to determine labor costs by using the collision estimating guides?

2. How many operations included in the refinishing times listed in the collision estimating guide?

3. What do the "hands-on" experiences mean?

4. How does betterment reduce the amount of the parts costs that an insurance company will cover?

参考译文

第二十五课 汽车维修工时费用估算

1. 作业工时

在做出进行更换损坏钣金的决定时,评估员会从碰撞修理指南表中查出工时定额。作业以小时和零点几小时列出。例如,拆卸和更换前照灯部件可能需要 0.4 个作业工时,也就是 24 分钟。3.5 个作业工时相当于 3 小时 30 分钟。

作业工时是以汽车制造商提供的信息和工时研究为基础的。制造商提供在普遍修理企业条件下可实现的时间定额。一般技师在平均劳动条件下按照制造商修理手册规定的工序,应该能在规定的时间内完成修理作业。作业工时研究包括收集工具和材料准备作业所花费的时间。

汽车制造商建议的作业工时,是指从新的、未损坏的汽车上拆卸和更换新的、未损坏的原装零件所用的时间。实际经验证明,修理损坏汽车时的实际用时有时与制造商提供的作业时间不符。因此,碰撞评估指南的出版商不断地从碰撞修理企业中收集数据,将其所列出的工时与修理作业的实际时间进行比较。在实际车身修理企业中进行时间研究以修正碰撞评估指南中所列的作业工时。这些工时研究中心遍及全国并覆盖了各种环境中的各类作业。这些实践经验以及行业调查和碰撞修理设备的技术数据,都被用来确定碰撞评估指南

中的工时定额。

2. 附加工时定额

作业时间的制定以安装新的、未损坏零件为独立作业为基础。这种工时仅仅适用于标准原装库存零件。这种工时不适用于装备非汽车制造商提供零件的汽车,制造商也不把该零件作为标准或常规产品选装来供货。如果其他零件或设备必须予以更换,作业工时就应该调整以弥补增加的劳动。例如,如果决定用市场配件或旧车拆解零件更换损坏零件,就会因调整和校正汽车零件而调整附加工时。

未列入工时定额的作业也需要计入附加工时。各种复杂的汽车状况和相差巨大的碰撞损失,是碰撞评估指南出版商们所无法简单预见的。所以,在计算作业工时时并未考虑下列情况。

(1)准备时间。切割、拉伸、压缩等方法拆卸严重损坏的零件。
(2)防腐抗锈材料。拆卸或应用可焊的锌底漆、石蜡、面漆、底漆等。
(3)碎玻璃的清理。
(4)细节。将车辆清洗到事故前的状况。
(5)电气元器件。
(6)必要的拆卸和安装时间,包括接线、线束和计算机模块。
(7)在断开蓄电池进行修理时,重新设置记忆模块功能的时间。
(8)车架调整。
(9)松动零件时间。将锈蚀在一起的零件松开所需的时间。
(10)测量和检验。承载式车身结构损伤。
(11)塞堵和修整孔。安装时塞堵零件上不需要的孔。
(12)修理或校准。更换类似零件。
(13)修复零件。适用于特定年款和车型(例如,钻车灯孔、修改散热器支架)。
(14)焦油和润滑脂。清洗这些或其他可能影响工作的材料。
(15)移装时间。将旧零件上的支架、托架或加强件焊接或铆接到新零件上。

撰写评估报告时参照评估指南全文说明是非常重要的。评估指南将解释包括哪些作业和不包括哪些作业时间。它们也会具体说明基于汽车附件和内饰件上的作业工时调整。其他条款给出了关于剖切、价格、定购零件和漆面修整的信息。

Lesson 26　Actual Cash Value of Automobile

Any vehicle is considered a "wear" item, with a definite lifespan. The average lifespan of American passenger cars, light trucks, and vans is 12 years. The average age of cars on the road today is about 6 years, and 80% of all vehicles are over 3 years of age.

1. ACV

In many cases, the value of a vehicle can significantly decrease with age and/or miles driven. This is even true when the vehicle has been properly maintained and serviced. For example, a vehicle that sold new for a list price of $15 000 several years ago can now have an average retail value of $8000 if it is still in good condition without excessive mileage. This $8000 figure represents the actual cash value(i.e., ACV) of the vehicle, and becomes a very important figure for determining if and how the repair will be made, particularly in insurance claims and evaluation of used vehicle. [1]

Excluding certain types of vehicle restoration, investing substantial sums of money into a vehicle will not significantly increase its market value. Investing $3000 into the collision repair of a $2000 vehicle will not result in a $5000 vehicle, or even a $3000 vehicle.

The ACV of a vehicle can be found using several sources. These include the NADA Official Used Car Guide, The Automobile Red Book published by Maclean Hunter Market Reports, Inc. , and the Kelley Blue Book, among others. These guides contain similar information, but prices and exact data listed can vary slightly between guides.

The NADA Official Used Car Guide lists the trade-in or wholesale value offered by car dealers for that particular make and model. It also gives the value of a loan that can be secured using the vehicle as collateral. The retail price given is the price that dealers would ask used car buyers to pay for that make and model. The retail value is the figure used in calculating the ACV.

The guide also lists the options available for the vehicle, including dollar amounts to add on or deduct for particular options. For example, power steering, air-conditioning, and other power and convenience features will increase the car's value. Features such as manual transmissions or diesel engines might reduce vehicle resale value. The guides also contain charts for determining value adjustments on vehicles with exceptionally high or low mileage.

Used car guides are continually updated and are normally obtained on a subscription basis. Because vehicle values may vary in different parts of the country, guide publishers often prepare regional editions reflecting these differences. In some cases, the average between two or more guides is used to determine the ACV.

Car dealership appraisals are also used as a source of determining ACV. Local dealers are often asked to determine a fair market value for vehicles, particularly true with "exceptional" vehicles. A good example would be an older vehicle with extremely low mileage that is in extraordinary condition. What would be the dealer's asking price if that car were on his or her lot? If the vehicle can easily be sold for greater than its "book" value, the insurance company is committed to settling at the higher ACV appraisal.

When determining the ACV of a vehicle, insurance companies do not normally consider recent mechanical repairs made at the expense of the vehicle owner. These are seen as normal operating and maintenance costs and do not increase ACV. For example, if a vehicle owner spends $1000 on mechanical repairs to a vehicle with an ACV of $2000, he or she might increase its lifespan, but the ACV remains at $2000.

2. Total Loss Vehicles

A vehicle's ACV is often an important factor when the repair involves an insurance claim settlement. For obvious reasons, insurance companies do not pay for repairs that exceed the actual cash value of the vehicle. Instead, the vehicle is declared a total loss.

Individual insurance companies have their own guidelines and formulas for determining "total" situations. Three of the most common formulas are as follows:

(1) when the total cost of repair equals or exceeds the ACV;

(2) when the total cost of repair equals or exceeds a fixed percentage of the ACV, such as 75% or 80%;

(3) when the total cost of repair, plus the salvage value of the vehicle, equals or exceeds the total ACV or a fixed percentage of the ACV.

As you can see, both formulas (2) and (3) will actually "total" a vehicle at less than its full ACV. In all cases, an insurance company adjuster must still appraise the damage to confirm that the cost of all reasonable repair methods exceeds the company's total loss guidelines.[2] Once this is proven, the vehicle owner receives a settlement check for the ACV amount. The title of the vehicle is transferred to the insurance company, who has effectively purchased the vehicle from the owner at the ACV price.

Any salvage value the vehicle might have now belongs to the insurance company. To minimize the time and effort needed to sell individual wrecks, some insurance companies sign yearly contracts with a single salvage yard in a given territory. This salvage yard agrees to purchase all wrecks from that company based on a certain percentage of their ACV. The range for late model wrecks is between 20% and 25%; with older models, the percentage is normally lower. Heavily damaged wrecks having less than three salvageable bolt-on parts are usually considered negotiable in terms of value. Such contracts are often awarded through competitive bidding.

New words

lifespan [laifspæn]	n. 使用年限
retail ['riteɪl]	n. 零售
	adj. 零售的
	ad. 以零售方式
	vt. 零售,细谈
	vi. 零售
restoration [restə'reiʃən]	n. 修复,恢复;归还
negotiable [ni'gəuʃieit]	vi. 谈判,协商,磋商定价;议定,处理,通过,做成

Phrases and Expressions

ACV	车辆现值
miles driven	行驶里程
NADA	美国汽车经销商协会
trade-in	折旧
wholesale value	批发价
salvage value	残余价值
competitive bidding	竞标

Notes to the Text

[1] This $8000 figure represents the actual cash value(i. e. , ACV) of the vehicle, and becomes a very important figure for determining if and how the repair will be made, particularly in insurance claims and evaluation of used vehicle.

这个 8000 美元即代表了这辆汽车目前的价值(即 ACV),其在确定是否和如何进行修理时很重要,特别是在保险公司索赔和旧车评估时。

[2] In all cases, an insurance company adjuster must still appraise the damage to confirm that the cost of all reasonable repair methods exceeds the company's total loss guidelines.

不论哪种情况,保险公司理赔员都必须对车辆的损坏程度进行评估,以确定所有合理的修理方法都会超过的公司规定的全损指标。

Review Questions

1. What is Actual Cash Value (ACV) of automobile?
2. How to determine a vehicle's ACV?
3. What is Total Loss Vehicles?

参考译文

第二十六课 车 辆 现 值

任何一辆汽车都是一件"消耗品",都有一定的使用年限。美国的乘用车、皮卡、货车的使用年限都是 12 年。现在公路上行驶的汽车平均寿命为 6 年,并且其中 80%的车辆已经超出额定寿命 3 年。

1. 车辆现值(ACV)

许多情况下,车辆的价值随着车龄或行驶里程的增加而显著下降。即使车辆维护得很好也一样。例如,几年前标价为 15000 美元的新车,假如现在运行状况仍然良好且没有超出额定行驶里程,其平均零售价格可能已经降至 8000 美元。这个 8000 美元即代表了这辆汽车目前的价值(即 ACV),其在确定是否和如何进行修理时很重要,特别是在保险公司进行索赔和旧车评估时。

除了某些特定的修复外,对车辆投入大批资金并不能够显著增加其市价。在原价 2000 美元的事故车辆上投资 3000 美元,并不会使其增值至 5000 美元,甚至其价值连 3000 美元也无法达到。

一辆汽车的现值可以从不同资料中查到。这些资料主要有 NADA 二手车官方指南、麦克林汉德市场报告公司(Maclean Hunter Market Report, Ir)出版的汽车红皮书以及凯利蓝皮书等。这些指南中的信息相似,但价格和一些确切数据略有不同。

NADA 二手车官方指南列出了由特定品牌和车型的汽车销售商提供的折旧价和批发价。同时还提供了如用车辆作抵押可贷款的数额。零售价是销售商就具体制造厂和车型给二手车买主的报价。这个零售价就是用来估算汽车现值的数据。

二手车指南也列出了车辆选配方案,包括特别选配需要增加或扣除的金额。例如,动力转向、空调和其他提供动力和便捷的选配将提高汽车的价值。汽车的另一些特点,如装备手动变速器或柴油机就会降低汽车的转卖价值。指南中还给出了价格调整表，以说明如何调整由行驶里程过多或过少引起的价格变动。

二手车指南内容在不断地更新，并且通常可以订阅。因为在一个国家的不同地区汽车的价格略有不同，所以二手车指南出版商印制了不同的版本，以反映各地区价格差别。某些情况下，其对汽车现价的定位是根据两个或多个手册的平均值来确定的。

汽车销售商的评估额也经常用于确定汽车的现值。当地销售商通常会给出一个公平的市场价格，尤其对"特殊"车辆的定价。比如，一辆看上去很旧的汽车，但行驶里程很短，就属特殊情况。如果这辆汽车在销售商那里，他（或她）会给出什么价位呢？如果这辆车能轻易地以比它在指南中的价格高许多的价格卖出，那么保险公司将由此给它一个较高的估价。

当确定一辆汽车的现值时，保险公司通常不会考虑车主近期支付的机械修理费用。这些被视为正常的管理和维护费用，不会提高汽车的现值。例如，如果车主花1000美元对一辆现值为2000美元的车进行机械修理，可能会延长该车的使用寿命，但是该车的现值仍然是2000美元。

2. 全损车

在车辆修理时如果涉及保险公司的一些条款，该车的现值就显得尤为重要。原因很明显，保险公司不会支付超出该车实际现值的修理费。当发生这类情况时，保险公司就会宣布这辆车全损。

每家保险公司都有一套关于全损情况的指标和公式。最常见三种如下：
（1）汽车修理总费用等于或超出该车现值；
（2）汽车修理总费用等于或超出了该车现值的一定比例，如75%或80%；
（3）汽车修理总费用加上残余价值的总和等于或超出了该车现值的一定比例。

由此可见，第（2）和第（3）种情况对于全损的定义标准低于其现值。不论哪种情况，保险公司理赔员都必须对车辆的损坏程度进行评估，以确定所有合理的修理方法也会超过的公司规定的全损指标。一旦确定全损，车主就将收到一张相当于该车现值总额的支票，汽车所有权将随之转给保险公司。在这种情况下，保险公司就以该车的现值从车主手中有效购买了这辆汽车。

汽车的残余价值现在属于保险公司。为了不在处理各个报废零件上浪费时间和精力，一些保险公司与各地的报废汽车停车场签订了年度协议。该报废汽车停车场同意从保险公司手中以事故车现值的一定比例购买这些报废车辆。较新的车辆按现值的20%到25%；旧的通常更低。损坏比较严重、不足三成可修旧零件的报废汽车残余价值通常可以磋商定价。这种合同通常是以竞标方式获得。

Unit 6　New Eenergy Vehicle and Connected Vehicle Technology

Lesson 27　The Electric Vehicles and Hybrid Power

1. Battery Electric Vehicle(BEV)

Honda has been installing 24 NiMH 12V batteries in its electric cars for export to the US, and Toyota has been using the same type of battery in its electric vehicles. Since 1971 Toyota has developed the TownAce, an electric van, and the RAV4.

The drive train of the RAV4, Fig. 27-1, consists of the battery pack, the electric motor and the control pack. Although it is a cumbersome installation as compared with that of an internal combustion engine powered vehicle, at least it has neither an exhaust system nor a conventional transmission; the electric motor transmits its drive through a simple reduction gear to the road wheels. [1] By virtue of optimisation of every aspect of this drive train, and the use of regenerative braking, a range of 124 miles per charge has, it is claimed, been attained.

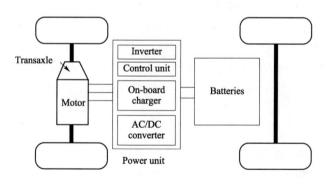

Fig. 27-1　The layout of the RAV4 electric vehicle

Nissan's Altra represents a major advance. It is powered by a water-cooled, permanent magnet, synchronous electric motor developing 62kW and 159N·m torque at 13 000 rev/min. [2] A key feature of this motor is the use of the highly efficient neodymium-iron-boron (Nd-Fe-B) magnet. The outcome is a motor weighing 39kg giving a power weight ratio of 1.6kW/kg. In addition, its speed is considerably higher than the average, which is 8000 to 9000r/min. Certain controller embodies twin CPUs to make the system fully redundant. Its input range is 216 to 400V. Its input is data on the state of charge of the batteries, temperatures, driving history, use of the regenerative braking system and the auxiliary systems. On the basis of this information, it can make accurate predictions of range of operation remaining available. It also controls relays in the battery cooling system, and determines the battery charging strategy.

The batteries are topped up by an external inductive charger plugged into a port in front of the car, which cannot be driven if the port is not closed afterwards.[3] A full charge takes 5 hours, and gives a maximum range of 193 km in ideal conditions, or 135 km in busy urban conditions.

For regenerative braking, the system cuts in when the driver lifts his foot off the accelerator pedal. If the driver then applies the brakes, it provides a considerably higher level of assistance. An electric power assisted steering system is employed, but it gives assistance only when really needed. The auxiliary systems are powered by a 12V lead-acid battery, which is charged from the main battery system by a water-cooled DC/DC transformer.

The lithium-iron battery pack was developed by Sony. Its nominal output is 345V from 12 modules each comprising 8 cells. The output from each cell is 36V fully charged and 20V discharged. With a gross weight of 350kg, the energy density is 90Wh/kg and power density 300W/kg. A nominal life of 1200 cycles, based on 5% reduction in energy density, is claimed, but lives in excess of 2000 cycles without significant further loss of efficiency have been obtained during tests.[4]

The batteries, mounted on a tray carried beneath the floor, approximately mid-way between the front and rear axels, have a dedicated cooling system with a fan.

2. Hybrid Power

For many years experiments have been carried out with diesel-or petrol-electric hybrid power units. All suffer the disadvantage that two power units are required: an internal combustion engine and an electric motor. The implications therefore are of complexity, high initial cost, two power units that could malfunction, and large bulk. In the past, controlling two power units for economical operation was difficult. However, the introduction of electronic engine management systems virtually eliminated this problem. Despite the high costs of these vehicles, it is possible that road users may be indirectly pressurised by legislation into buying them.

Several strategies can be employed for the management of such power combinations. With an internal combustion engine as the primary source of power, batteries are not essential, although the whole system becomes much more flexible with batteries. In any case, at least one battery is needed for starting the engine and serving the electric equipment in general. Currently, the most economical and practicable arrangements are those in which a diesel engine drives in series a generator to charge the batteries, which drive the electric motor, Fig. 27-2.

Alternatively, in a parallel hybrid system(Fig. 27-3)the electronic power management system can be employed to switch the drive from the batteries alone, over to combined battery and electric drive for acceleration or climbing hills. The diesel or gasoline engine can be stopped for operation at light load, and automatically started again when either the batteries must be recharged or the torque output has to be supplemented by either direct power from the generator, or by power from both the batteries and generator or internal combustion engine, or even from all three simultaneously. [5]

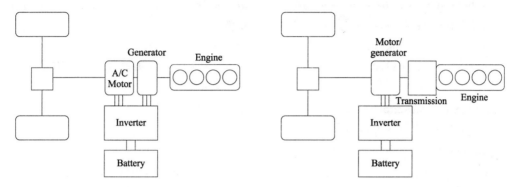

Fig. 27-2　The series hybrid system　　　　Fig. 27-3　The parallel hybrid system

3. The Prius Hybrid Vehicle

Toyota is producing the Prius car for sale in Japan and China. A four-cylinder in-line engine of 1.5 litres swept volume is employed. Operating at a high expansion ratio (with variable valve timing), it develops 42.6kW at 4000rev/min, at which speed its torque rating is 101.8Nm. Its output is split, by a planetary gear set, between a high efficiency permanent magnet synchronous AC generator and the final drive gear, Fig. 27-4. The ratio of the split, which varies, is dependent on the instructions given by the computer control and the relative resistances to rotation presented by the final drive gear and generator. [6]

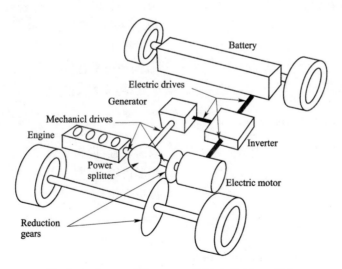

Fig. 27-4　Layout of Toyota parallel hybrid drive vehicle

To limit both fuel consumption and emissions, the engine is kept running within its most efficient speed range. If the vehicle is moving under very light load or is stationary, the fuel supply to the engine is cut and battery power only used. When more torque is needed, the engine is restarted and supplements the power from the electric motor. The change from IC engine to electric power is claimed to be so smooth that drivers are unaware of it.

New Words

cumbersome [ˈkʌmbəsəm]	adj. 笨重的
combustion [kəmˈbʌstʃən]	n. 燃烧
synchronous [ˈsiŋkrənəs]	adj. 同时的，同步的
transaxle [trænsˈæksl]	n. 驱动桥（与变速箱连成一体，用于前轮驱动的车）
converter [kənˈvɜːtə(r)]	n. 转换器
neodymium [ni(ː)əˈdimiəm]	n. 钕
lithium [ˈliθiəm]	n. 锂
module [ˈmɔdjuːl]	n. [计算机] 模块, 组件
nominal [ˈnɔminl]	adj. 名义上的，有名无实的
auxiliary [ɔːgˈziljəri]	n. 帮助者，辅助物，助动词
	adj. 附加的，辅助的
inductive [inˈdʌktiv]	adj. 归纳的，动人的，感应的
transformer [trænsˈfɔːmə(r)]	n. 变压器
simultaneous [ˌsiməlˈteinjəs]	adj. 同时发生的
malfunction [mælˈfʌŋkʃən]	n. 故障
	v. 发生故障，不起作用
pressurized [ˈpreʃərazd]	adj. 加压的，受压的
parallel [ˈpærəlel]	adj. 平行的
	ad. 平行地
	n. 平行线
	vt. 与……平行
series [ˈsiəriːz]	n. 连续，系列

Phrases and Expressions

reduction gear	减速装置（齿轮）
ring gear	环形齿轮，齿圈
splitter gear	行星齿轮

Notes to the Text

[1] Although it is a cumbersome installation as compared with that of an internal combustion engine powered vehicle, at least it has neither an exhaust system nor a conventional transmission: the electric motor transmits its drive through a simple reduction gear to the road wheels.

相比于由内燃机驱动的汽车，它虽然比较笨重，但它至少没有排气系统，也没有传统的传动系统：电动机只需一个简单的减速装置将其驱动力传至车轮。

[2] Nissan's Altra represents a major advance. It is powered by a water-cooled, permanent magnet, synchronous electric motor developing 62kW and 159N·m torque at 13 000 rev/min.

尼桑公司的 Altra 车有一个显著的优势。它由一个水冷、永磁同步电动机驱动,该电机在转速为 13000r/min 时输出功率 62kW,转矩 159N·m。

[3] The batteries are topped up by an external inductive charger plugged into a port in front of the car, which cannot be driven if the port is not closed afterwards.

蓄电池通过一个外部感应充电器充电,这个感应充电器插入汽车前部的插孔,充电后如果插孔不关闭,汽车就无法运行。

[4] With a gross weight of 350kg, the energy density is 90 Wh/kg and power density 300 W/kg. A nominal life of 1200 cycles, based on 5% reduction in energy density, is claimed, but lives in excess of 2000 cycles without significant further loss of efficiency have been obtained during tests.

电池组总质量为 350kg,能量密度为 90Wh/kg,功率密度为 300W/kg。据称,它的额定循环寿命为 1200 次,能量密度减少为 5%,但是,试验过程中,循环寿命超过 2000 次,效率并没有进一步明显的下降。

[5] The diesel or gasoline engine can be stopped for operation at light load, and automatically started again when either the batteries must be recharged or the torque output has to be supplemented by either direct power from the generator, or by power from both the batteries and generator or internal combustion engine, or even from all three simultaneously.

在小负荷下,柴油或汽油内燃机可以不工作,当蓄电池必须充电或输出转矩增大时,内燃机会自动起动投入工作,通过带动发电机直接输出电能,或者蓄电池和发电机或发动机共同输出动力,甚至三者共同输出动力。

[6] Its output is split, by a planetary gear set, between a high efficiency permanent magnet synchronous AC generator and the final drive gear, Fig. 27-4. The ratio of the split, which varies, is dependent on the instructions given by the computer control and the relative resistances to rotation presented by the final drive gear and generator.

在高效率的永久磁体同步交流发电机和主减速器之间有行星齿轮,通过行星齿轮分配动力,如图 27-4 所示。分配比例的变化取决于计算机的控制指令和主减速器、发电机运转阻力矩的相对大小。

Review Questions

1. Try to list some famous electric vehicles.
2. What are the main advantages of the RAV4?
3. What information is needed for Nissan's Altra to make accurate predictions of range of operation remaining available?
4. What are the main strategies employed for the management of power combinations?
5. Please briefly describe the working principle and advantages of the Prius.

参考译文

第六单元 新能源汽车与车联网技术

第二十七课 电动汽车和混合动力

1. 电动汽车(BEV)

本田公司在其向美国出口的电动汽车上安装了 24 块 12V 的镍化氢电池,丰田公司也在其电动汽车上采用了相同类型的电池。自 1971 年起,丰田公司已开发了电动小型货车 TownAce 和 RAV4。

如图 8-1 所示,RAV4 的驱动装置包括电池组、电动机和控制装置。相比于由内燃机驱动的汽车,它虽然比较笨重,但它至少没有排气系统,也没有传统的传动系统:电动机只需一个简单的减速装置将其驱动力传至车轮。凭借该驱动装置的每个部件的最优选择和制动能量的回收,据称每次汽车充电后续航里程 124 英里。

尼桑公司的 Altra 车有一个显著的优势。它由一个水冷、永磁同步电动机驱动,该电机在转速为 13000r/min 时输出功率 62kW,转矩 159N·m。电动机主要特征是高效率钕铁硼磁铁(Nd-Fe-B)的使用。实现了重为 39kg 的电动机其功率密度为 1.6kW/kg。另外,它的速度远高于一般电机 8000~9000r/min 的转速。有的控制器由两个 CPU 组成,使系统实现完全冗余。它的输入电压在 216~400V 之间。系统的输入信息包括:蓄电池的充电情况、温度、行驶里程、再生制动系统和附件系统的应用。基于这些信息,它可以对以后运行情况进行精确的预测,也可以控制蓄电池冷却系统继电器,决定蓄电池充电策略。

蓄电池通过一个外部感应充电器充电,这个感应充电器插入汽车前部的插孔,充电后如果插孔不关闭,汽车就无法运行。一个完整的充电过程需要 5 小时,理想情况下的最高续航里程为 193km,在繁忙的城市路况下的最高续航里程为 135km。

对于能量再生,当驾驶员的脚离开加速踏板时,(再生制动)系统开始工作。如果驾驶员踩下制动踏板,就会产生一个很大的辅助力。采用了电动助力转向系统,但是只有在真正需要时,该系统才产生助力作用。辅助系统由一块 12V 的铅酸电池驱动,该铅酸电池由主电池组通过水冷 DC/DC 转换器进行充电。

索尼公司开发了一种锂铁电池组。8 个单格串联成一块电池,12 个电池组成额定输出为 345V 的车用电池组。每个电池在充满电时输出电压为 36V,放电后输出电压为 20V。电池组总质量为 350kg,能量密度为 90Wh/kg,功率密度为 300W/kg。据称,它的额定循环寿命为 1200 次,能量密度减少为 5%,但是,试验过程中,循环寿命超过 2000 次,效率并没有进一步明显的下降。

电池组安装在地板下面的托盘上,置于前后桥大约中间的位置,有一个带风扇的专门冷却系统。

2. 混合动力

柴油混合动力装置和汽油混合动力装置都已经经过多年实验。但其都存在这样的缺点,即需两套动力装置:内燃机和电动机。这就意味着复杂、成本高、两套动力装置故障多、体积大。在过去,控制两套系统实现经济运行是难点。但是,发动机电子管理系统的出现彻底解决了这一问题。尽管这些车辆的造价很高,但由于立法的存在,间接迫使购买者购买这种车成为可能。

可以采用不同策略对混合动力系统进行管理。内燃机是主要的动力源,尽管蓄电池使整个系统更加高效,但它不是最主要的。不论何种方式,至少需要一块电池来起动发动机并为电动设备日常运行供电。目前,最经济实用的方式是利用柴油机来驱动串联式发电机,发电机为蓄电池充电,蓄电池为电动机供电,如图 27-2 所示。

相对而言,在并联式混合动力系统中(图 27-3),车辆加速或爬坡时,电子管理系统可将蓄电池单独提供动力转换成由电池和发动机驱动的发电机共同提供动力。在小负荷下,柴油或汽油内燃机可以不工作,当蓄电池必须充电或输出转矩增大时,内燃机会自动起动投入工作,通过带动发电机直接输出电能,或者蓄电池和发电机或发动机共同输出动力,甚至三者共同输出动力。

3. Prius 混合动力汽车

丰田公司正在生产 Prius,其将在日本和中国出售。Prius 采用直列四缸发动机,其排量为 1.5L。保持高的膨胀比运行时,(采用可变气门正时),在 4000r/min 时输出功率为 42.6kW,输出转矩为 101.8N·m。在高效率的永久磁体同步交流发电机和主减速器之间有行星齿轮,通过行星齿轮分配动力,如图 27-4 所示。分配比例的变化取决于计算机的控制指令和主减速器、发电机运转阻力矩的相对大小。

为了控制燃料消耗量和排放量,发动机保持在最有效的速度范围内运行。车辆如果负荷很小或处于静止状态,将中止发动机的燃油供给,只由蓄电池驱动。当需要更大转矩,发动机重新起动,和电动机共同驱动。据说发动机和电力之间的转换非常平稳,不会使驾驶员觉察到。

Lesson 28   Plug-in Hybrid Electric Vehicle

China's BYD Auto launched the world's first dual-mode electric vehicle F3DM on December 15, 2008, in Shenzhen. The price of the F3DM is, announced Zhibing Xia, general manager of BYD Auto Sales Co, Ltd, ¥149 800($21 700). The founder and chairman Chuanfu Wang explained:"Currently the cost of the battery pack, electric motors, drive controls and other equipment is high until volume production. But compared with the Toyota Prius that is sold in China for ¥280 000, the F3DM is almost half of the cost but it can work in electric made for 100 km."

The F3DM can travel for 100km with a full charge. When the battery pack is depleted, its 1.0-liter BYD371QA gasoline engine kicks in. The all-aluminum engine has a power exceeding 50kW/L and works with a 75kW electric motor. Maximum speed is 150 km/h. The battery pack can be recharged using a home power plug in 9 hours. But with special industrial charging equipment, it takes only 15 minutes to bring the capacity up to 80%.

The F3DM is the world's first commercial plug-in hybrid electric car that does not depend on a professional charging station. The F3DM is a milestone showing that the world has entered the era of electric cars.

Plug-in hybrid electric vehicles (PHEV) extend the vehicle technology of hybrid cars to replace a portion of petroleum-powered personal vehicle travel with electric power. As the word "plug-in" and the letter "P" is included in its names, plug-in hybrid electric vehicles are designed for external electrical recharge, it get the electricity from the grid and store it in an on-board battery, while other HEV are not.

Like currently commercialized HEV, PHEV use a power train that combines an electric motor with an internal combustion engine. However, conventional HEV are charge-sustaining: while driving they maintain their batteries at a roughly constant state of charge (SOC, a percentage of the electric capacity of the battery), and recharging occurs only from on-board electricity generation by the engine fueled by.[1] In contrast, PHEVs can operate in either charge sustaining or charge-depleting mode.

Nevertheless, PHEV also face many challenges. Although the batteries required are not as costly as those required by pure EVs, the capacity still needs to be high and that means higher production costs than conventional cars. The battery capacity is one of the main problems that hybrid and pure electric vehicles face.

The government requires passenger carmakers to cut their average fuel consumption from 6.9L/100km in 2015 to 5.0L/100km by 2020, with the average annual reduction standing at about 6.2%. To meet this stringent requirement, many carmakers have turned to hybrid technologies, which ensure high fuel economy and a long driving range. Among hybrid cars, plug-in hybrid models have been hotly pursued by carmakers including luxury car companies.

Global leading car manufactures have already spent a large amount of time and energy in the development and industrialization of PHEV. Some PHEVs are already on the market, such as Audi A3 e-tron, Toyota Prius, BMW X5 xDrive40e, Benz C350 eL and others. Chinese BYD has made developing a new generation of PHEV also, while its plug-in hybrid sedan, the Qin, has already proved popular, with 31-895 units sold in China in 2015. An industry insider predicts that new energy cars will see rapid growth between 2016 and 2020, and PHEV remains as the major force in the new energy car market.

According to the State Council's 2012—2020 energy-saving and new energy vehicle development plan, the overall production output and sales of pure electric and plug-in hybrid electric vehicles are expected to surpass 5 000 000 units by 2020.

China has rolled out measures to promote new energy vehicles in a bid to save energy and combat pollution, including tax exemptions, subsidies for new energy vehicles(NEV) by government.[2] The government's subsidies cover a variety of NEVs, including battery BEV, PHEV, and fuel cell vehicles (FCV).

However, the remarkable increases in both the production and sales of NEV were coupled with frequent consumer complaints about quality problems. Because many Chinese NEV manufacturers are keen on obtaining government subsidies as well as orders from the government, instead of strengthening their research and development(R&D) efforts.

The Chinese government will gradually cut down on its NEV subsidies over the next five years. The government will adjust its subsidy policies according to technological advancement, industrial development, promotion scale, and cost effectiveness, among others. It is necessary for Chinese regulators to make the NEV market competitive.

New Words

launch[lɔːntʃ]	*vt.*	发射；发动；开展（活动、计划等）
	vi.	投入；着手进行；投掷
	n.	大船上的小艇；
volume [ˈvɒljuːm]	*n.*	体积；卷；音量；量，大量
	adj.	大量的
	vi.	成团卷起
	vt.	把……收集成卷
depleted[dɪˈpliːtɪd]	*adj.*	废弃的
	v.	<正>使大大地减少，使空虚；耗尽，使枯竭
aluminum[əˈljuːmɪnəm]	*n.*	铝
stringent [ˈstrɪndʒənt]	*adj.*	严格的
surpass[səˈpɑːs]	*vt.*	超过；优于
subsidy[ˈsʌbsədi]	*n.*	补贴；津贴；助学金；奖金

Phrases and Expressions

dual-mode	双重工作状态的，两种工作方式的
State Council	国务院
rolled out	推出；铺开；转出
tax exemptions	免税

Notes to the Text

[1]However, conventional HEV are charge-sustaining: while driving they maintain their batteries at a roughly constant state of charge (SOC, a percentage of the electric capacity of the battery), and recharging occurs only from on-board electricity generation by the engine fueled by.

但是，常规的混合动力电动汽车采用电量保持模式：行驶时，它们保持电池在大致恒定的荷电状态（SOC，电池容量的百分比），需要充电时，电能只能由发动机燃烧燃料驱动车载发电机提供。

[2]China has rolled out measures to promote new energy vehicles in a bid to save energy and combat pollution, including tax exemptions, subsidies for new energy vehicles (NEV) by government.

为节约能源和控制污染，中国已经推出了新能源汽车的推进措施，包括税收减免、政府部门给予的新能源汽车补贴。

Review Questions

1. What advantage does PHEV have in comparison with conventional HEV?

2. What are the government subsidies to new energy vehicles?

参考译文

第二十八课　插电式混合动力电动汽车

2008年12月15日，中国的比亚迪汽车公司在深圳推出世界首款双模电动汽车F3DM。

比亚迪汽车销售有限公司总经理夏治冰在现场公布了F3DM的价格为149800元（21700美元）。比亚迪汽车公司创始人兼董事长王传福解释说"在投入大批量生产前，我们目前的电池组、电机、传动控制以及其他一些设备的成本比较高。但是与丰田在中国卖28万元的普锐斯相比，F3DM的价格只有它的一半，然而电动模式却可以续航100km。"

电池组充满电后F3DM续航里程可达100km。电量耗尽后，F3DM搭载的1.0L的BYD371QA汽油发动机就会起动。全铝发动机功率在50kW/L以上，电机功率75kW。（该车）最高时速150km/h。电池组使用家用电源插座9小时即可完成充电。但在专业充电站里只需15分钟就可充电80%。

F3DM车是世界上第一辆实现商业化的不依赖专业充电桩的插电式电动汽车。F3DM是宣告世界进入电动汽车时代的一个里程碑。

插电式混合动力电动汽车（PHEV）扩展了混合动力车辆技术，以便汽车运行中用电力取代部分燃油动力。正如单词"插入"和字母"P"被包含在其名称中，插电式混合动力电动汽车可以利用外部电力为车辆充电，PHEV从电网取电并储存在车载电池中，而其他HEV则不能。

和目前商业化的HEV一样，PHEV也使用电动机与内燃机结合的动力系统。但是，常规的混合动力电动汽车采用电量保持模式：行驶时，它们保持电池在大致恒定的荷电状态（SOC，电池容量的百分比），需要充电时，电能只能由发动机燃烧燃料驱动车载发电机提供。但是，插电式混合动力电动汽车既可以在电量保持模式下运行，也可以在电量消耗模式下运行。

然而，PHEV也面临着许多挑战。虽然其所需的电池不像纯电动汽车所需的电池昂贵，但电池容量仍需很高，这意味着PHEV比传统汽车生产成本高。电池容量是混合动力和纯电动汽车面临的主要问题之一。

政府要求乘用车制造商将燃油平均消耗量从2015年的6.9L/100km降低至2020年的5.0L/100km，年平均降低约6.2%。为了满足这一严格要求，许多汽车制造商已经转向混合动力技术，以确保高燃油经济性和长续航路程。在混合动力汽车中，插电式混合动力车型一直受到包括豪华车公司在内的汽车制造商的追捧。

全球领先的汽车制造商在插电式混合动力电动汽车的开发和产业化方面已经花费了大量时间和精力。一些插电式混合动力电动汽车已经上市，如奥迪A3 e-tron、丰田普锐斯、宝马X5 xDrive40e、奔驰C350 eL及其他车型。中国比亚迪也已研发新一代插电式混合动力车，它的插电式混合动力轿车——秦，2015年在中国销售了31895台，已经证明其受市场青睐。一位业内人士预测，新能源汽车将在2016至2020年间快速增长，插电式混合动力车仍将是新能源汽车市场的主力。

根据国务院2012—2020节能和新能源汽车发展规划，至2020年，纯电动和插电式混合动力电动汽车的整体产量和销售预计将超过 5 000 000 台。

为节约能源和控制污染,中国已经推出了新能源汽车的推进措施,包括税收减免、政府部门给予的新能源汽车补贴。政府的补贴涵盖各种新能源车,包括 BEV、PHEV 和燃料电池汽车(FCV)。

然而,新能源车在产量和销售额显著增加的同时,消费者有关质量的投诉也频繁发生。因为中国的许多新能源制造商都热衷于获得政府补贴以及政府的订单,而非加大研发力度。

在接下来的五年,中国政府将逐步减少对新能源汽车的补贴,政府将根据技术进步、产业发展、推广规模、成本效益等调整补贴政策。中国监管机构有必要对新能源电动车市场竞争进行监管。

Lesson 29　Basic Knowledge of Electric Vehicle

1. Overview of Electric Vehicle

With the development of society and economy, vehicles have become an important means of transport for us. The environmental problems caused by traditional fuel car and demand for petroleum resources have attracted our attention. Electric vehicles have a significant energy saving and environmental advantages of great significance to promote the application of electric vehicles to reduce foreign oil dependence, the nation's energy security and achieve sustainable economic and social development.

However, electric vehicles have many categories, such as BEVs, HEVs, extended-range electric vehicles(EREVs), PHEV and FCV. At present, BEVs, HEVs, EREVs, PHEVs,and FCVs are categorized as new energy vehicles in China. HEVs are categorized as energy-saving vehicles.

1)BEV

BEV is propelled by one or more electric motors powered by rechargeable battery packs or energy storage to comply with road traffic and safety regulations with the requirements of the vehicle.

2)HEV

HEV is the vehicle which can acquire power from the following two types of on-board storage energy:consumable fuel and storage device which can be charged electric or energy.

According to the structure of HEVs, it can be divided into series HEVs, parallel HEVs,series-parallel HEVs.

(1)Series HEV: the driving force of this type of HEV can only get driving force from motor.

(2)Parallel HEV: the driving force of this type of HEV can be supplied by motor or engine or motor and engine at the same time.

(3)Series-parallel HEV: this type of HEV has both series and parallel driving mode. The most famous production of HEV is the Toyota Prius.

2. Electric Motors

Electric motors are at the heart of electric vehicles. It is the electric motor (or motors) which turns electrical power from batteries into mechanical power to turn the wheels. Motors are divided into two broad classes—AC and DC machines. The AC motors are simpler devices than the DC machines and are generally more efficient, but they need complex and expensive controllers (which, among other things) converts the DC output of the battery into the AC needed by the motors.

There are many different types of electric motor but there are probably four types available for purchase today that are potential candidates for propelling an EV: permanent magnet brushless DC motor, AC asynchronism motor, permanent magnet synchronous motor, and switched reluctance motor.

3. Electric Vehicle Battery
1) Types of Electric Vehicle Battery

There are three main kinds of batteries which are commonly used on electric vehicle: lead-acid battery, nickel metal-hydride battery, and lithium ion battery.

(1) Lead-acid battery.

All lead-acid batteries use the same basic electrode materials-a lead anode and a lead dioxide cathode. This combination produces just over 2V per cell. In most lead-acid batteries, the electrodes are not pins or rods but flat plates. The electrolyte is sulfuric acid.

(2) Nickel metal-hydride battery.

The nickel metal-hydride battery which has superior features of higher power density, lighter weight and longer life is applied to the electric vehicle. Until recently, most volume manufactures of hybrid vehicles used nickel metal-hydride batteries. These have a better specific than lead-acid batteries, but far lower specific energy than lithium ion batteries.

(3) Lithium ion battery.

Lithium ion battery has huge advantages over lead acid. They have three or four times the specific energy of lead acid and can in some cases deliver good specific power and long cycle life.

2) Basic Terminology

There are several battery parameters which it is important to understand if you are going to do a good job of choosing batteries for your vehicle.

(1) Capacity.

Under certain discharge conditions, the quantity of electricity that battery discharges is defined as capacity of battery. We can use capital letter "C" to denote Capacity. And the unit of it is denoted by "A·h".

The A·h ("Amp-hour", not "Amps per hour") is the prime measure of the capacity of the battery. As the term implies the A·h is the number of amps (A) multiplied by the length of time. In a perfect world, a 20 A·h battery would provide 1A for 20 hours or 20 A for one hour.

(2) State of charge.

State of charge is called SOC for short. It describes the remaining capacity of battery and it is an important parameter in the using process of battery. State of charge is a percentage and its value range is [0,1].

(3) Depth of discharge.

Depth of discharge is called DOD for short and is defined as a percentage of the ratio of discharge capacity to the rated capacity. The mathematical relation of DOD and SOC is:

$$DOD = 1 - SOC$$

The value of DOD has great influence to the battery service life. Generally speaking, the deeper DOD of secondary battery is, the shorter its service life is. If you routinely run your batteries completely flat, you may shorten their life. Discharging down to 70% or 80% of maximum capacity is probably a good compromise with many types of cell. Therefore, we should avoid deep-discharge in the courses of using.

(4) Cycle life.

Battery charges and discharges one time, we can call this process as one time of cycle. The unit of battery cycle life is "time". Battery has a limit on the number of times they can be charged and discharged. Beyond this limit either the performance will have degraded to unacceptable level or it will be liable to sudden failure-or both.

(5) C Rate.

The C rate is an important parameter of lithium ion battery. The maximum C rate of a battery multiplied by its A·h rating gives the maximum current that can be drawn from the battery. So, for example, a 100A·h battery with a maximum C rate of 3 can safely provide 300A, but a 40A·h battery with the same maximum C rate can only provide 120 (40×3)A safely.

New Words

electrolyte[ɪˈlɛktrəlaɪt]	n. 电解液
asynchronism[eˈsɪŋkrənɪzəm]	n. 不同时,异步
switch[swɪtʃ]	vt. & vi. 转换
	n. 开关
reluctance [rɪˈlʌktəns]	n. 磁阻
nickel [ˈnɪkl]	n. 镍
hydride[ˈhaɪdraɪd]	n. 氢化物
lithium [ˈlɪθɪəm]	n. 锂元素
ion[ˈaɪən]	n. 离子

Phrases and Expressions

electric vehicle	电动汽车
blade electric vehicle	纯电动汽车
hybrid electric vehicle	混合动力(电动)汽车
extended-range electric vehicle	增程式电动汽车
plug-in hybrid electric vehicle	插电式混合动力(电动)汽车
fuel cell vehicle	燃料电池(电动)汽车

new energy vehicle	新能源汽车
energy-saving vehicle	节能汽车
series hybrid electric vehicle	串联式混合动力(电动)汽车
parallel hybrid electric vehicle	并联式混合动力(电动)汽车
series-parallel hybrid electric vehicle	混联式混合动力(电动)汽车
lead-acid battery	铅酸电池
nickel metal-hydride battery	镍氢电池
lithium ion battery	锂离子电池
capacity	容量
state of charge	荷电状态
depth of discharge	放电深度
cycle life	循环寿命
A·h	安时
C rate	充放电倍率

Review Questions

1. What is electric vehicle?
2. What is hybrid electric vehicle? Can you come up with an example?
3. What do you call "state of charge" for short?
4. Can you tell me any type of motors for electric vehicles?
5. What is the unit of battery capacity?

参考译文

第二十九课　电动汽车基本知识

1. 电动汽车概述

随着经济社会的发展,汽车已经成为人们重要的代步工具。传统燃油汽车对石油资源的需求以及带来的环境问题已引起人们的关注。而电动汽车具备显著的节能减排和环保优势,推广应用电动汽车可以减少对外石油依赖,保障国家能源安全,实现经济社会可持续发展。

然而,电动汽车的种类很多,主要包括纯电动汽车、混合动力汽车、增程式电动汽车、插电式混合动力汽车和燃料电池汽车等。目前在我国,纯电动汽车、增程式电动汽车、插电式混合动力电动汽车和燃料电池电动汽车被归为新能源汽车。混合动力电动汽车被划为节能汽车。

1)纯电动汽车

纯电动汽车是指以可充电蓄电池组或蓄能器为动力,用一个或多个电动机驱动行驶,符合道路交通、安全法规和各项要求的车辆。

2)混合动力汽车

混合动力汽车是指能够从下述两类车载能源中获得动力的汽车:可消耗的燃料和可再充电能/能量储存装置。

混合动力汽车按结构分类,可分为串联式混合动力汽车、并联式混合动力汽车和混联式混合动力汽车。

(1)串联式混合动力汽车:指车辆的驱动力只来源于电动机的混合动力汽车。

(2)并联式混合动力汽车:指车辆的驱动力由电动机或发动机单独供给或二者同时供给的混合动力汽车。

(3)混联式混合动力汽车:指同时具有串联式、并联式两种驱动方式的混合动力汽车。当前最著名的量产混合动力汽车是丰田的普锐斯。

2. 电动机

电动机是电动汽车的核心。它将电池中的电能转换成机械能来驱动车轮。电动机分为两大类——交流电动机和直流电动机。交流电动机比直流电动机简单而且通常效率更高,但它们需要复杂、昂贵的控制器来将电池输出的直流电转换成电动机所需的交流电。

电动机有很多种,但现在能买到的、有望作为电动汽车动力的有四种类型:永磁无刷直流电动机、交流异步电动机、永磁同步电动机和开关磁阻电动机。

3. 电动汽车电池

1)电动汽车电池种类

电动汽车上常用的电池主要有三种:铅酸电池、镍氢电池和锂离子电池。

(1)铅酸电池。

所有铅酸电池都使用相同的基本电极材料——铅阳极和二氧化铅阴极。这种结合使每个电池单元产生了刚好超过 2V 的电压,大多数铅酸电池的电极不是针状或杆状而是平板。电解液是硫酸。

(2)镍氢电池。

镍氢电池因其众多的功率高、质量轻、使用寿命长等性能被应用在电动汽车上,时至今日,大多数批量生产混合动力汽车的制造商也开始使用镍氢电池。这些电池优于铅酸电池,但比能远低于锂离子电池。

(3)锂离子电池。

锂离子电池相对于铅酸电池有巨大的优势。它们的比能量是铅酸电池的三四倍,在某些情况下,还可以提供良好的比功率和长的循环寿命。

2)基本术语

为车辆选择电池时,弄明白以下几个电池参数是很重要的。

(1)容量。

电池在一定的放电条件下所能放出的电量称为电池容量,以其英文单词的首字母 C 表示,其单位用安时(A·h)表示。

安时(是"安培小时",而不是"安培每小时")是电池容量的主要度量方式。顾名思义,安时等于安培数乘以时间长短。在理想的情况下,一个 20A·h 的电池可以将 1A 的电流工作 20 小时或以 20 安时电流工作 1 小时。

(2)荷电状态。

荷电状态简称"SOC"。它描述了电池的剩余电量,是电池使用过程中的重要参数。荷电状态一般用百分比表示,取值范围为[0,1]。

(3)放电深度。

放电深度简称 DOD,是放电容量与额定容量之比的百分数。DOD 与 SOC 之间存在如下数学计算关系：

$$DOD=1-SOC$$

放电深度的高低对电池的使用寿命有很大的影响。一般情况下，二次电池常用的放电深度越深，其使用寿命就越短。如果您经常将电池中的电全部放完，这可能会缩短其寿命。对多数电池放电至最大容量的 70%～80% 或许是不错的选择，因此在电池使用过程中应尽量避免深度放电。

(4) 循环寿命。

蓄电池经历一次充电和放电，称为一次循环。循环寿命的单位是"次"。电池有一个充放电次数上的极限。超出这个极限，它们的性能会退化到不可接受的程度，或者有可能突然失效，或者兼而有之。

(5) 充放电倍率。

充放电倍率是锂电池很重要的一个参数。一个电池的最大充放电倍率乘以其安时数就是电池所能提供的最大电流。例如，一个最大充放电倍率是 3、容量为 100A·h 的电池可以稳定提供 300A 的电流，而具有相同最大充放电倍率、容量为 40A·h 的电池只能稳定提供 120(40×3)A 的电流。

Lesson 30 Paris Show Points the Way to the Future of Electric Cars

Paris-when 18th century sailors saw the first birds in the air after a long ocean crossing, they knew that land was finally getting close. For the future automotive industry that will be based on electricity, the 2008 automotive show in Paris is like seeing that first bird in the air.[1]

While there are important new motorized cars unveiled at the show, like the new Renault Megane and Volkswagen Golf, the look at the future came from 19 different electric cars proposed by large and small automakers.

In a way, the European battery-powered car industry is like the car industry in China. There are many players who hope to succeed, and experience shows that in the end, they will not all arrive.

Some of the new entrants are well financed, like Bollore, which makes batteries and super capacitors, and has a partnership with Italian engineer and designer Pininfarina. They introduced their B-zero car that they expect to begin selling next year.

Others are small hopeful players, like the South African company Optimal Energy, which has an idea for a 6-passenger minivan designed by a former Jaguar designer. And all the new entrants will have competition with the major automakers.

"The future of the automobile lies in the zero emission", said Renault chairman Carlos Ghosn, who introduced the Z. E. electric concept car based on the Kangoo van. He said that the Renault-Nissan Alliance is spending a third of its R&D money on clean vehicles, with the priority given to electric cars.

Renault expects to sell between 20 000 and 40 000 electric vehicles in 2011, when it starts a program of electric Meganes in Israel, Portugal and Denmark, and 100 000 in 2012. Renault has joined with the other members of ACEA, the European automaker organization, to establish technical standard for electric vehicles, especially batteries.

Some major automakers showed concept ideas for electric cars, like Citoren's C-Cactus, but other automakers have electric cars already ready for the road. Mitsubishi showed its iMiEV, a 4-seat electric car. Smart already has 100 electric versions being tested in London, and it showed its version to the press and public. Both cars could be driven on a small test track at the Paris auto show, along with the battery-powered sports car.

The taste for electric power is especially keen in France, which produces 80% of its electricity in nuclear power plants that emit no CO_2. Thus, electric cars in France will be good to the local environment, with zero emissions, and good for the planet.

The key to electric cars is the battery, and most automakers have made arrangements with a particular battery supplier. At first, carmakers demanded that battery makers meet difficult targets of capacity, power and cost, and it was almost impossible to do so. [2] Toyota was the first to link with a battery maker, and its Prius has been a success.

Batscap and Bollore are in a similar position to BYD in China, which began as a battery maker and went into the automotive business. Warren Buffet, a U.S. Investor, took a 9.9% stake in BYD in 2008, September, and one of his executives behind the investment, David Sokol, said that Chinese companies are emerging as important centers for R&D and technology.

Batscap has developed lithium metal polymer batteries, with a solid electrolyte, and combined with its own super capacitors, it will give the B-zero car a range of 250 km and a lifetime of 200 000 km.

Of course, the future of the electric cars was not the only element of the auto show, but the glitter of the new cars was sometimes over shadowed by the gloom of the economic environment in the United States and West Europe.

Renault introduced its new Megane sedan and coupe. The Megane family accounts for 30% of Renault's sales, and 40% of its profits according to some analysts.

Opel introduced its upper medium car—the Insignia. [3] While sales of large cars have been declining, the company expects the car to do as well in its first year as the Vectra—the car it replaces—did when it was introduced in 2002. "We will have the sporty 1.6 liter turbo Tourer in spring, and we will have a 190 hp version later to complete the range," said Andreas Hafele, director of the global Delta platform.

Volkswagen introduced the sixth generation of its Golf, which has been the usual volume leader in the lower medium segment in Europe. Ford showed the Ka, its new small car based on the same platform as the popular Fiat 500. And luxury brands showed cars that clearly indicate their path down market. The Audi A1 concept and the BMW X1 concept are both prototypes that will come to production in a very similar form.

Luxury brands are presenting smaller cars, because the market is moving in that direction under pressure from the European Union, which wants to limit fuel consumption. [4]

Infiniti, the luxury brand of Nissan, arrived in Europe at the Paris show going in the opposite direction. It counts on its FX37 sports utility to account for 80% of its sales, and the car will emit about 280g of CO_2 per km, more than twice as much as the European goal of 130 g/km.

The V6 diesel engine is by far a most popular engine choice for big luxury cars. The gloomy current outlook does not discourage the automakers, it just makes them cautions.

"The auto industry is complex. There is no one remedy," said Jean-Pierre Collin, general manager of Peugeot,"when you sail upwind, you keep your destination the same, even if you tack to get there."

But suppliers see a rough time ahead. The eve of the show, directors of supplier organizations from Japan, Europe and North America were gathered together.

New Words

battery-powered [ˈbæt(ə)rɪ-ˈpaʊəd]	adj. 靠电池驱动的
capacitor [kəˈpæsɪtə]	n. 电容器
minivan [ˈmɪnɪvæn]	n. 小型面包车
polymer [ˈpɑlɪmɚ]	n. 聚合物；聚合体
coupe [ˈkʊpe]	n. 双座轿式马车；双门小轿车
segment [ˈsɛgmənt]	n. 部分；部门
turbo [ˈtɝbo]	n. 涡轮增压器
hp. (horsepower) [ˈhɔrsˈpaʊɚ]	n. 马力
remedy [ˈrɛmədi]	n. 治疗；疗法；药物
upwind [ˈʌpˈwɪnd]	adj.&adv. 逆风的(地)；迎风的(地)；顶风的(地)
rebound [rɪˈbaʊnd]	v. (使)弹回,跳回 n. 回弹；返回
mobility [moˈbɪləti]	n. 运动性；机动性；灵活性
adaptation [ˈædæpˈteʃən]	n. 适应；适合；适应性变化

Phrases and Expressions

in a way	从某种意义上说
have a partnership with	与……合伙
with the priority	优先考虑
be keen in	对……着迷；喜爱
link with	与……想联系；有关系

Notes to the Text

[1] For the future automotive industry that will be based on electricity, the 2008 Automotive show in Paris is like seeing that first bird in the air.

犹如第一次看到空中的飞鸟那样，2008年巴黎车展首次展示了将基于电力的未来汽车业。

[2]At first, carmakers demanded that battery makers meet difficult targets of capacity, power andcost, and it was almost impossible to do so.

起初,汽车制造商要求电池制造商在电池容量、功耗和成本等方面达到难以企及的目标,而这些几乎是做不到的。

[3]Opel introduced its upper medium car— the Insignia.

欧宝推出了高档中型汽车——徽章。

[4]Luxury brands are presenting smaller cars, because the market is moving in that direction under pressure from the European Union, which wants to limit fuel consumption.

豪华品牌展示的是小型汽车,因为迫于欧盟限制燃油消耗的压力,市场正朝着这一方向前进。

Review Questions

1. What is the key of the future of the automobile said by Renault chairman Carlos Ghosn?
2. What is the key to electric cars?
3. Illustrate how many automakers showed concept ideas for electric cars.
4. What is developed by Batscap with a solid electrolyte?

参考译文

第三十课 巴黎车展显示电动汽车的未来

巴黎——当18世纪的水手远涉重洋第一次看到天空中出现飞鸟时,他们知道船快要靠近陆地了。犹如第一次看到空中的飞鸟那样,2008年巴黎车展首次展示了将基于电力的未来汽车业。

尽管展会上有许多重要的新车亮相,如雷诺梅甘娜和大众高尔夫等,从大小汽车制造商提供的19辆风格迥异的电动汽车可以看出汽车未来发展的端倪。

从某种意义上说,欧洲电池驱动的汽车产业很像中国的汽车行业。参与者众多,他们都希望获得成功,但经验表明不可能人人如愿以偿。

一些新加入者资金雄厚,如制造电池和超级电容器的博洛雷,已经与意大利工程师和设计师宾尼法利纳建立了合作伙伴关系。他们推介的B-0汽车打算明年销售。

其他一些小企业很有希望,如南非的优化能源公司,打算生产由前捷豹设计师设计的6座位轻型客车。所有的新加入者都将与主要汽车制造商进行竞争。

"未来的汽车关键在于零排放,"雷诺总裁卡洛斯·戈恩在介绍一款基于Kangoo轻型客车研发的Z.E.电动概念车时说。雷诺日产联盟将用三分之一的研发资金开发清洁车辆,优先考虑电动汽车。

雷诺在以色列、葡萄牙和丹麦启动梅甘娜电动汽车计划,预计在2011年出售20 000至40 000辆电动汽车,到2012年销售1 000 000辆。雷诺已经同欧洲汽车制造商组织ACEA的其他成员一起为电动车辆制定技术标准,特别是电池方面。

一些主要的汽车制造商展示了电动汽车的概念理论,如雪铁龙的 C-Cactus,但其他汽车制造商的电动汽车已经准备上路了。三菱展示了一款 4 座位的电动汽车 iMiEV。Smart 已经有 100 个电动汽车版本正在伦敦测试,而且已经公诸于众。这两款汽车和其他电动跑车一样,都可以在巴黎车展小型测试车道上试驾。

法国对尝试电动汽车的兴致特别浓厚,因为 80% 的电力来自核电厂,无 CO_2 排放。因此,法国电动汽车实现零排放,对保护当地环境和全球环境有益。

电池是电动汽车的关键,大多数汽车制造商都曾和某个电池供应商协作过。起初,汽车制造商要求电池制造商在电池容量、功耗和成本等方面达到难以企及的目标,而这些几乎是做不到的。丰田是第一家和电池制造商联手的汽车制造商,其研发的普锐斯获得了成功。

巴斯凯普和博洛雷与中国的比亚迪处境相似,比亚迪开始是电池生产商,后来进入汽车产业。2008 年 9 月,美国的投资家沃伦·巴菲特投资比亚迪,买下 9.9% 的股份,协助巴菲特投资的高管大卫·索科尔说,中国企业正在崛起,成为重要的研发和技术中心。

巴斯凯普利用固体电解质已经开发出锂金属聚合物电池,结合原有的超级电容器,可使 B-0 汽车最大行程达到 250km,使用寿命 20 万 km。

当然,电动汽车的未来并不是巴黎车展的唯一看点,那些闪闪发光的新车有时会蒙上美国和西欧经济环境悲观的阴影。

雷诺推出了新款梅甘娜轿车和小客车。据一些分析师透露,梅甘娜家族汽车占雷诺汽车销售的 30%,而利润占到了 40%。

欧宝推出了高档中型汽车——徽章。虽然大型轿车销售一直在下滑,该公司预计这个后续产品会像 2002 年推出维达汽车时那样,在第一年就走红。欧宝全球三角洲平台主管安德烈斯·哈菲利说:"我们将在春季推出 1.6 升涡轮增压运动车 Tourer,以后还推出一款 190hp 车型来完善这个系列。"

大众汽车公司推出的第六代高尔夫,高尔夫在欧洲中低档车中通常产量最高。福特展示汽车 Ka 是与流行的菲亚特 500 基于同一平台生产的新型小汽车。豪华汽车品牌展示清楚地表明了市场的走向。奥迪 A1 概念车和宝马 X1 概念车都是汽车原型,将来投产的方式也非常相似。

豪华品牌展示的是小型汽车,因为迫于欧盟限制燃油消耗的压力,市场正朝向这一方向前进。

在欧洲巴黎车展上,日产豪华车英菲尼迪显示了相反的发展方向。FX37 运动型多用途车销售业绩良好,占到其销量的 80%,该车每千米会排放约 280g CO_2,比欧洲标准每千米 130g 的两倍还多。

V6 柴油发动机是目前大型豪华轿车最为流行的一种发动机选择。如今汽车制造商并不因为大排量车前景暗淡而泄气,他们只是变得谨慎而已。

"汽车工业很复杂,没有统一的补救良方",标志总经理让·皮埃尔·科林说,"当逆风行船时,你只要把握目的地的方向不变,即使左冲右突都无所谓"。

但许多供应商意识到时世艰难,日本、欧洲和北美的供应商纷纷赶在车展前夜来到巴黎。

Lesson 31　The Car of the Future: It Talks, It Thinks, and It Can Drive Itself

Monday morning, August 17, 2020, and you are off to work. You hop into the driver's seat, which, like the cabin temperature, is adjusted precisely to your liking. Even though your daughter used it to go to a friend's house last night, the car knowns it is your driving now. So the satellite radio has switched from R&B (your daughter's favorite) to your preferred all-news station. The car's electric motor runs on hydrogen, and has already been topped off, automatically, from an appliance in your garage. So far, so good.

You glide onto the freeway ramp and decide to get a jump on the workweek. Setting the automatic pilot, you call up the office e-mail through the on-board computer. Guided by advanced cruise control, GPS, and sensors embedded in the roadway, the car stays in its lane, maintains a safe distance from other vehicles, and alerts you to your exit. Once in the parking lot, you check the fuel gauge and figure you have got more than enough juice to make it home. So you plug into the city's power grid to feed it electricity generated by your car—for which you will get an energy credit later on.

Sounds great, doesn't it? What this cheery vision of a morning commute hides is a growing sense of urgency on the part of the world's automakers. [1] The current model for making and selling cars in the United States—big vehicles with big fuel tanks and sky-high costs—has almost driven the auto industry off the road. No one's predicting that gasoline prices will come down dramatically anytime soon, if ever. The pollution and energy consumption, plus the traffic, created by so many cars will simply force the industry to change.

The questions are what, and how soon. Experts generally agree that we are on the verge of an era of new fuels. "We have to find alternatives," says Larry Burns, vice president of Research and Development and Strategic Planning for General Motors Corp., and one of the industry's most optimistic visionaries. "By 2020, we are expecting 1.1 billion cars and trucks on the planet, compared to 750 million today. Imagine 125 freeway lanes running side by side, bumper to bumper, going all the way round the world."

The leading candidate to replace good old smelly gasoline is hydrogen, the most plentiful and available element on the planet. [2] No one geographical region has a monopoly on it—so there is little chance of a production cartel, like OPEC. And in theory at least, hydrogen will deliver superior fuel efficiency with no air pollution. Already, the major automakers are working on hydrogen-fed fuel cells.

Others, however, believe hydrogen cars are much further in the future, maybe even a half-century away. For starters, the fuel cells made with today's technology are hugely expensive. Science knows how to make them—just not how to make them cheaply. Add to that the lack of a hydrogen-fueling infrastructure, and technical difficulties of storing and handing hydrogen, and you are looking at years of work ahead.

"Fundamentally, we see no game-changing technology available by 2020," says Bob Rivard, vice president of Advanced Technology and Product Marketing for automotive supplier Robert Bosch Corp, "we will see evolutionary steps, not a paradigm shift."[3] Among the stages he envisions are cleaner, more fuel-efficient gasoline-powered vehicles, along with alternative fuels and new propulsion systems.[4] Gasoline-electric hybrids, like the Toyota Prius, Ford Escape, and Honda Civic and Insight, will be more common. "As much as we would like to be getting around in flying saucers, the reality is that by 2020 we will still be driving vehicles that use fossil fuels," says Mary Ann Wright, Ford Motor Co.'s director of Sustainable Mobility Technologies and Hybrid Vehicle Programs. "But I do think there will come a point in time when every vehicle will have some kind of hybrid technology".

Within the next decade, we expect to see more clean diesel-powered engines, like those available from Volkswagen and Mercedes-Benz. These vehicles are up to 40% more fuel-efficient than gasoline cars, and produce about 15% less CO_2. The downside of diesel? Oxides of nitrogen-known as NOx-are potent irritants. Other new gasoline replacements to watch for biofuel, biodiesel and natural gas.

If there is disagreement over just what will power the car of the future, there is no debate about how cool the actual vehicles will bevery, very cool. Picture this: it is 2020 and you are driving home from work on the freeway. But there are no road signs anywhere, not for stores, gas stations, restaurants or even the local exits and interchanges. There is no need for them—your car's computer keeps you oriented and on track (it also knows the speed limit, so you'll have no excuses with the local cop). Can't recall if you need milk for breakfast? Your car's computer contacts your home inventory system to check. Sure enough, you need milk-and orange juice too. The interactive systems take over. Your car spots a convenience store at the next and zaps your grocery list ahead. When you arrive, everything is bagged and ready for pickup. "By 2020, it will no longer be a big deal to have Internet connectivity almost anywhere, anytime," Says K. Venkatesh Prasad, technical leader in Ford's Infotronics Technologies Department.

New Words

automatically[ˌɔːtəˈmætikəli]　　*adv.* 自动的;机械的
glide[glaɪd]　　*v.* 轻快平稳地行驶;滑行;滑翔
cruise[kruːz]　　*n.* 巡游;巡航
sensor[ˈsensə]　　*n.* 传感器;感应器;探测装置
gauge[geɪdʒ]　　*n.* 测量仪表;检测表
grid[grɪd]　　*n.* 系统网络(输电线路);网格;坐标方格
commute[kəˈmjuːt]　　*n.* 上下班交通;通勤路程
bumper[ˈbʌmpə]　　*n.* 缓冲器;减振器
propulsion[prəˈpʌlʃən]　　*n.* 推进;推进力
sustainable[səˈsteɪnəbl]　　*adj.* 能持续的;能维持的

interchange[ˈɪntətʃendʒ]	n. 交互,交换;(公路等)立体交叉;交换道
spot[spɑt]	vt. 认出;发现
zap[zæp]	v. 快速传递;迅速移动

Phrases and Expressions

on the roads	在路途上;在转变过程中
cabin temperature	驾驶时温度
freeway ramp	高速公路匝道
automatic pilot	自动驾驶仪
cruise control	巡航控制

Notes to the Text

[1] What this cheery vision of a morning hide is a growing sense of urgency on the part of the world's automakers.

但对世界各国的汽车制造商而言,在这幅令人愉快的上班图背后却隐藏着一种不断增长的紧迫感。

[2] The leading candidate to replace good old smelly gasoline is hydrogen, the most plentiful and available element on the planet.

最有可能替代气味浓烈、历史悠久的汽油的物质是氢气,它是地球上最丰富的可用元素。

[3] "Fundamentally, we see no game-changing technology available by 2020," says Bob Rivard, vice president of Advanced Technology and Product Marketing for automotive supplier Robert Bosch Corp, "we will see evolutionary steps, not a paradigm shift."

"在2020年前,我们根本看不出生产技术会有突破。"汽车供应商罗伯特·博世集团先进技术和产品市场副总裁鲍勃·里瓦尔德说,"我们会看到前进的步伐,但不是方法的典范转移。"

[4] Among the stages he envisions are cleaner, more fuel-efficient gasoline-powered vehicles, along with alternative fuels and new propulsion systems.

他预计下个阶段会研制出更加清洁、更加节能的汽油机车,并伴有替代燃料和新的汽车驱动系统。

Review Questions

1. What is the cheery vision of a morning commute?
2. What will simply force the industry to change?
3. What are the advantages and disadvantages of the hydrogen?
4. Why there is no debate about how cool the actual vehicles will be?

参考译文

第三十一课　未来汽车:会说、会想、会驾驶

2020年8月17日,星期一的早晨,你要去上班。当你跳上驾驶座,车内立刻为你调好

你喜欢的温度。即使你女儿昨晚开着它去过朋友家,但它知道现在驾车的是你。因此,卫星广播也从(你女儿喜欢的)R&B自动切换到你爱听的新闻台。汽车的电力发动机由氢气驱动,早已在车库里自动把气充好了。到目前为止,一切良好。

你平稳的驶上高速公路匝道,下决心要把本周工作干得更为出色。设定自动驾驶仪后,你打开车载电脑接收办公邮件。汽车有先进的巡航控制系统、全球定位系统以及埋设在道路两旁的传感探测器导航,行进在自己的车道上,与其他车辆保持安全的距离,并提示你将驶到出口处。到了停车场后,你检查燃油表,估算一下,一定要备有充足的油量开回家。于是,你可以接通市政电源为汽车充电——为此,将会收到一张电费账单。

听上去很棒,不是吗?但对世界各国的汽车制造商而言,在这幅令人愉快的上班图背后却隐藏着一种不断增长的紧迫感。如今美国制造和销售的汽车款式——大车身拖着大油箱的天价车——几乎使汽车工业走向末路。即使汽车价格下跌,也没有人会知道在近期内的哪一天会大幅下跌。如此庞大的汽车数量导致大气污染、能源消耗以及城市交通日趋恶化,这些严重问题只会迫使汽车工业发生改变。

但问题是需要变革什么?何时才能实现这些变革?专家一般认为,我们正在步入新燃料时代。通用汽车公司研发及战略规划部副总裁拉里·伯恩斯说:"我们必须找到汽车的替代品。"他是汽车工业最为乐观的预言家之一。"现在有7.5亿辆汽车,到2020年预计全世界会有11亿辆乘用车和货车。设想一下,世界各地的汽车在125条车道的高速公路上一列挨着一列、一辆接着一辆穿梭行驶将会是何种的景象。"

最有可能替代气味浓烈、历史悠久的汽油的物质是氢气,它是地球上最丰富的可用元素。任何地域都无法垄断它,因而不会出现类似OPEC的垄断集团。至少从理论上讲,氢气燃料的效能极高,无空气污染。为此,汽车业的巨头早已开始研究氢燃料电池。目前相关示范性的汽车已在道路上试运行。

然而,也有人认为现在谈论氢动汽车还为时过早,至少还要等半个世纪。对开拓者而言,以今天的工艺制造的燃料电池汽车价格不菲。科学制作方法已有了,但无法廉价生产。此外,由于缺乏施加氢燃料的基础设施,储存和处理氢气也还有技术难度,需要经过多年的努力才能使之变为现实。

"在2020年前,我们根本看不出生产技术会有突破。"汽车供应商罗伯特·博世集团先进技术和产品市场副总裁鲍勃·利瓦尔德说,"我们会看到前进的步伐,但不是方法的典范转移。"他预计下个阶段会研制出更加清洁、更加节能的汽油机车,并伴有替代燃料和新的汽车驱动系统。油电混合动力车型将更为普及,如丰田的普瑞斯、福特的翼虎、本田的思域和远见系列。"诚然我们喜欢乘坐飞碟四处游玩,但现实是到2020年我们还只能开化石燃料汽车。"福特汽车续动技术和混合动力车项目总监玛丽·安·莱特说道,"不过我坚信总有一天,每一辆车辆都可以运用某种混合动力技术。"

在今后十年里,我们期待着更多的清洁柴油发动机面世,如同现在大众和梅塞德尔-奔驰汽车的发动机一般。这些汽车比一般的汽油机车节能达40%以上,而CO_2排放量降低15%左右。为什么柴油的使用越来越少?因为氮氧化合物NO_x具有强烈的刺激味。其他值得注意的汽油代用品还有生物燃料、生物柴油和天然气。

尽管对于未来汽车的驱动燃料众说纷纭,但对未来汽车的性能非常酷这一点是没有异议的。让我们设想一下:2020年的某一天,你下班回家开着车在高速公路上驰骋。但道路两旁没有任何商店、加油站和餐馆的路标,甚至连当地出口和交换道的指示牌都没有。因为已经没有必要设置了——汽车上的电脑随时随地为你导航(车速限制也会显示,所以面对交警再也找不到借口了)。是否记得还有早餐牛奶?车载电脑会连接到你家里的盘存系统查看。如果你真需要牛奶还有橙汁,互动通信系统便自动联系。你的汽车帮你找到下个出口附近的一家便利店,并把你的购物清单快速传送到该商店。当你到达店铺的时候,一切都已经打包完毕,只等你取货了。"到了2020年,随时随地进行网络连接不再是什么难事。"福特汽车电子信息技术部总监K·旺卡特·普拉斯德说。

Lesson 32　The First Internet Vehicle

Back in 2015, Alibaba and SAIC Motor Corporation, China's largest automaker, established a fund of one billion yuan (150 million dollars) for building an "Internet vehicle" under their strategic partnership—SAIC to do manufacturing, and Alibaba to support in technology.

In late April 2016, they released Roewe RX 5, a sport utility vehicle (SUV). Roewe RX5 what they are calling the world's first "Internet vehicle". The companies describe an Internet vehicle as a vehicle that is fully connected to the Internet, featuring various functions including navigation, music, social networking, entertainment, and etc.. They envision people-to-vehicle communication that will expand to areas of vehicle-to-vehicle, vehicle-to-road, and vehicle-to-infrastructure communication. The Internet related features will increase the value of the vehicle. Jack Ma, founder of the Alibaba Grou called it a new milestone, to create the first mass-produced Internet vehicle in China.

"We want to introduce the Internet as an infrastructure to vehicle. With this infrastructure, the vehicle is really running on the Internet and have more follow-up functions and more extensions." Alibaba Group Chief Technology Officer Jian Wang said.

The smart vehicle is connected to an Internet of Things (IOT) ecosystem to provide customized user experiences. YunOS for vehicles is a comprehensive operating system developed specifically for smart vehicle, aiming to make the interaction between the driver and the vehicle more efficient.

YunOS for vehicles allows RX5 to not only inform drivers of the state of vehicle's components, such as the tire pressure, but also to make it work like a smartphone that creates reminders, calculates an optimal route from A to B, and reserves and pays for a parking space via Alipay.[1] Yet as a wholesome operating system, YunOS for Vehicle does not require a smartphone to work, because everything is run on the cloud.

Each driver of RX5 has a unique ID. Using driver-input data such as music, restaurants, or other driver destinations, the data is used to recommend customized user experiences for the driver. In addition, it can be based on driver's history routes and driving habits, and suggest new routes if the road ahead is blocked or even if a traffic jam is expected. The SUV also supports 360-degree cameras and Advanced Driver Assistance Systems (ADAS).

Jian Wang said: "What we are creating is not 'Internet in the vehicle', but a 'vehicle on the Internet'. This is a significant milestone in the automobile industry. Smart operating systems become the second engine of vehicle, while data is the new fuel. Going forward, vehicle will become an important platform for internet services and smart hardware innovation. We will be embracing a world where everything is closely connected," said Wang Jian.

Alibaba is far from the only Chinese Internet firm to get into vehicle. LeEco is backing U. S. project Faraday Future and building a vehicle of its own, while Baidu is one of the front runners testing self-driving vehicles in both China and the U. S.[2]

The new internet technology will allow the joint venture to quickly adapt its vehicle to become self-driving. Now, in an attempt to keep up with emerging technology, the companies will soon be implementing self-driving features into their vehicles.

But the race to commercialise self-driving vehicle is far from over. There are five levels of automation and experts predict a fully autonomous vehicle will not hit the market until 2020 or later.

FIVE LEVELS OF AUTOMATION:

Level One—Small amount of control is accomplished by the system such as adaptive braking if a vehicle gets too close.

Level Two—The system can control the speed and direction of the vehicle allowing the driver to take their hands off temporarily, but they have to monitor the road at all times and be ready to take over.

Level Three—The driver does not have to monitor the system at all times in some specific cases like on the high ways but must be ready to resume control if the system requests.

Level Four—The system can cope with all situations automatically within defined use but it may not be able to cope With all weather or road conditions. System with rely on high definition mapping.

Level Five—Full automation. System can cope with all weather, traffic and lighting conditions. It can go anywhere, at any time in any conditions.

New Words

navigation [ˌnævɪˈgeɪʃn]　　　　　　　　n. 航行(学);航海(术);海上交通
entertainment [ˌentəˈteɪnmənt]　　　　　n. 娱乐节目;娱乐,消遣;招待,款待
envision [ɪnˈvɪʒn]　　　　　　　　　　vt. 想象,预见,展望
infrastructure [ˈɪnfrəstrʌktʃə(r)]　　　　 n. 基础设施;基础建设
ecosystem [ˈiːkəʊsɪstəm]　　　　　　　n. <生>生态系统
interaction [ˌɪntərˈækʃn]　　　　　　　 n. 互动;一起活动;合作;互相影响

Phrases and Expressions

Advanced Driver Assistance Systems (ADAS)　　先进的驾驶辅助系统
emerging technology　　　　　　　　　　　　新兴技术

self-driving 自动驾驶

Notes to the Text

[1] YunOS for Cars allows RX5 to not only inform drivers of the state of car's components, such as the tire pressure, but also to make it work like a smartphone that creates reminders, calculates an optimal route from A to B, and reserves and pays for a parking space via Alipay.

RX5车载YunOS系统不仅告知驾驶员车辆的部件状态,如轮胎气压,也使它像智能手机一样可以创建提醒,计算从A到B的最优路径,并通过支付宝预定停车位和支付相关费用。

[2] LeEco is backing U.S. project Faraday Future and building a vehicle of its own, while Baidu is one of the front runners testing self-driving vehicles in both China and the U.S.

乐视支持法拉第未来的美国项目并建造自己的汽车,百度是在中国和美国测试无人驾驶车辆的领跑者之一。

Review Questions

1. What are the features of the first Internet car?
2. What are the five levels of commercial self-driving cars?

参考译文

第三十二课　第一辆互联网汽车

早在2015,阿里巴巴和中国最大的汽车制造商上汽集团成为战略合作伙伴,建立了一个十亿元人民币(1.5亿美元)基金建造"互联网汽车"——上汽负责制造,阿里巴巴提供技术支持。

2016年四月下旬,阿里巴巴和上汽集团发布了荣威RX 5,它是一个运动型多功能车(SUV)。荣威RX 5被他们称之为世界上第一个"互联网汽车"。他们描述互联网汽车是完全连接到互联网的汽车,具有导航、音乐、社交、娱乐等多种功能。他们设想人与车通信,可扩展到车与车通信、车与路通信、车与基础设施通信。互联网相关功能将增加车辆的价值。阿里巴巴创始人马云称这是一个新的里程碑,是中国第一款大批量生产的互联网汽车。

阿里巴巴集团首席技术官王健说:"我们希望将互联网作为基础设施引入汽车。有了这个基础设施,汽车真正的运行在互联网上,并有更多的后续功能和更多的扩展。"

智能汽车可连接到物联网(IOT)生态系统以提供定制的用户体验。车载YunOS系统是专门为智能汽车开发的综合操作系统,旨在让驾驶员和汽车更高效地互动。

RX5车载YunOS系统不仅告知驾驶员车辆各部件状态,如轮胎气压,也使它像智能手机一样可以创建提醒,计算从A到B的最优路径,并通过支付宝预定停车位和支付相关费用。然而作为一个健全的操作系统,车载YunOS系统不需要智能手机工作,因为一切都是在云系统运行。

每个RX5车主都有一个特定的ID。使用驱动程序的输入数据,如音乐、餐厅或其他驾驶员的目的地,数据用来向驾驶员推荐定制的用户体验。此外,它可以依据驾驶员的历史路线和驾驶习惯,如果前面的道路被封锁或者出现交通堵塞预期,将建议新的路线。该车还支持 360°摄像头和先进的驾驶辅助系统(ADAS)。

王健说:"我们创造的不是'汽车上网',而是'互联网上的汽车'。这是汽车工业的一个重要里程碑。智能操作系统成为汽车的第二个发动机,而数据是新的燃料。展望未来,汽车将成为互联网服务和智能硬件创新的重要平台。我们将拥抱一个一切紧密相连的世界。"

阿里巴巴是迄今为止唯一一家进入汽车行业的中国互联网公司。乐视支持法拉第未来的美国项目并建造自己的汽车,百度是在中国和美国测试无人驾驶车辆的领跑者之一。

新的互联网技术将让合资公司使他们的汽车迅速实现自动驾驶。现在为试图跟上新兴技术,各公司将很快将自动驾驶功能应用到他们的汽车上。

但商业化的自动驾驶汽车竞赛还远未结束。有五个层次的自动化,专家预测一个全自动化的汽车直到 2020 或更晚才会进入市场。

五级自动化:

一级——系统完成少量的控制,如车辆太接近时车辆主动制动。

二级——系统可以控制车辆的速度和方向,可让驾驶员暂时将他们的手移开,但他们必须实时监测道路,随时做好接管的准备。

三级——在某些特殊的情况下,如在高速路上,驾驶员无须时时监视系统,但如果系统要求,必须随时准备恢复控制。

四级——该系统可以根据设置应付所有情况,但它可能无法应付全部天气或道路情况。系统工作情况将取决于**高清地图**。

五级——全自动化。系统可以应付任何天气、交通和照明情况。它可以在任何时间、任何条件下,去任何地方。

Vocabulary

A

absorption [əb'sɔːpʃn]   n. 吸收
abbreviation [əˌbriːviˈeɪʃn]   n. 缩写,缩短,缩写式
abreast [ə'brest]   ad. & adj. 朝同方向并列(的),并肩(的)
accessibility [əkˌsesəˈbɪlətɪ]   n. 易接近,可到达的
accommodate [əˈkɑməˌdeɪt]   v. 给方便,使适应,供给……住宿,照应,招待,调节,和解
accuracy [ˈækjərəsi]   n. 准确,精确,准确度
acoustics [əˈkustɪks]   n. 声学,音响效果
actuator [ˈæktʃʊˌeɪtə]   n. 促动器
adaptation [ˌædæpˈteʃən]   n. 适应;适合;适应性变化
adapter [əˈdæptər]   n. 适配器
adherence [ədˈhɪrəns]   n. 粘着[附,结],粘着(力)
adhesion [ədˈhiʒ(ə)n]   n. 附着,粘着,固定
administrative [ədˈmɪnɪˌstreɪtɪv]   adj. 行政的,管理的
aforementioned [əˈfɔrˌmenʃənd]   adj. 上述的,前述的
aforesaid [əˈfɔrˌsed]   adj. 上述的
aggravate [ˈægrəˌveɪt]   v. 使……恶化,使……更严重
aldehyde [ˈældəˌhaɪd]   n. [化]醛,乙醛
alignment [əˈlaɪnmənt]   n. 调整,定位
allot [əˈlɑt]   vt. (按份额)分配,分派
alternator [ˈɔltərˌneɪtər]   n. 交流发电机
altus [ˈæltəs]   adj. 高的
aluminum [əˈljuːmɪnəm]   n. 铝
ambient [ˈæmbiənt]   adj. 周围的,外界的
amicable [ˈæmɪkəb(ə)l]   adj. 友好的,和睦的
amplitude [ˈæmplɪˌtud]   n. 广阔,广大,充足,丰富,(思想的)广度,(天体)出没(磁)方位角,(交变电流的)幅度,(无线电波)波幅,调幅,(音波场中空气压力的)振幅,(钟摆持的)摆幅

analyzer [ˈænəˌlaɪzə]	n. 分析仪
anticipate [ænˈtɪsɪˌpeɪt]	v. 预期,期望,过早使用,占先,预订,预见,可以预料
application [ˌæplɪˈkeɪʃ(ə)n]	n. 申请,应用软件程序
appraiser [əˈpreɪzə(r)]	n. 评估鉴定员
approximation [əˌprɒksɪˈmeɪʃ(ə)n]	n. 接近,近似,近似值
arbitration [ˌɑː(r)bɪˈtreɪʃ(ə)n]	n. 仲裁,公断,(国际法)调停,鉴定,检验,判优法
armrest [ˈɑrmrest]	n. 椅子扶手
ascertain [æsərˈteɪn]	v. 确定,探知,认定
assault [əˈsɔlt]	n.&v. 攻击,突袭,袭击,突袭
assembly [əˈsembli]	n. 集合,集会,装配
assert [əˈsərt]	vt. 宣称,断言,声明,维护,坚持
associate [əˈsoʊʃɪət]	n. 同伴,伙伴
	v. 联合,联想
	adj. 副的
asynchronism [eˈsɪŋkrənɪzəm]	n. 不同时,异步
atmospheric [ˌætməˈsferɪk]	adj. 大气的
atomise [ˈætəumaɪz]	vt. (=atomize)使化为原子,使雾化,使粉化
authentic [ɔˈθentɪk]	a. 可靠的,可信的,真的,真正的
automatically [ˌɔːtəˈmætɪkəli]	adv. 自动地;机械地
auxiliary [ɔɡˈzɪljəri]	n 帮助者,辅助物,助动词
	adj. 附加的,辅助的
axially [ˈæksɪəli]	ad. 轴向地

B

bagel [ˈbeɪɡ(ə)l]	n. 百吉饼(一种点心)
battery [ˈbæt(ə)ri]	n. 电池,殴打
battery-powered [ˈbæt(ə)rɪ-ˈpauəd]	n. 大海;海洋
berth [bərθ]	n. (船与灯塔,沙滩等之间留出的)安全距离,(船、车、飞机等的)座[铺]位 卧铺,停泊地,锚[泊]位,船台,(轮船上的)住舱
beverage [ˈbev(ə)rɪdʒ]	n. 饮料(如茶、酒、牛奶、汽水、低度汽水等),[英方]餐费,酒费
blissful [ˈblɪsfəl]	adj. 有福的,极乐的
bonnet [ˈbɑnət]	n. 发动机罩
borne [ber]	v. 生,负荷
brace [breɪs]	n. 支柱,支架,摇钻,大括号,带子

	vt. 振作精神,拉紧,支住,激励,加强,使经受锻炼
	vi. 支持,撑牢,振作起来,奋起,打起精神,做好准备
	adj. 曲柄的
brackets [ˈbrækət]	*n.* 托架;括号;(收入额等的)等级,档次,给……装托架;把……括在括号内;把……相提并论把……围住;把……放在考虑之外
	vi. 对……作界定
brittle [ˈbrɪt(ə)l]	*adj.* 易碎的,老化的
bulge [[bʌldʒ]	*n.* 凸出部分,膨胀
bumper [ˈbʌmpər]	*n.* 防撞物,缓冲器,减振器;防撞器;(汽车前后部的)保险杠;消音器,阻尼器
butterfly [ˈbʌtəˌflaɪ]	*n.* 蝴蝶,蝶式,蝶形

C

candidate [ˈkændɪˌdeɪt]	*n.* 候选人,求职者
capacitor [kəˈpæsɪtər]	*n.* 电容器
carbonize [ˈkɑːbənaɪz]	*vt.* 碳化
carburetion [ˌkɑːbjuˈreʃən]	*n.* 渗碳作用,化油作用
casting [ˈkæstɪŋ]	*n.* 投掷,钓鱼,投掷的技巧或动作,铸造品,铸件,铸型法
categorise [ˈkætɪɡəˌraɪz]	*v.* 加以类别,分类
cater [ˈkeɪtər]	*vi.* 承办酒席,提供食物[娱乐节目],迎合,投合,特殊照顾
certificate [sərˈtɪfɪkət]	*n.* 证(明)书,执照
	vt. 批准
chamber [ˈtʃeɪmbər]	*n.* 室,房间,会所,枪膛
	v. 放在枪膛内,关在室内
charge [tʃɑrdʒ]	*n.* 费用,充电
chassis [ˈʃæsi]	*n.* (pl. chassis, chassises)底盘,底架,底板[座];机架[壳,箱],框[车,炮,起落]架
chest [tʃest]	*n.* 胸腔,胸膛,箱,柜
circumstance [ˈsərkəmstəns]	*n.* 环境,状况,事件
clamp [klæmp]	*n.* 夹子,夹钳
clutch [klʌtʃ]	*v.* 抓住,攫住
	n. 离合器
coefficient [ˌkoʊəˈfɪʃ(ə)nt]	*n.* 系数;率
collision [kəˈlɪʒən]	*n.* (车、船的)碰[互]撞,(利益,意见的)冲突,

	抵触,(政党派系之间的)倾轧,振动,跳跃,颠簸,打[冲]击,截击(空中目标)
combustion [kəm'bʌstʃən]	n. 燃烧(有机体内营养料的)氧化
commission [kə'mɪʃ(ə)n]	n. 委任状,任官令,佣金
	v. 委任,委托,使服役
commute [kə'mjut]	n. 上下班交通;通勤路程
competent ['kɑmpɪtənt]	adj. 有能力的,胜任的,足够的
compiling [kəm'paɪl]	n. 编纂
comply [kəm'plaɪ]	v. 顺从,答应
component [kəm'poʊnənt]	n. 部件,构件
comprehensive [ˌkɑmprə'hensɪv]	adj. 综合的,广泛的,理解的
compression [kəm'prɛʃən]	n. 压缩
comprise [kəm'praɪz]	v. 包含,由……组成
conceive [kən'siv]	v. 构思,以为,怀孕
concentration [ˌkɑnsən'treɪʃ(ə)n]	n. 集中,集合,专心,浓缩,浓度
configuration [kənˌfɪgə'reɪʃ(ə)n]	n. 结构,布局,形态,[计算机]配置
confiscate ['kɑnfɪˌskeɪt]	v. 没收,充公,查抄
conformity [kən'fɔrməti]	n. 适合,一致,相似
confuse [kən'fjuz]	v. 混乱,狼狈,困惑
consent [kən'sent]	n. 同意,许可
	vt. 同意,承诺
console ['kɑnˌsoʊl]	n. 控制台
constantly ['kɒnstəntli]	ad. 坚定地,坚决地,始终如一地,忠诚地,不断地
consumption [kən'sʌmpʃ(ə)n]	n. 消费(量),消尽,消耗
contaminate [kən'tæmɪˌneɪt]	v. 污染
contingency [kən'tɪndʒənsi]	n. 意外,意外事故,可能,可能性,偶然,偶然性,临时费,应急费,意外费用,偶然误差,偶然错误
conversion [kən'vɜrʒ(ə)n]	n. 变换,转化
converter [kən'vɜrtər]	n. 转换器
correlation [ˌkɔrə'leɪʃ(ə)n]	n. 相互关系,相关,关联
corrosion [kə'roʊʒ(ə)n]	n. 腐蚀,侵蚀,(渐渐的)损坏,消损,铁锈;【植】溶蚀
corrosive [kə'roʊsɪv]	adj. 腐蚀的,腐蚀性的,蚀坏的
	n. 腐蚀物
coupe ['kupe]	n. 双座轿式马车;双门小轿车
cowling ['kaʊlɪŋ]	n. 发动机罩
crevice ['krevɪs]	n. 裂缝
cruise [kruz]	n. 巡游;巡航

cumbersome ['kʌmbərsəm]　　　　　　　adj. 笨重的

D

decoration [ˌdekə'reɪʃ(ə)n]　　　　　n. 装饰，装饰品
deduct [dɪ'dʌkt]　　　　　　　　　　v. 扣除
deductible [dɪ'dʌktəb(ə)l]　　　　　adj. 可扣除的
defective [dɪ'fektɪv]　　　　　　　　adj. 有缺陷的
deformation [ˌdefər'meɪʃ(ə)n]　　　n. 变形，变态，形变，畸变；在绘画中由于明暗、色调不准而歪曲了原来的形象
defray [dɪ'freɪ]　　　　　　　　　　v. 支付，支出
deliberately [dɪ'lɪb(ə)rətli]　　　　ad. 故意地
demanding [dɪ'mændɪŋ]　　　　　　adj. 要求多的，吃力的
depleted [dɪ'plitɪd]　　　　　　　　adj. 废弃的
　　　　　　　　　　　　　　　　　v. <正>使大大地减少，使空虚；耗尽，使枯竭
deposit [dɪ'pɑzɪt]　　　　　　　　　vt. 放下，寄存，存放储蓄，贮存 沉淀，淤积
deposition [ˌdipə'zɪʃ(ə)n]　　　　　n. 沉积物
deregister [di'redʒɪstə]　　　　　　vt. 撤销……的登记
deteriorate [dɪ'tɪəriəreɪt]　　　　　vt.&vi. (使)恶化；(使)恶化，【化】变质
deviate ['diviət]　　　　　　　　　v. 偏差
diagnose ['daɪəɡ.noʊz]　　　　　　vt. 诊断
diagnostic [ˌdaɪəɡ'nɑstɪk]　　　　　adj. 诊断的
diesel ['dizl]　　　　　　　　　　　n. 柴油；柴油机，内燃机车
　　　　　　　　　　　　　　　　　adj. 柴油机的，内燃机的
differential [ˌdɪfə'renʃ(ə)l]　　　　adj. 差别的，微分的，【机，物】差动的，差速的
diffuse [dɪ'fjuz]　　　　　　　　　　v. 散播
dipstick ['dɪp.stɪk]　　　　　　　　n. 机油尺，量油计
disassemble [ˌdɪsə'semb(ə)l]　　　v. 解开，分解，[计算机]反汇编
discontinued [ˌdɪskən'tɪnjud]　　　adj. 不连续的
discretionarily [dɪskreʃənərili]　　ad. 任意地，自由决定地
disparate [dɪ'sperət]　　　　　　　adj. 不同的，全异的，乖离的
dispute [dɪ'spjut]　　　　　　　　　n.&v. 争论
dissidence ['dɪsɪdəns]　　　　　　　n. (意见等的)不同，不一致，异议
domestic [də'mestɪk]　　　　　　　adj. 国产的，国内的，家庭的
downstream [ˌdaʊn'strim]　　　　　ad.&adj. 下游地；下游的
drain [dreɪn]　　　　　　　　　　　n.&vi. 排水
dribble ['drɪb(ə)l]　　　　　　　　　vt. 使点滴流下；使淌(口水)；使逐渐落下
driveability [ˌdraɪvə'bɪləti]　　　　n. (汽车的)驾驶性能，操纵性能，操纵灵活性
driveline ['draɪvlaɪn]　　　　　　　n. 传动系统，驱动管路
duct [dʌkt]　　　　　　　　　　　　n. 管，输送管，排泄管，通过管道输送

dulcet ['dʌlsət]   *adj.* 优美的，美妙的，美味的
dummy ['dʌmi]   *n.* 哑巴，傀儡，假人，假货
                    adj. 虚拟的，假的，虚构的
duration [dʊ'reɪʃ(ə)n]   *n.* 持续；持久，持续时间，延续性，期限[间]，存在时间，波期；宽度
dynamic [daɪ'næmɪk]   *adj.* 动力的，动态的

E

ecosystem ['iːkəʊsɪstəm]   *n.* ＜生＞生态系统
electrolyte [ɪ'lektrəlaɪt]   *n.* 电解液
electromagnetic [ɪˌlektroʊmæg'netɪk]   *adj.* 电磁的；电磁学的
elimination [ɪˌlɪmə'neʃən]   *n.* 除去，消除
embody [ɪm'bɑdi]   *vt.* 包括，包含，收录，概括；使具体化，使形象化，体现；配备，连接，接合，补充
empathetic [empə'θetɪk]   *adj.* (＝empathic)移情作用的，感情移入的
endeavor [ɪn'devər]   *n. & v.* 努力，尽力
engagement [ɪn'geɪdʒmənt]   *n.* 接合，咬合
enmesh [ɪn'meʃ]   *vt.* 使陷入
entertainment [ˌentə'teɪnmənt]   *n.* 娱乐节目；娱乐，消遣；招待，款待
envision [ɪn'vɪʒn]   *vt.* 想象，预见，展望
epicyclic [ˌepi'saiklik]   *adj.* [数]周转圆的，[天]本轮的
equivalent [ɪ'kwɪvələnt]   *v.* 扩大，升高，增强
evaluate [ɪ'væljuˌeɪt]   *vt.* 估价
evaporate [ɪ'væpəˌreɪt]   *vt.* 使蒸发；通过升华使(金属等)沉淀
evaporative [i'væpərətɪv]   *adj.* 相等的，相当的，同意义的
                    n. 等价物，相等物
escalate ['eskəˌleɪt]   *adj.* 蒸发的
exemption [ɪg'zempʃən]   *n.* 免除
exert [ɪg'zɜrt]   *n.* 竭尽全力
expansion [ɪk'spænʃ(ə)n]   *n.* 扩展
expire [ɪk'spaɪr]   *v.* 期满，失效，终止，断气

F

fault [fɔlt]   *n.* 故障
fender ['fendər]   *n.* 防御者，防御物，防撞者；火炉围栏；炉格子；(车辆的)挡泥板，[英](电车、机车等的)缓冲装置，救护装置；碰垫，叶子板，翼子板，护舷木

foothold [ˈfut.hould]	n. 立足处,据点,根据地
foray [ˈfɒreɪ]	n.&v. 侵略,劫掠,侵掠,侵略,攻击
foregoing [ˈfɔr.gouɪŋ]	adj. 前面的,先前的,前述的
forfeit [ˈfɔrfɪt]	vt.(因被罚而)丧失(所有权);(因犯罪等而)失去(职位、生命等);(因过劳等而)失掉(健康等)
forge [fɔːdʒ]	n. 熔炉,铁工厂
	v. 打制,想出,伪造
formulate [ˈfɔrmjə.let]	v. 用公式表示,明确的叙述
fortitude [ˈfɔrtɪ.tud]	n. 坚强意志,坚忍,刚毅
frame [freɪm]	n. 骨架结构,框架,框子;【机】架,座身;(人或物的)骨骼,身躯
frayed [freɪd]	n. 磨破的
friction [ˈfrɪkʃ(ə)n]	n. 摩擦,摩擦力
frighten [ˈfraɪt(ə)n]	vt&vi. 使惊恐,吓唬,惊恐,害怕,受惊吓
frozen [ˈfrəuz(ə)n]	adj. 结冰的;冻死的,冻伤的;严寒的;冷藏的;不能动用的;冷淡的
fulcrum [ˈfulkrəm]	n. 支点
fundamental [fʌndəˈment(ə)l]	adj. 基本的,根本的

G

gallop [ˈgæləp]	n.(马等的)疾驰,飞奔;骑马,奔跑,快步;用最大速度跑
gauge [gedʒ]	n. 测量仪表;检测表
glazed [gleɪzd]	n. 磨光的
glide [glaɪd]	v. 轻快平稳地行驶;滑行;滑翔
gradient [ˈgreɪdiənt]	n. 倾斜度,坡度,升降率;梯度
	adj. 倾斜的,步行的
gravel [ˈgræv(ə)l]	n. 砂砾
grid [grɪd]	n. 系统网络(输电线路);网格;坐标方格
grille [grɪl]	n.(银行,邮局柜台上的)铁栅
grime [graɪm]	n. 尘垢,污点
groove [gruv]	n. 凹槽,惯例
ground [graund]	vt. 使……接地(搭铁)
gulp [gʌlp]	v. 吞,一口吞(下),忍住,抑制,吞咽
	n. 吞咽

H

harness ['hɑrnəs]	n. 导线,配线
haze [heɪz]	n. 薄雾,疑惑,阴霾
	v. 使变朦胧,使变糊涂,使劳累,变朦胧,变糊涂
hereinafter [ˌhɪrɪn'æftər]	ad. 在下文,以下
heyday ['heɪdeɪ]	n. 全盛时期;最高潮
homogeneous [ˌhɑmə'dʒiniəs]	adj. 同种的,同类的,相似的 纯一的,均质的
hood [hʊd]	n. 车盖、车篷;(汽车的)发动机罩;(机)罩整流罩;(机身)成形架
hospitalization [ˌhɑspɪtələr'zeɪʃ(ə)n]	n. 医院收容,住院治疗
hp. (horsepower) ['hɔrs'paʊə]	n. 马力
hybrid ['haɪbrɪd]	n. 混合物;混合动力车
hydride ['haɪdraɪd]	n. 氢化物
hydrocarbon [ˌhaɪdroʊ'kɑrbən]	n. 烃,碳氢化合物
hydrodynamic [ˌhaɪdroʊdaɪ'næmɪk]	adj. 水力的;水压的,液力的;流体动力学的
hydrostatic [ˌhaɪdrə'stætɪk]	adj. 流体静力学的;流体静压力的

I

identification [aɪˌdentɪfɪ'keɪʃ(ə)n]	n. 鉴定,证明
idle ['aɪd(ə)l]	adj. 空闲的,懒惰的,停顿的,无用的,无价值的
	vt. 虚度,使空闲,使空转
illogical [ɪ'lɑdʒɪk(ə)l]	adj. 异常的,不合理的
illuminate [ɪ'lumɪ.neɪt]	v. 照明,阐释,说明,照亮
illustration [ˌɪlə'streɪʃ(ə)n]	n. 说明,图解;例证,实例,插图
imaginary [ɪ'mædʒɪ.neri]	adj. 假想的
immunity [ɪ'mjunəti]	n. 免疫,免疫性,免除
impact [ɪm'pækt]	n. 碰撞,冲击,冲突,影响,效果
	vt. 挤入,撞击,压紧,对……发生影响
impart [ɪm'pɑrt]	v. 给予(尤指抽象事物),传授,告知
inaccurate [ɪn'ækjərət]	adj. 不精确的,不准确的,错误的
incentives [ɪn'sentɪv]	n. 动机
	adj. 激励的
inclusive [ɪn'klusɪv]	adj. 包含……在内的;[计算机]包括的
indemnify [ɪn'demnɪ.faɪ]	vt. 保护[障,险](against,from);赔偿,偿付,付还(for)使安全;使免受伤害
indemnity [ɪn'demnəti]	n. 保护[障,险];赔偿,补偿;[pl.]赔偿金;赔

款;免罚,赦免;免除债务

index ['ɪn.dɛks] n. 索引,指针,指数
v. 编入索引中,指出

indicate ['ɪndɪ.keɪt] vt. 指出,显示
indicative [ɪn'dɪkətɪv] adj. 指示的
indicator ['ɪndɪ.keɪtər] n. 指示器,指示剂
inductive [ɪn'dʌktɪv] adj. 引入的;诱进的;吸入的;感应的;电感的;入门的,绪论的;诱人的,动人的,感人的,归纳的

inertia [ɪ'nɜrʃə] n. 惯性,惰性
inevitably [ɪn'ɛvɪtəbli] ad. 不可避免地
infrastructure ['ɪnfrəstrʌktʃə(r)] n. 基础设施;基础建设
inflate [ɪn'fleɪt] v. 充气
initial [ɪ'nɪʃ(ə)l] adj. 最初的,初始的
initiate [ɪ'nɪʃi.et] v. 开始,发起
inspection [ɪn'spɛkʃ(ə)n] n. 检查,检验,检阅,视察
instantaneous [.ɪnstən'teɪniəs] adj. 即刻的,瞬间的,立刻做成的,立即发生的
insurance [ɪn'ʃʊrəns] n. 保险
intake ['ɪn.teɪk] n. (水管、煤气管等的)入口,进口,通风口,(在一定期间的)引入的量

integral [ɪn'tɛgrəl] n. 构成整体所必需的,组成的,主要的,必备的;完整的,整体的;综合的
adj.【数】整的;积分的;累积的;全悬挂的,[数学]积分,完整,部分

integrate ['ɪntə.greɪt] v. 整合,使……成整体
adj. 真诚的

integration [.ɪntə'greɪʃ(ə)n] n. 整合,集成
intentionally [ɪn'tɛnʃənli] ad. 有意地,故意地
intently [ɪn'tɛntli] ad. 一心一意地,心无旁物地,专心地
interaction [.ɪntər'ækʃən] n. 相互作用,相互影响
interactive [.ɪntər'æktɪv] adj. 交互式的
interchange [ɪntə'tʃendʒ] n. 交互,交换;(公路等)立体交叉;交换道
intermittent [.ɪntər'mɪt(ə)nt] adj. 间歇性的
intermittently [ɪntər'mɪtəntli] ad. 间歇地
interpretation [ɪn.tɜrprə'teɪʃ(ə)n] n. 解释,演出,翻译,互动
interruption [.ɪntə'rʌpʃən] n. 打岔,中断,中断之事
inventory ['ɪnvən.tɔri] n. 详细目录,存货清单
inverted [ɪn'vɜrt] adj. 反向的,倒转的
investigate [ɪn'vɛstɪ.get] v. 调查,研究
invoice ['ɪnvɔɪs] n. 发票,发货单;货单托运物品

ion [ˈaɪən]	n. 离子
irrevocable [ɪˈrevəkəb(ə)l]	adj. 不能取消的,不能撤回的,不能改变的,不能挽回的
item [ˈaɪtəm]	n. 项目

J

junction [ˈdʒʌŋkʃən]	n. 连接,会合处,交叉点

K

knock [nɑk]	n. & v. 敲打,敲击,敲缸

L

laconic [ləˈkɑnɪk]	adj. 简洁的
laggardly [ˈlæɡədli]	adj. 缓慢的,落后的
	ad. 行动缓慢地
lagniappe [lænˈjæp, ˈlænjæp]	n. 小赠品
lash [læʃ]	n. 间隙
launch [lɔːntʃ]	vt. 发射;发动;开展(活动、计划等)投入
	vi. 着手进行;投掷
	n. 大船上的小艇;
lawfully [ˈlɔːfəli]	ad. 依法地,法定地,合法地
leakage [ˈlikɪdʒ]	n. 泄漏,渗漏
legacy [ˈleɡəsi]	n. 祖先传下来之物,遗赠物
leverage [ˈlev(ə)rɪdʒ]	n. 杠杆作用;杠杆机构;杠杆(效)率,杠杆臂长比;扭转力矩
liable [ˈlaɪəb(ə)l]	adj. 有(法律)责任的,应受(罚)的,应付(税)的,应服从的
lifespan [ˈlaɪf.spæn]	n. 使用年限
lithium [ˈlɪθiəm]	n. 锂
litigation [lɪtɪˈɡeɪʃ(ə)n]	n. 诉讼,起诉
longevity [lɑnˈdʒevəti]	n. 使用寿命,耐久性
longitudinal [.lɑndʒɪˈtud(ə)nəl]	adj. 经度的,经线的;纵的;长度的
loyalty [ˈlɔɪəlti]	n. 忠诚,忠心
lubricate [ˈlubrɪ.keɪt]	v. 润滑,涂油
lucrative [ˈlukrətɪv]	adj. 有利的,赚钱的,合算的,待遇好的,值得作为目标的
luminance [ˈluːmɪnəns]	n. 亮度

M

magnitude [ˈmæɡnə.tud]   n. 大小,重要,光度,(地震)级数
maintenance [ˈmeɪntənəns]   n. 维修;维护
majeure [mæˈʒɜː]   n. 压倒的力量(不可抗力)
maldistribution [ˌmældɪstrɪˈbjuːʃən]   n. 分布不均
malfunction [mælˈfʌŋkʃ(ə)n]   n. 故障
    v. 发生故障,不起作用
manifold [ˈmænɪfəʊld]   n. 复印本
    adj. 多种多种形式的,有许多部分的,多方面的
    vt. 复写,繁殖,增多
manufacturer [ˌmænjəˈfæktʃərər]   n. 制造商
markedly [ˈmɑːkədli]   ad. 显著地,醒目地,明显地
mechanic [məˈkænɪk]   n. 机修工,机械师
medium [ˈmiːdiəm]   n. 媒体,方法,媒介
    adj. 适中的,中等的
mentholated [ˈmenθəleɪtɪd]   adj. 含薄荷醇的
meticulous [mɪˈtɪkjələs]   adj. 细心的,注意细节的,一丝不苟的,精确的
mileage [ˈmaɪlɪdʒ]   n. 英里数
misalign [ˈmɪsəlaɪn]   v. 不对正
miscellaneous [ˌmɪsəˈleɪniəs]   adj. 混杂的,多方面的
mobility [moʊˈbɪləti]   n. 运动性;机动性;灵活性
module [ˈmɑdʒul]   n. 模块,组件,模数
momentum [moʊˈmentəm]   n. 动力,动量
mortgage [ˈmɔːrɡɪdʒ]   n.&v. 抵押
muffler [ˈmʌflər]   n. 消声器,消音器
multimeter [ˈmʌltɪmiːtə]   n. 万用表
multiplicity [ˌmʌltəˈplɪsɪti]   n. 多样性
multitude [ˈmʌltɪ.tud]   n. 大量,多倍
mushroom [ˈmʌʃ.rum]   n. 草,蘑菇
mutual [ˈmjutʃuəl]   adj. 共同的,相互的

N

navigation [ˌnævɪˈɡeɪʃn]   n. 航行(学);航海(术);海上交通
neatness [ˈnitnɪs]   n. 整洁,干净
negotiable [nəˈɡoʊʃiəb(ə)l]   v. 谈判,协商,磋商,定价,议定,处理,通过,做成

neodymium [ˌnioˈdɪmɪəm]	n. 钕
neutralise [ˈnutrəˌlaɪz, ˈnju-]	vt. 中和(使……中立,使……失效)
nickel [ˈnɪkl]	n. 镍
nipple [ˈnɪp(ə)l]	n. 接头
nominal [ˈnɑmɪn(ə)l]	adj. 名义上的,有名无实的
nonuniformly [ˈnɑnjuːnɪfɔːmlɪ]	ad. 不一致地,不均匀地

O

obligation [ˌɑblɪˈgeɪʃ(ə)n]	n. 义务,责任
obnoxious [əbˈnɑkʃəs]	adj. 不愉快的,讨厌的
obsolescent [ˌɑbsəˈlɛsənt]	adj. 逐渐被废弃的,废退的,萎缩的
obviate [ˈɑbvɪ.eɪt]	vt. 消除,排除(危险、障碍等),回避,预防,避免
occidental [ˌɑksɪˈdɛntl]	adj. 欧美人的,西方人的;欧美国家的
	n. 西方人,欧美人
optimum [ˈɑptɪməm]	n. 最适宜
	adj. 最适宜的
ornament [ˈɔrnəmənt]	n. 装饰品,点缀品
	vt. 装饰,美化,为……增光
oscilloscope [əˈsɪlə.skoup]	n. 示波器
ovality [əuˈvælɪti]	n. 椭圆度,椭圆形
overfill [ˌovəˈfɪl]	vt. 装得过满
overture [ˈouvər.tʃur]	n. [常用复]建议,提议,提案,开端,序幕【音】序曲,前奏曲,序诗
oxidation [ˌɑksɪˈdeɪʃ(ə)n]	n. [化]氧化
oxide [ˈɑk.saɪd]	n. [化]氧化物
ozone [ˈou.zoun]	n. 新鲜的空气,[化]臭氧

P

parallel [ˈpɛrə.lel]	adj. 平行的
	ad. 平行地
	n. 平行线
	vt. 与……平行
pelvis [ˈpɛlvɪs]	n. [解]骨盆
penetration [ˌpɛnəˈtreɪʃ(ə)n]	n. 渗透,浸透,侵入
periphery [pəˈrɪf(ə)ri]	n. 周边(边缘,圆周,圆柱体表面)
perpendicular [ˌpɜːrpənˈdɪkjələr]	adj. (与另一线或面)成直角的,垂直的,正交的(to)

	n. 直立的垂直线,垂直的位置
personnel [ˌpɜrsəˈnel]	n. 人员,专门人才
phased [feɪz]	adj. 定相的
photochemical [ˌfəʊtəʊˈkemɪkl]	adj. 光化学的
pinpoint [ˈpɪnˌpɔɪnt]	vt. 为……正确定位
plethora [ˈpleθərə]	n. 过剩,过多
polymer [ˈpɑlɪmɚ]	n. 聚合物;聚合体
preaccident [ˈpriæksɪdənt]	n. 出事前
premium [ˈprimiəm]	n. 额外费用,奖金,保险费
pressurized [ˈprɛʃəraɪzd]	adj. 加压的,受压的
prevailing [prɪˈveɪlɪŋ]	adj. 流行的;通行的,普遍的;占优势的;主要的;有力的
primary [ˈpraɪm(ə)ri]	adj. 第一位的,主要的,初步的,初级的,原来的,根源的
procedure [prəˈsidʒər]	n. 程序,工序
profitable [ˈprɑfɪtəb(ə)l]	adj. 有益的,有用的
programmability [ˈproɪˌgræməˈbɪləti]	n. 可编程序性
proportional [prəˈpɔrʃn(ə)l]	adj. 成比例的,相称的
	n. [数]比例项
proposition [ˌprɑpəˈzɪʃ(ə)n]	n. 建议,命题,主张
	v. 向……提议,向……调情
propulsion [prəˈpʌlʃən]	n. 推进(力);推进器
prototyping [ˈproʊtətaɪp]	n. 原型机制造,样机研究
provenance [ˈprɑvənəns]	n. 出处,起源
provision [prəˈvɪʒ(ə)n]	n. 供应品,供给[应];准(预、防)备,(预防)措施;设备,装置,构造,规定,条款,食物
prudent [ˈprud(ə)nt]	adj. 慎重的,智慧的,稳健的,节俭的
psychic [ˈsaɪkɪk]	adj. 灵魂的,精神的,心灵的,对超自然力敏感的,通灵的
	n. 巫师,灵媒,心灵研究
purchase [ˈpɚtʃəs]	vt. & n. 买,购买
pursuant [pərˈsuənt]	adj. (= according to) 按照(根据,与……一致,合乎,和……一致)

Q

quality [ˈkwɑləti]	n. 品质,性质
quench [kwentʃ]	v. 结束,熄灭,猝熄,平息
quote [kwoʊt]	n. 引用
	v. 引述,举证,报价

R

rag [ræg]   n. 抹布

ramp [ræmp]   n. 斜坡,坡道,诈欺

v. 狂跳乱撞,乱冲,造倾斜路面

rampant ['ræmpənt]   adj. 猖獗的,蔓延的,奔放的

rapport [ræ'pɔr]   n. 关系,同意,一致

raster ['ræstə]   n. 光栅波形

ratify ['rætə.faɪ]   v. 批准,认可

rebound [rɪ'baʊnd]   v. (使)弹回,跳回

n. 回弹;返回

n. 单据;进款;人款

reciprocate [rɪ'sɪprə.keɪt]   v. 互换,交换,报答,【机】使往复运动,上下移动

recombine [ˌrikəm'baɪn]   vt. 再结合,重组

regulations [ˌrɛgjə'leɪ(ə)n]   n. 规章,法规

reimbursement [ˌriːɪm'bɜːsmənt]   n. 偿还(偿付,赔偿)

reinforce [ˌriɪn'fɔrs]   n. 加固物

v. 增援,加强

reinforcement [ˌriɪn'fɔrsmənt]   v. 增援,支援,增强,增加,加强,加固,援军,求援,得到,加强

n. 加固物

reinspect [ˌriːɪn'spɛkt]   v. 重新检查

reissue [ˌri'ɪʃu]   v. 再发出,重新发行

n. 新发行本

relevant ['rɛləvənt]   adj. 有关的,相应的

reliability [rɪˌlaɪə'bɪləti]   n. 可靠性

reluctance [rɪ'lʌktəns]   n. 磁阻

remedy ['rɛmədi]   n. 治疗;疗法;药物

resale [ˌri'seɪl]   n. 再贩卖,转售,零售

residue ['rɛzɪdu]   n. 残余,残渣

resilience [rɪ'zɪljəns]   n. 恢复力

resistance [rɪ'zɪstəns]   n. 抵抗力,反抗,反抗行动;阻力,电阻;反对

restoration [ˌrɛstə'reɪʃn]   n. 修复,恢复;归还

retail ['riteɪl]   n. 零售

adj. 零售的

ad. 以零售方式

v. 细谈

retain [rɪ'teɪn]   vt. (=keep)保留[持],不忘,记住,雇用,聘请(律师等)

retardation [ˌriːtɑːˈdeɪʃ(ə)n]	n. 智力迟钝,精神发育迟缓
retention [rɪˈtenʃ(ə)n]	n. 保存(保持力,包装牢固,记忆力,保留物)
retrieve [rɪˈtriːv]	vt. 读取
	n. 检索
reveal [rɪˈviːl]	v. 显示,透露
revised [rɪˈvaɪzd]	adj. 修订过的,改订的
rigidity [rɪˈdʒɪdəti]	n. 硬,劲直,硬度
rival [ˈraɪv(ə)l]	n. 对手,竞争者
	adj. 竞争的
	vt. 与……相匹敌,比得上
rivet [ˈrɪvɪt]	n. 铆钉
	v. 固定
robust [roʊˈbʌst]	adj. 强壮的,强健的
rollover [ˈroʊl.oʊvər]	n. 翻滚
rust [rʌst]	n. 铁锈,铁锈色
	v. (使)生锈,(脑子等)发锈,衰退

S

scatter [ˈskætə]	n. 散播之物,散布
	v. 散开,散布,散播
scavenge [ˈskævəndʒ]	v. 打扫,排除废气,到处觅食
schedule [ˈskedʒəl]	n. 计划表,日程表
secure [sɪˈkjʊr]	adj. 无虑的,安心的,安全的
	v. 固定,获得,使……安全
seepage [ˈsiːpɪdʒ]	n. 渗透
segment [ˈsɛgmənt]	n. 部分;部门
semantic [səˈmæntɪk]	adj. 语义的,语义学的
semiconductor [ˌsɛmikənˈdʌktə]	n. 半导体
seminar [ˈsemɪ.nɑr]	vt. (大学的)研究班,研讨会
sensor [ˈsensər]	n. 传感器
sequentially [sɪˈkwenʃəli]	ad. 继续地;顺序地
series [ˈsɪriz]	n. 连续,系列
severally [ˈsevərəli]	ad. 各自地,各个地
shelter [ˈʃeltə(r)]	n. 庇护所,避难所,庇护
	v. 庇护,保护,隐匿
simultaneous [ˌsaɪm(ə)lˈteɪniəs]	adj. 同时发生的
simultaneously [ˌsaɪməlˈteɪniəsli]	adj. 同时存在[发生]的
	ad. 同时地
slot [slɑt]	n. 水沟,细长的孔,狭缝,硬币投币口,组织、系

              统中的一个位置或空位
              v. 留细长的孔

smear [smiə]   v. 涂,擦上,抹擦使变模糊
              n. 油迹,污点,诋毁,诽谤
socket ['sɒkət]   n. 插座,插口
soot [sʊt]   n. 煤烟,烟灰
              v. 用煤烟弄脏
sound [saʊnd]   adj. 可靠的,正常的
specific [spə'sɪfɪk]   adj. 详细而精确的,明确的,特殊的
specification [,spesɪfɪ'keɪʃ(ə)n] n. 规格,详述,详细说明书,规范
spot [spɒt]   vt. 认出;发现
spray [spreɪ]   n. 喷雾,飞沫
              vt. 喷射,喷溅
sprung [sprʌŋ]   adj. 支在弹簧上的
stall [stɔl]   v. (使)停转,(使)停止
static ['stætɪk]   adj. 静态的,静力的
statistics [stə'tɪstɪks]   n. 统计,统计数字,统计学
sternward ['stɜːnwəd]   adj. 船尾的,后面的
              ad. 在船尾
stethoscope ['steθə,skoʊp]   n. 听诊器
stimulate ['stɪmjə,leɪt]   vt. 刺激,激励,鼓舞
stringent ['strɪndʒənt]   adj. 严格的
stipulate ['stɪpjə,leɪt]   vt. 要求以……为条件,规定,约定
stringency ['strɪndʒənsi]   n. 迫切,银根紧
strive [straɪv]   vi. 努力,奋斗,力求;斗争,反抗
strut [strʌt]   n. 高视阔步,支柱,抗压材
              v. 趾高气扬地走,用支柱支撑
stuffing ['stʌfɪŋ]   n. 填塞物,填料
subdivide [,sʌbdɪ'vaɪd]   vt. 细分(细区分,再划分,重分,叠分,分小类)
subrogate ['sʌbrə,ɡeɪt]   vt. 取代,接替(别人);【律】(担保人清偿债务后)取代(债权人)
subsequent ['sʌbsɪkwənt]   adj. 随后的,后来的
subsidy ['sʌbsədi]   n. 补贴;津贴;助学金;奖金
subtle ['sʌt(ə)l]   adj. 微妙的,敏感的,精细的,狡猾的
succinct [sək'sɪŋkt]   adj. 简洁的
supervise ['supər,vaɪz]   v. 监督,管理,指导
surpass [sə'pɑːs]   vt. 超过;优于;
susceptible [sə'septəb(ə)l]   adj. 易受影响的,容许……的
              n. (因缺乏免疫力而)易得病的人
suspension [sə'spenʃ(ə)n]   n. 悬挂,未决,中止

sustainable [sə'stenəbl]	adj. 能持续的；能维持的
swirl [swɜrl]	n. (水、风等的)旋转；旋涡
switch [swɪtʃ]	vt. &v. 转换
	n. 开关
symmetrical [sɪ'metrɪk(ə)l]	adj. 对称的
symptom ['sɪmptəm]	n. 症状；故障现象
symptomize ['sɪmptəmaɪz]	vt. 表明
synchronous ['sɪŋkrənəs]	adj. 同时的，同步的

T

tactility [tæk-'tɪləti]	n. 触知性，触感
tappet ['tæpɪt]	n. (气门)推杆
tarlike [tɑrlaɪk]	adj. 像炭一样的
technician [tek'nɪʃ(ə)n]	n. 技术员，技师
terminate ['tɜrmɪ.neɪt]	adj. 有结尾的，有限的
	v. 结束，终止，满期
testimonial [.testə'moʊnɪəl]	n. (品格、行为、资格等的)证明书；推荐书；奖状[品、金]，感谢信，纪念品
thereof [ðer'ɔv]	ad. 关于……，将它，它的
thermal ['θɜrm(ə)l]	adj. 热的，热量的
	n. 上升的热气流
thermostat ['θɜrmə.stæt]	n. 自动调温器，温度调节装置
threshold ['θreʃ.hoʊld]	n. 限值
tipper ['tɪpə]	n. 自(动倾)卸车，翻斗车，倾卸装置
tire [taɪr]	n. 轮胎
tolerant ['tɑlərənt]	adj. 宽容的，容忍的
top-up ['tɒpʌp]	vt. 加注，注满
torsion ['tɔrʃ(ə)n]	n. 扭，捻，捻率，【物】【机】扭转，转矩
tradeoff ['treidɔːf]	n. 权衡(折中，换位，比较评定，放弃，交换)
transaxle [træns'æksəl, trænz-]	n. 驱动桥(与变速箱连成一体，用于前轮驱动的车)
transferable [træns'fɜrəb(ə)l]	adj. 可转移的
transformer [træns'fɔrmə]	n. 变压器
transient ['trænzɪənt]	adj. 短促的，片刻的，一瞬间的；易逝的，虚无的；不稳定的；过渡的
transition [træn'zɪʃ(ə)n]	n. 转变，转换，跃迁，过渡，变调
transmission [træns'mɪʃən, trænz-]	n. 传递；移转；传播；传播之物；【机】传动装置；变速器[箱]；联动机件；【无】传送；发射[送]；播送；通话；通信，传输

transshipment [træns'ʃɪpmənt]	n. 转运
transverse [trænz'vɜrs]	n. 横向[截];横梁[材,骨];横墙;横放物
tread [tred]	n. 轮胎花纹,轮胎胎面
troubleshooting ['trʌblʃu:tɪŋ]	n. 故障诊断
tune-up ['tunˌʌp,'tjun-]	n. 维护
turbine ['tɜr.baɪn]	n. 涡轮
turbo ['tə:bəu]	n. 涡轮增压器
turbulence ['tɜrbjələns]	n. 骚乱,动荡,(液体或气体的)紊乱
tyre ['taɪr]	n. 轮胎

U

ultimate ['ʌltɪmət]	adj. 最后的,最终的,根本的
	n. 最终
undercoating ['ʌndəˌkəutɪŋ]	n. (涂在车辆底部、通常以柏油打底的)防水底涂层
undo [ʌn'du]	vt. 解开,松开
unrealistic [.ʌnrɪə'lɪstɪk]	adj. 不切实际的,不实在的
unremitting [.ʌnrɪ'mɪtɪŋ]	adj. 不歇的,不断的,坚忍的
unresponsive [.ʌnrɪ'spɑnsɪv]	adj. 无反应的
unsprung ['ʌn'sprʌŋ]	adj. (车、椅等)不支承在弹簧上的
upstream [ʌp'strim]	ad. 上游
upwind [,ʌp'wɪnd]	adj.&ad. 逆风的(地);迎风的(地);顶风的(地)

V

vacuum ['vækjum]	n. 真空,空间,真空吸尘器
	adj. 真空的,产生真空的,利用真空的
vague [veɪg]	adj. 模糊的,不明确的,无表情的
van [væn]	n. 运货车,前卫,先头部队,先锋
	vt. 用车搬运
vaporizer ['veɪpəˌraɪzə]	n. 汽化器
vendor ['vɛndə(r)]	n. 小贩;法卖方,卖主(亦作:vender)
ventilate ['vent(ə)l.eɪt]	vt. 使……空气流通
vertical ['vɜrtɪk(ə)l]	adj. 垂直的,直立的,顶点的,[解]头顶的
	n. 垂直线,垂直面,竖向
via ['vɪə]	prep. 经,通过,经由
vibration [vaɪ'breɪʃ(ə)n]	n. 震(颤、振)动,摆动,振荡,(思想情绪的)激动,摇摆,犹豫

vital [ˈvaɪt(ə)l]	adj. 致命的，极其重要的
volatility [ˌvɒləˈtɪləti]	n. 挥发性[度]，轻快，快活
volume [ˈvɒljuːm]	n. 体积；卷；音量；量，大量
	adj. 大量的
	vi. 成团卷起
	vt. 把……收集成卷
volumetric [ˌvɒljəˈmetrɪk]	adj. 测定体积的

W

warranty [ˈwɔrənti]	n. 担保，保证，根据，授权，授权，担保
wear [wer]	v. 磨损
weldable [ˈweldəbl]	adj. 可焊的
whirl [hwɜrl]	v. (使)旋转，急动，急走
	n. 旋转，一连串快速的活动
windshield [ˈwɪn(d).ʃild]	n. (汽车)风窗玻璃
wiring [ˈwaɪrɪŋ]	n. 配线，接线
wobbly [ˈwɑbli]	adj. 摆动的
workshop [ˈwɜrk.ʃɑp]	n. 车间
wow [waʊ]	n. 巨大的成功
	int. 唯

Z

zap [zæp]	v. 快速传递；迅速移动

Reference
参 考 文 献

[1] Michael Crandell. Estimating for Collision Repair. Delmar Publishers. 2000.
[2] 陈焕江,徐双应. 交通运输专业英语[M]. 北京:机械工业出版社,2002.
[3] 李俊玲,罗永革. 汽车工程专业英语[M]. 北京:机械工业出版社,2005.
[4] 英华大字典[M]. 北京:商务印书馆,1987.
[5] 王锦俞,闵思鹏. 图解英汉汽车技术词典[M]. 北京:机械工业出版社,2002.
[6] 英国培生教育出版有限公司. 朗文当代高级英语词典[M]. 北京:外语教学与研究出版社,2004.
[7] Proceedings of 2005 Shanghai International Symposium on Automotive Electronics & Advanced Technology. Shanghai, 2005.
[8] 卢思源. 汽车英语[M]. 南京:东南大学出版社,2010.